D1605068

A TRAILS BOOKS GUIDE

THE GREAT INDIANA TOURING BOOK

20 SPECTACULAR AUTO TOURS

Thomas Huhti

TRAILS BOOKS
Black Earth, Wisconsin

Library of Congress Control Number: 2001097359
ISBN: 1-931599-09-2

Editor: Stan Stoga
Photos: Thomas Huhti
Production: Sarah White
Cover design: John Huston
Cover photo: Michael Shedlock

Printed in the United States of America.

07 06 05 04 03 02   6 5 4 3 2 1

Trails Books, a division of Trails Media Group, Inc.
P.O. Box 317 • Black Earth, WI 53515
(800) 236-8088 • e-mail: info@wistrails.com
www.trailsbooks.com

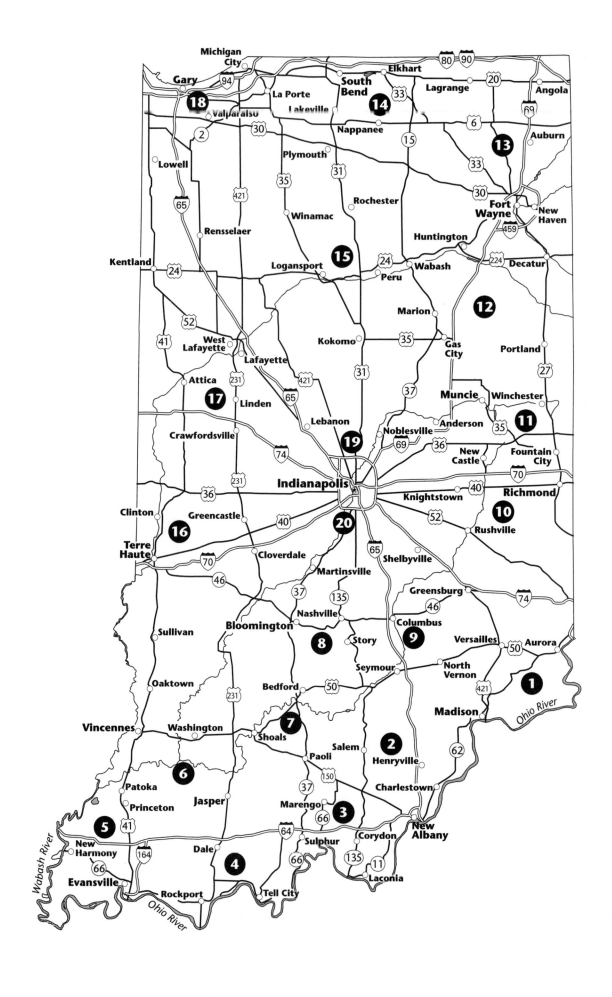

Contents

Introduction

A marvelous state treasure, one of Indiana's many parks.

To preface our journey, an admission: I am not a native son of Indiana and, before I began this book, had no special attachment to it. But I am a born-and-bred Midwesterner, an American. I am also a Traveler, with a capital T, one with a trusty Taurus— my endlessly faithful Running Bull—who hungers again for the little highways as I type these words.

Millions of words have been written about the American love for—perhaps devotion to—our cars. No matter what you call it, this is a sentiment I'm in harmony with. I simply think that the "Road does rule." We are a nation endlessly restless, always wondering what is there, not here. We snoop, we explore, we follow our individual manifest destiny from within by driving away from something, but in the end always toward something else. I'm a Midwesterner by birth and a vagabond by choice.

Allow me to tell a little more about myself. If we're to be road trippers together, seat mates on long roads into the horizon, please allow me a bit more biography, a little method to the madness, as it were.

About the time I got my driver's license—the mark of adulthood in this culture—I serendipitously came across some musty, dog-eared volumes that were to change my life. They were the mother of all guidebooks, the Works Progress Administration's highway-by-highway guides to every state in the Union, numbering 48 at the time. I devoured them all in order and knew someday that I had to do some grand and sweeping journey like the ones they described. Written circa-World War II, they were the product of some of this country's most talented writers; they augured the future of American auto travel decades before it exploded into what it is today. (What a grand and edifying thing it is, I thought, to be a writer and a wanderer and the government gives you a job for it!)

Later, I read William Least-Heat Moon's *Blue Highways*. I read it about once a year now and still find it the best overview of the compulsion to *move* I've ever found. Like anyone else who is disconcerted by the endless swells of mad travelers on the interstates—quite possibly the worst inven-

A weathered advertising sign on a barn—classic Indiana rural architecture.

tion our culture has ever produced (an "ugly necessity")—the book compels me to search for the real part of America.

When I first started these journeys, I confused an appreciation of country and culture with transcontinental mad dashes, the mileage clicking mercilessly as I did the sea-to-shining-sea thing in a numbed state of hyperdrive. I was addicted to movement, all the while feeling guilty that fellow travelers would take me for one of those unfortunate visa collectors you meet backpacking around the world. Like any addict, I could not stop the moving, the *driving*.

This compulsion led me to spend years working on books detailing the dozen early national highways linking all points of the U.S. compass. They were fine and I adored all those hundreds of thousands of miles. Yet at one point I found myself trying to "do" all of Canada and wound up at my own Land's End, in St. John's, Newfoundland, pretty much out of highway. Then I knew. I wasn't going to find myself if I did not stop once in a long while to think things through. And it was high time to return home to the Midwest. And by serendipity again, this project and I met and decided to form a partnership to explore Indiana, one of the region's hallmark states.

And now the window's open, the dog's panting in the back. The tent's dry and the gazeteer's riding shotgun. It's time to explore what we don't know yet or, even, what we might think we know already.

The Highways and Byways
The routes and roads followed in this book are mostly of my own choosing, and I take full respon-

sibility for them. Some follow topographical maneuverings, others historical, still others a methodology even I'm not quite sure of. But most were chosen using the process I have always found best: careful research followed by fortuitous blundering in all its majestic forms. It's amazing, truly unbelievable, how the Road always just . . . works somehow. That's what the Road in this book is all about: one state, more than five million people, and infinite varieties of experience.

What generally happens with guidebooks (of any sort) is that the trip is preceded by many, many months of planning. Uncounted Indiana-themed brochures, glossy PR media kits, and printed pages—and a gajillion Web sites—are pored over. Box upon box of state tourism department publications are deposited daily with a thud on the doorstep by decreasingly cheery delivery drivers. Friendships are formed with those wondrously chatty and solicitous employees of state/county/ city/town/village visitors offices or chambers of commerce. They never seem to tire of being peppered with questions about who/what/where/ when/why.

The preparation continues. Lists are compiled and a network of map routes, variously outlined in the yellows, greens, oranges, and pinks from highlighter pens, begins to take shape. Out of all this a couple of conditions for the tours emerged: they had to be loops, and they had to be of a reasonable length, so that each could be finished in a day. Now this sounds fine on paper, but one must remember that one person's leisurely jaunt is another person's maniacal daylong rush. Obviously, cartographic considerations had to come first. I started by plotting a set of tours that could conceivably be

linked together day by day. As it turned out, topography and history were my primary considerations in fashioning the original tour outlines. Along the way, pure happenstance flavored the route—a detour here and there, a full U-turn on more than one occasion to take in something new and unique, a half-day stop where none was planned. It was always my hope that each tour have at least one historical sight, one spot for nature lovers, maybe a village for antiquers or shopping buffs, and lots of great back roads for the behind-the-wheel fans.

One essential foundation did underpin all planning and execution: *Avoid interstates at all cost.* I will be the first to acknowledge the extraordinary efficiency with which these transnational veins swoosh us kinetic Americans about. Yet if you're reading *this* book, I'm likely preaching to the choir if I mention the interstates' impersonal vacuum of existence, the disconnect from the very context of a trip, that pervades on those occasionally awful drag strips. Too much white-knuckled, white-noise-laden isolation there. Although I made strong efforts to route away from these claustrophobic channels, a few were unavoidable. So, during those infrequent times, let's consider their mileage as a respectful doff-of-the-cap to the American spirit and transportation engineering.

The idea was to head for the nearest exit and start scouting out roadways with nomenclature containing myriad numbers and letters, an indication that the trip was going to be full of twists and bends. (A personal observation: the greater the number of digits or letters in a road's name, the narrower the road—likely in graceful disrepair—and the greater the charm of the land and people; and the greater the curvature, the more worthy in all likelihood.) Indiana, like most Midwestern states, has an extraordinary network of byways and back roads, thanks to its extensive farm-to-market trails from the nineteenth and early twentieth centuries. Later these would widen somewhat, become paved, enabling modern vagabonds to get an up-close glimpse at the "real" Indiana. That's providing you've got a full tank of gas and a very, very good gazeteer, although even the best could not hope to capture the wide array of the state's county roads.

It is by keeping an open mind and being happy to drift off a planned route onto the more obscure of any state's roads that the real adventure of travel begins, that the traveler experiences many of his or her most precious travel moments. I have to admit that many of this book's smaller and subtler back-road sights found their way into these pages by pure dumb luck allowed by little sleep and an incurable case of wanting to be anywhere-but-here. If other guidebook writers tell you otherwise, they are shading the truth—we're professional snoopers more than all else. You can plan all you want to: the Road will give up what it wishes. Soon enough, any guidebook writer's airtight plan goes right out the window. Some hold on longer; others—like this author—are always

hoping to get a lead on someplace different. My favorite sources of information—clerks in convenience stores and gas stations—rarely disappoint. A case in point: after just 20 miles had elapsed on the very first tour of this book, the ad-libbing started. Serendipity showed up in the form of some teenagers filling up in a gas station. They mentioned my license plate and dusty car, seemed intrigued by the project, and soon were filling a tape recorder with ideas. Cool. We all benefit.

Many of these tours hardly resembled those on the master plan when I returned home. Many, many times, a proposed 60-mile tour turned into an exhausting 200-mile day, rife with drifting down roads for no real reason other than curiosity and a total loss of direction. Consider the partial list of happily accidental discoveries I made, those places I saw on no brochure or map despite voracious reading: all those nature preserves/wildlife areas; *lots* of parks (the nation's most underappreciated assets are its county parks, I believe); memorials and museums of all sorts (my favorite: Ernie Pyle's memorial/museum in Dana); tiny Boggstown, wonderfully isolated and wonderful for its musical attractions (probably the book's best of example of "What in the world is this doing here?"); the amazing steepled vistas of Oldenburg; Jug Rock in Shoals (thanks to the gravel truck driver who pointed it out at the wayside well pump as I washed up); the glass museum of Dunkirk; a Tibetan retreat (of all things) south of Bloomington; my all-time favorite forest fire lookout tower (won't tell you where yet!); the incredible architecture—and antiques—of the U.S. 40 alley; the *Hoosiers* legacy of New Richmond; Mentone's concrete egg; and on and on and on.

Some of you will come upon your own finds. If you do, cultivate karma by sharing so we may all experience the beneficial vagaries of traveling the Road. That is, after all, part of its ethos and its travelers—a shared, special experience.

One of the many bridges of Parke County, part of the charm of Indiana.

Indiana

Still one more admission (I promise it will be the last!): I was one of the guilty ones. I fell prey to the prejudices and stereotypes haunting the "bland and boring" Midwest. I grew up here perhaps feeling guilty because maybe there was something to those stereotypes. Also, I never had given much thought to Indiana before, outside of a few quizzical and cursory glances, wondering, "I wonder what's there." I am guilty of having overlooked the garden just beyond my own backyard.

I have written many pages in many books and have filled volumes with assorted scribblings and musings on travel. I can quite honestly say that this book was one of the most enjoyable I've ever researched. I was given virtually free reign by the publisher. The people of Indiana, like the folks of Wisconsin, my home, do live up to the stereotype: they're among the nicest, most wonderful people in the world. Just meeting them would have made the trip worthwhile.

For people "passing through" Indiana, give it a shot; a nickel gets you a dime you stay longer than you thought you would. Even if you think you're an Indiana "expert," there's so much here that you could never cover it all. And native Hoosiers should never take their state for granted—and I suspect that many of them don't.

I'm still awed by every little thing I discovered in Indiana. I have seen things I never dreamed existed in the Midwest. Long a lover of the Great Lakes, with its whitecapped vistas and stinging freshwater spray, I came to regard Indiana's brief but precious national lakeshore as one of my favorite respites in the world.

And I'm now a self-confirmed river rat, having become addicted to the soft, rolling, chocolate-drop hills and wildly serpentining roads that trace Old Man River—the mighty Ohio. He and the other Old Man, the Mississippi, may get all the credit, but I have a fresh appreciation for the Wabash River valley and its crucial importance to the expansion and history of this country.

Southern Indiana's undulations and epic swaths of green will always beckon me. Caves, rivers, old-growth forest, farmland, diverse ecology—it's got it all. Northern Indiana is truly the Crossroads of America, with cities that were once the gateways to an expanding frontier. Here, bucolic agrarian communities stand side by side with historic industrial cities in typically Midwestern fashion. A side note to this is the amazingly important role the state played in the development of the automobile, an ironic fact given the mandate of our journey. And exactly how many covered bridges are there in the state? Not enough, as far as I'm concerned.

You could spend your entire trip just checking out the historic towns and cities along Indiana's ribbony roads and rivers; it's home to presidents and could be called a barometer of America. It's as if there's almost too much history to use, to quote a Midwestern poet. And the Amish will always have

The Amish, a living link to Indiana's past.

a soft spot in my heart not only for their culture but also for their buggies, which link the past to the task at hand in this book.

And so this book is ultimately about Indiana's people. As the roads decrease in width, it seems the charm of the people increases in direct proportion. As forest gives way to river country, then gives way to classic pastoral farmland before the road rolls into friendly city, everywhere I go I met people who will keep me coming back. I hope you'll have the same experience.

Practical Stuff

Tourist information: The main office of the Indiana Tourism Development Division, (800) 289-6646, www.enjoyindiana.com, One N. Capitol, Suite 70, Indianapolis, IN 46204, has just about anything you need. State information centers are located on I-65 North near the Kentucky state line; I-69 South near the Michigan state line; I-70 East near the Illinois border; I-70 West near the Ohio state line; I-74 East near the Illinois state line; I-74 West near the Ohio state line; and I-64 West near the Illinois state line.

Hoosier National Forest: For recreation information, contact the Hoosier National Forest, (812) 275-5987, 811 Constitution Avenue, Bedford, IN 47421.

State parks and forests: Contact the Division of State Parks and Reservoirs, (317) 232-4124, www.ai.org/dnr, 204 W. Washington Street, Room W298, Indianapolis, IN 46204. The Division of Wildlife (same address, Room W273) can be reached at (317) 232-4080; the Division of Forestry (Room W296) is at (317) 232-4105.

One of the many things for kids to do in Indiana.

Camping: A variety of campsites ($5–13) can be reserved at state facilities, except for those at Harmonie, Shades, Summit Lake, and Tippecanoe State Parks. Sadly, the Department of Natural Resources is still not Web friendly for reservations. A two-week limit is enforced on campsites. When in doubt that a campsite will be available, always head for federal land since you can camp anywhere *following strict backcountry rules*. A highlight of Indiana's state park system is its popular set of inns and housekeeping cabins.

A bridge over the historic canal at Metamora.

On the Road

Seat belt/child restraint laws: Seat belts are required for driver and front-seat passenger; child restraints mandatory for children under 5.

Radar detectors: Permitted

Helmet law: Required for motorcycle riders under 18

Vital Statistics

Population: 5,900,000 (approximate), 14th largest

Capital: Indianapolis

Area: 36,291 square miles, 38th largest

Admitted to the Union: December 11, 1816 (19th state)

Nickname: Hoosier State

Flower: Peony

Motto: The Crossroads of America

Bird: Cardinal

Tree: Tulip tree

Highest point: 1,257 feet, near Fountain City

Lowest point: 320 feet, Ohio River

Holidays: January 1; Martin Luther King Jr's Birthday (third Monday in January); Lincoln's Birthday (February 12); Washington's Birthday (third Monday in February); Good Friday; Election Day (May); Memorial Day (last Monday in May); Labor Day (first Monday in September); Veterans Day (November 11); Thanksgiving; Christmas Day (December 25).

Time zones: Mostly on eastern and central standard time. No daylight savings time in the zones around Cincinnati and Louisville and near Chicago and Evansville.

Taxes: State tax is five percent, with local options adding one percent more. Counties can add more to that.

Brown County State Park—one of the Midwest's natural gems.

20 SPECTACULAR AUTO TRIPS

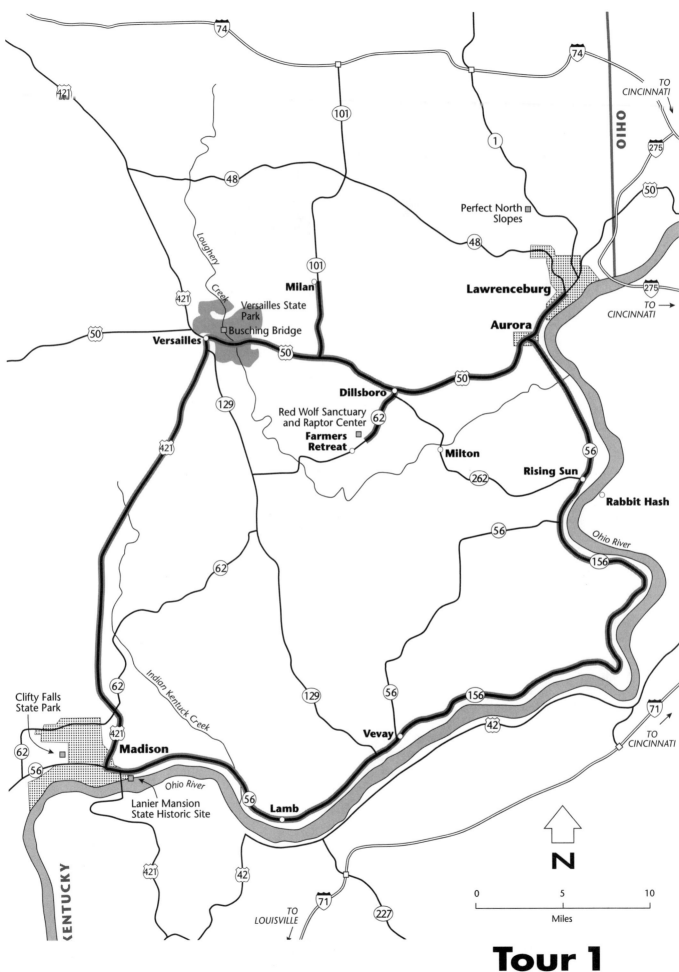

OHIO

TO CINCINNATI

TO CINCINNATI

TO CINCINNATI

TO CINCINNATI

Perfect North Slopes

Lawrenceburg

Aurora

Milan

Versailles State Park

Busching Bridge

Versailles

Dillsboro

Red Wolf Sanctuary and Raptor Center

Farmers Retreat

Milton

Rising Sun

Rabbit Hash

Ohio River

Clifty Falls State Park

Madison

Indian Kentuck Creek

Loughery Creek

Vevay

Lanier Mansion State Historic Site

Ohio River

Lamb

KENTUCKY

TO LOUISVILLE

N

0   5   10

Miles

Tour 1

Tour 1
River Country

Aurora–Rising Sun–Vevay–Madison–Versailles–Dillsboro–Lawrenceburg–Aurora

Distance: 116 miles

The wondrous stylings of Hillforest Mansion, Aurora.

This lovely tour begins in the southeast corner of Indiana, in classic river country, offers some of the best features of auto touring, and focuses on one of southern Indiana's crown jewels. Lean back and let the miles spin. Take in tranquil river towns filled with nineteenth-century architecture and shopping galore. Madison may be southern Indiana's most perfectly preserved town and is a gem on any itinerary. But wait! We've just started. We bend north from the river to take in some wondrous natural beauty as we roll toward Versailles State Park. These regions display some of Indiana's oldest—and youngest—geology, so keep your eyes open.

Start your tour in Aurora on Highway 50 overlooking the Ohio River. Highway 50 has been called the Loneliest Road, but here it's the gateway to one of the most picturesque road trips anywhere.

Aurora is an eye-catching town set off from the river against a modestly aggressive bluff line. The town's early architecture was well known for having sidewalks that sometimes reached up to the second stories of buildings in order to deal with the rises and falls of the river. The old WPA guide noted that "for several miles up and down the Ohio River, the river banks are peopled with families who live in shacks or houseboats. They raise a small patch of tobacco for their own use, and subsist mainly on catfish and greens, accepting the periodical high waters with philosophical calm."

The town was founded in 1819 by Jesse Holman, one of the first justices of the Indiana Supreme Court. Today its architectural highlight is the restored antebellum *Hillforest Mansion*, a gem of historic "Steamboat Gothic" architecture. (Actually it's Italian Renaissance but that sounds so academic; the steamboat nickname stems from its steamboat-resembling add-ons, which include round central colonnades and a "pilot house" belvedere.) It has all the trappings of a historic

Madison's train depot, one of the city's many classic structures.

lock. The boat still holds the record for the fastest time between Cincinnati and Louisville (267 minutes, 49 seconds, set in 1923). Hours are 11 a.m.–4 p.m., every day but Wednesday; and they are subject to change. Admission.

Along slightly different lines is the *Oak Tree Herb Farm,* 2023 Brown Road, (812) 438-3742, which specializes in growing medicinal, culinary, and other herbs. The farm also has an English cottage garden and a rare tree trunk house.

Two unique festivals in town are the *Blue Jeans Festival* the last weekend in June and a *Navy Bean Fall Festival* the first weekend in November. At the legendary *Rising Sun Regatta* the second weekend in September hydroplanes race on the river. All are great fun.

structure, but perhaps most appealing is the view of three states from inside. Just reading about the renaissance man who built the place is fascinating; Thomas Gaff was an industrialist and businessman who just about did it all, and he pulled out all the stops on this baby. Located at 213 Fifth Street, it is just a couple blocks north of downtown (signs are prevalent), (812) 926-0087. Hours are 1–5 p.m. Tuesday–Sunday, April 1–late December, and also 1–5 p.m. Monday, Memorial Day–Labor Day. Admission.

Other notable local residents include Edwin Hill and Elmer Davis, who were popular radio commentators in the early twentieth century.

If you want to rest your weary bones, the paddlewheel replica *Dottie G,* offers lunch, dinner, and sightseeing cruises on the Ohio River, (812) 438-4595.

From Aurora, head south along Highway 56 for 9 miles to Rising Sun. The road wends and rolls through riverine loveliness to the aptly named Rising Sun. If you take the road in the early morning, the views to the port side can be extraordinary, quite possibly the best along the Ohio River. The sun rises above the Kentucky town of Rabbit Hash, a quaint name if there ever was one.

One of the best-preserved towns in all of Indiana, Rising Sun is filled with revitalized warehouses and commercial buildings and spacious residential spreads. Trim and pleasant, the town extends long and narrow along the river's edge. For information, visit the Rising Sun/Ohio County Convention and Tourism Office, 120 N. Walnut Street, (888) RSNG-SUN, www.risingsun-in.org. Hours are Monday to Saturday, 8:30 a.m. to 5 p.m.

The Ohio County Courthouse is the oldest in continuous operation in the state. History buffs will also love the *Ohio County Historical Museum,* 212 S. Walnut Street, (812) 438-4915, with displays on nineteenth-century river life and mock-ups of the *Hoosier Boy,* a hydroplane invented in the town by furniture builder J. W. Whit-

Go south on Highway 56 for 2.5 miles to Highway 156. Turn onto 156 and go for about 30 miles to Vevay. The road does some serious serpenting as it parallels the river, so it's a good time to throttle back and enjoy the scenery. You pass through a few micro-sized river towns in various stages of historic preservation before arriving in Vevay (pronounced "Veevee"), seat of Switzerland County, in honor of its ethnic history.

The story goes that in 1801 Swiss immigrants were so taken with the area and its temperate climate that they put down permanent roots to establish a still-thriving wine industry; in fact, vineyards once encircled the town. The wines were this country's first commercial domestic wines and were even carried to President Thomas Jefferson. The historic downtown has more than 300 nineteenth-century buildings, and many of them bear markers detailing their historic significance. Stretch your legs with a walking tour; the visitors center has brochures to guide you.

The first stop for travelers should be the *Hoosier Theater,* 209 Ferry Street, (800) HELLO-VV, as it's the local welcome center as well as a historic jewel in its own right. Built in 1837, this grand dame has been completely restored and now holds live theater and musical performances. It's well worth a look if you have the time. The architectural cornerstone is the 1864 *Switzerland County Courthouse,* in 1864 Classical Revival style; on the grounds are an original six-sided privy and the old jail. The small *Switzerland County Historical Museum* is located in a wonderful old Presbyterian church at Main and Market Streets. Hours are noon–4 p.m. daily, April–October. Admission. You'll find many other historic structures in town.

Vevay was the home of Edward Eggleston, who penned *The Hoosier Schoolmaster,* which details his brother's experiences here as a 16-year-old teacher. Many literary historians considered the book one of the first serious literary works to emerge from the Midwest, though most preferred Eggleston's later works. His *First of the Hoosiers*

The Ohio River

The mighty Mississippi may get more press, but the Ohio River has been just as important as Old Man River. In a sense the first U.S. east-west "highway," the Ohio played a crucial role in this nation's policy of westward expansion. Towns that started as supply "nodes" grew into prosperous commercial or manufacturing centers. Some of the state's most precious extant architecture and historical landmarks are found among the rolling valleys and hills; geologically, it contains some of the state's oldest—and newest—topography.

It's as fickle as any river anywhere. Geological analysis shows it has six distinct terraces, indicating it has jumped its banks a lot. In fact, it hardly resembles itself 150 years ago. Ohio River towns that once had shoreline properties now sit isolated some distance away. Vevay once had an island (I sure missed it). Rising Sun somehow lost more than 100 yards of shoreline. Hardinsburg was once a port.

And then there are the floods, those savage, epic, alluvial invasions that periodically remind us just exactly who is in charge. When the river gets its dander up, waves roll into town, deposit tons of silt and other detritus, leave unsanitary conditions and disease, kill enough to be feared, then retreat. It's not hard to consider a river like this an omnipotent creature.

Floods have been plaguing the Ohio River valley settlers of Indiana since they arrived in the late eighteenth century. In fact it didn't seem to cause much of a fuss since folks pretty much used the time to socialize and the towns hadn't much infrastructure. But no one had ever seen anything like the great flood of 1937 and its lasting effects on the valley.

This Noah-esque deluge ruined much of the Ohio River valley. It was the result of more than a foot of rain over a two-week period mixed with an early snow melt along streams that fed into the Ohio. It rose so high that Coast Guard cutters could patrol the waters. On January 31, 1937, the river reached its highest level ever. Eventually more than 15,000 square miles encompassing 12 states were inundated. A massive relief effort was launched to help locals and to prevent outbreaks of disease. Thousands were evacuated to northern Indiana. No one knows how many people died—certainly hundreds. Waters crested at 80 feet in Cincinnati, 54 feet in Evansville, 57 feet in Tell City and New Albany. Evansville had experienced a flood in 1913 but this one was devastating. It affected more than 10,000 homes; 46 percent of the town was covered with fetid water.

At New Albany the river crested more than 10 feet over the previous record. Half the town's nearly 7,000 houses were ruined; martial law was declared. At Tell City it crested 17 feet above record stage, and more than half the town was destroyed. Leavenworth was so badly damaged that it completely relocated to higher ground. Previously it had been on a beautiful but dangerous river bight backed up against a cliff; waters raced in, hit the bluff, then raced back through. This town that was famed for its boatyard (it had never closed for a single day) lost over 60 homes; it had already begun to lose its importance as a river hub with the arrival of railroads, and this flood pretty much finished the job. Horrified crowds watched from bluffs as the waters swallowed up the towns of Jeffersonville and New Albany. Several relief workers died from flood-related disease.

One positive result was that the state thereafter seriously began looking at reforestation and flood control—as well as the interaction of humans and river—and constructed many dams and levees.

was perhaps more evenly drawn; it too focused on the experiences of Eggleston and his brother in the educational milieu of the region.

In Vevay, rejoin Highway 56 and continue southwest for 19 miles to Madison. Few communities show up along this stretch of the road. After passing through Lamb, a few appealing aeries appear to the right. Some intrepid travelers have reported commanding views (more than 10 miles) of the river valley from these imposing heights; of course, remember to respect all private property laws. What comes next is the linchpin of this stretch of the Ohio River in Indiana—the city of Madison, ensconced on a narrow peninsula between the river and some serious bluff rises.

The city was settled in 1805 on land purchased by John Paul, a Revolutionary War soldier who had fought in George Rogers Clark's campaign to control Vincennes, north of Evansville. Its prime location for river transportation encouraged a thriving shipbuilding industry and drew many workers; by 1850 the city had more than five thousand residents and was, for five wondrous years, the largest city in Indiana. It later became the eastern terminus of the first railroad west of the Allegheny Mountains, thus establishing itself as a gateway to the Northwest Territory.

The architecture is so well preserved that the city, in its entirety of 133 blocks, is listed on the National Register of Historic Places and has been dubbed "Prettiest Town" and "Best Preserved Town," among other superlatives bestowed by boatloads of national media. Stop at the *Madison Visitor Center,* 301 E. Main Street, (812) 265-2956; www.visitmadison.org, which has excellent walking tour brochures. If walking isn't your thing, on summer weekends a wonderful historic trolley tour takes in many of the attractions in town. And on Tuesday, Thursday, and Saturday mornings, the city hosts a lovely farmers market.

The *Lanier Mansion State Historic Site,* 511 W. First Street, (812) 265-3526, is an 1840s Greek Revival home designed for James F. D. Lanier, railroad baron. The city-block-long estate includes a restoration of a "cutting and necessary garden," along with perennials and dwarf fruit trees. Hours are 9 a.m.–5 p.m. Tuesday–Saturday, 1–5 p.m. Sunday; last tour departs at 4:30 p.m.

The *Madison Railroad Station and Historical Society Museum*, 615 W. First Street, (812) 265-2335, is housed in a restored 1895 railroad depot. Its prominent octagonal shape makes it a likely photo-op. In addition to historical railroad artifacts and exhibits is an antique caboose that can be clambered onto. Hours are 10 a.m.–x4:30 p.m. Monday–Friday, 1–4 p.m. Sunday, late April to Thanksgiving; reduced times rest of year. Admission.

The *Jeremiah Sullivan House*, 204 W. Second Street, (812) 265-2967, is considered Madison's first mansion and it features the only known restored Federal serving kitchen on record in the country. Jeremiah Sullivan was one of the original Indiana Supreme Court justices, a Presbyterian elder, and original local Mason, and he is credited with naming Indiana's capital "Indianapolis." Hours are 10 a.m.–4:30 p.m. Monday–Saturday, 1–4:30 p.m. Sunday, mid April–late October. Admission.

If you're not historically or architecturally oriented, a great recreation option exists. A mile west of town along the north edge of Highway 56 sits *Clifty Falls State Park*, (812) 265-1331, a superb park with more than 13 miles of challenging hiking trails that pass close to waterfalls and offer great views for wildlife watchers. Prominent hiking magazines rate these trails as some of the Midwest's best. Be very careful; some of these hikes are truly rugged. Of the ten trails, a personal favorite is Trail 10, because it's easy. Trail 1 is likely most popular since it leaves from the nature center. It also offers a wonderful photo-op, a 200-foot high escarpment called Devils Backbone. Four waterfalls draw thousands (and thousands and thousands) of shutterbugs. Equally impressive are the explosions of wildflowers in spring. For wildlife lovers, hawks abound here, along with hard-to-see black vultures. Even budding geologists will love the place. The park has a campground with reservable sites that sometimes are booked early and an inn for those not wanting to rough it. Both are popular places to stay.

The park's features were formed during the Ice Age when the south-flowing waters of Clifty Creek met the newer Ohio River in an enormous plunge, probably 200 feet high. Since then a two-mile-long cut has been formed through the 425-million-year-old shale and limestone. These formations were so daunting that they thwarted an attempt to build a railroad link from Madison to the Ohio River; dubbed "Brough's Folly" this quixotic project gives you an indication of what kind of geology you're dealing with here. *Clifty Canyon Nature Preserve* within the park contains some of southern Indiana's most precious plant and animal species. Fossil hunting is superb here but remember that all fossils are protected and none may be removed.

On the east edge of Madison, get on Highway 421 and head north for 25 miles to Versailles. This highway, with its multilanes and belching trucks, isn't as pretty as the river road, but it is geologically significant. You can even espy some of the 300 feet of sedimentary rock—Silurian dolomite and limestone—that underlie the region and helped make southern Indiana famous. In fact, the town of Versailles sits at the eastern edge of Indiana's karst region, a zone of freakish limestone sinkholes and upthrust. Totally fascinating! Abandoned limestone quarries can be found throughout the region.

The highway leads into the town with the lovely name, Versailles (pronounced "Vur-SAILS" locally). It's friendly enough but doesn't offer much in the way of aesthetics. A unique downtown attraction is the *Tyson United Methodist Church*, one block north of Highway 50 at the corner of Tyson and Adams Streets, (812) 689-6976. Ultra-modern and eclectic describe this church. A cast-aluminum, openwork spire rises more than 100 feet; all angles—roof, columns, corners—have been rounded; the interior was originally painted to resemble the sky; parts of the Taj Mahal have been emulated in the interior design. Wonderfully different.

The town hosts the wonderful *Versailles Pumpkin Show* the last weekend of September and a *bluegrass festival* the first weekend of September. Both are great fun!

From Highway 421 in Versailles, go east on Highway 50/129 a short distance to *Versailles State Park*. This sublime retreat, Highway 50 E, (812) 689-6424, offers a host of activities within its gently rolling hills. A 230-acre lake lies smack in the middle. These regions show the residual geological effects this area of Indiana is so famous for; the park sits at the west end of the Dearborn upland and affords good views of the shales, silts, moraines, and sinkholes, along with the limestone bedrock. Many trails trace these geological formations and provide an instant millennial primer. Lookouts grace the tops of ridges and provide an overview of this, one of Indiana's most popular parks. In autumn, almost unbearably resplendent in

The Rebels Are Coming

Versailles's moment in history came during the Civil War. In July 1863 Confederate troops under the command of General John Hunt Morgan rode throughout the area, looting and terrorizing the locals. After robbing a couple of stores in nearby Rexville, the armed men marched into town, threatened to raze the downtown area if the local militia put up a fight, and emptied the county treasury of its $5,000 (though other money had been buried), for loot to support the South's war effort. Or so they thought. The local help they expected for a drive toward Indianapolis never materialized, and the Confederates were mostly lost or captured in their doomed march.

riotous color, this is one of my favorite views in the world. You can even see lingering effects of the farmland that once was here.

If you're out to view wildlife, you've come to the right place: soaring hawks, turkey vultures, and more. Rare black vultures are also found here. One of the more precious wildlife species here is the gray fox; it's a gorgeous animal indeed. Rent a canoe and explore the creeks to get up-close glimpses of herons and other waterborne waterfowl. Fishing is good for bass and bluegill, and the odd channel catfish tastes pretty good fried up.

Note that the park's popular campground can get pretty crowded. Its 225 sites often fill up, so reservations are recommended. At the gate you're met by another piece of Indiana eye-candy: the 1865 *Busching Covered Bridge*. For hikers there are three moderately challenging trails. A personal favorite is Trail 1; it's less than 2.5 miles but passes through some of the park's great oddball topography and isn't too ambitious. If you've brought your bicycle you can hop on the 27-mile *Hoosier Hills Bicycle Route* nearby. The aforementioned lake is popular; rentals of canoes, paddleboats, and rowboats are available. You'll even find a swimming pool with waterslide.

Continue east on Highway 50/129 for approximately 9 miles to Highway 62 just east of Dillsboro, then turn right. A short distance south on Highway 62 brings you to the Red Wolf Sanctuary and Raptor Center, (812) 667-5303, which is operated as a refuge and rehabilitation center for animals indigenous to the Ohio River valley, including, among many other species, deer, mountain lion, red fox, great horned owl, and everyone's favorite, the eponymous red wolves—gray wolves are here, too. Reservations are required.

Quick Trip Option: This being Indiana, and thus hoops heaven, basketball aficionados will find an excellent side trip option. Approximately halfway between Versailles and Dillsboro, Highway 101 leads north from Highway 50/129 for 5 miles to Milan, a flyspeck community famous throughout Indiana (and now perhaps the world) for its 1954 high school basketball team. Coming from a high school of 150 students, this scrappy group went all the way to the state championships, where they knocked off a highly touted Muncie Central team—creating a frenzy in small burgs throughout the state and inspiring the Hollywood film *Hoosiers*.

The eye-catching spire of the Tyson United Methodist Church, Versailles.

Return to Highway 50/129 and go east on Highway 5/421 for about 11 miles back to Aurora, your starting point. For a bonus trip, you can continue for about three miles past Aurora to Lawrenceburg, home of the *Argosy Casino and Hotel,* (888) 771-1711, the world's largest riverboat casino, with more than 1,700 slot machines and an enormous 200,000-square-foot dining pavilion underneath the world's largest stained-glass dome. Northeast of town along Highway 1 are the ski slopes of *Perfect North Slopes,* 19640 Perfect Lane, (812) 537-3754; a dozen or so slopes of varying degrees of difficulty line the 70 acres. They offer a wide variety of package deals so you're sure to find one to suit you.

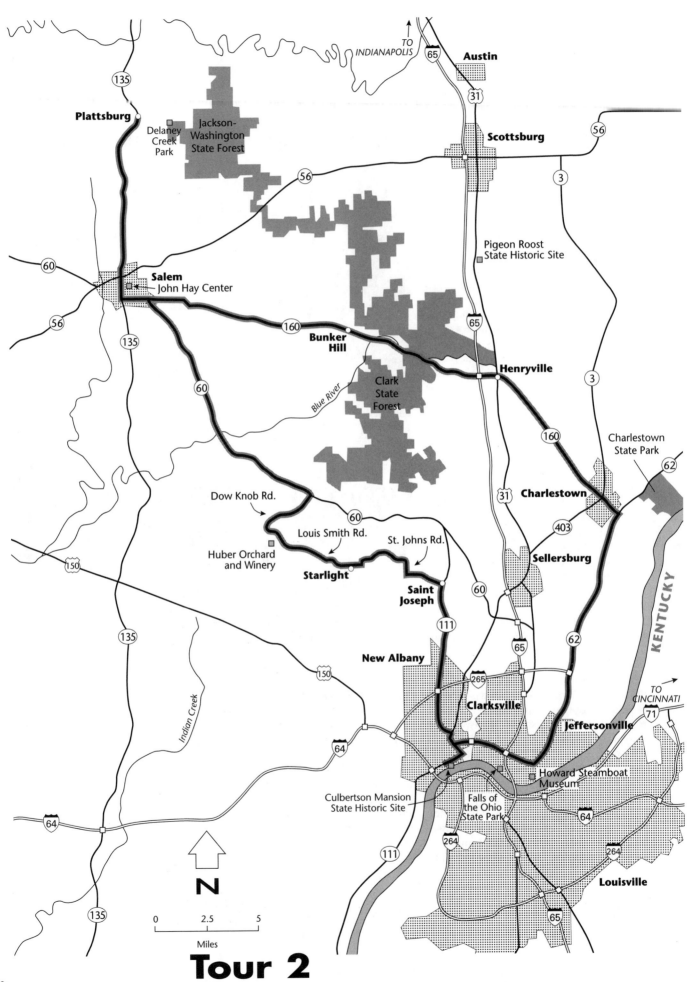

Austin

TO
INDIANAPOLIS

Plattsburg

Delaney
Creek
Park

Jackson-
Washington
State Forest

Scottsburg

Pigeon Roost
State Historic Site

Salem
John Hay Center

Bunker
Hill

Henryville

Blue River

Clark
State
Forest

Charlestown
State Park

Dow Knob Rd.

Louis Smith Rd.

Charlestown

St. Johns Rd.

Huber Orchard
and Winery

Starlight

Sellersburg

Saint
Joseph

New Albany

Clarksville

Jeffersonville

TO
CINCINNATI

Indian Creek

Culbertson Mansion
State Historic Site

Howard Steamboat
Museum

Falls of
the Ohio
State Park

KENTUCKY

Louisville

N

0   2.5   5

Miles

Tour 2

8

Tour 2
Rivers and Forests

Charlestown–Jeffersonville–Clarksville–New Albany–Starlight–Salem–Henryville–Charlestown

Distance: 91 miles

On this tour you'll experience both Ohio River ambience and Indiana's oldest state forest, offering unparalleled bucolic hiking and wildlife viewing. We start out in several of the classic river towns southern Indiana seems to specialize in. No less than 400 million years of geological time is on display at the Falls of the Ohio, one of southern Indiana's prime draws. We learn of steamboats and Louisville Sluggers, then of some backroom misdealings that took place in the area. We get a glimpse of history at sites dedicated to a figure in Abraham Lincoln's administration and to a battlefield. And don't forget that you're still rolling along the mighty Ohio River. The stretches along here aren't the most epic or lengthy, but they may be the most important, historically and geologically.

It's probably best to start this tour in Charlestown, 28 miles southwest of Madison. Charlestown appears to be a phlegmatic little town. It was settled after the turn of the nineteenth century and was the seat of Clark County from 1811 to 1878. It boomed in population and size in 1940 when the federal government contracted to build an enormous smokeless powder plant nearby. The $25 million contract went to E. I. du Pont de Nemours, and it was estimated that up to 5,000 people would find employment there. Real estate went through the roof, but the project never reached its potential.

Today it's the home of one of the state's newest state parks, the appealing and diverse *Charlestown State Park,* Highway 2E, (812) 256-5600. It surrounds the Fourteenmile Creek valley and has splendid vistas of the area from its 200-foot promontories. Freakish karst sinkhole topography is a rarity and worth a visit (hiking trails give access to Devonian fossil outcroppings); birders are drawn by the 75 species of birds including bluebirds, black vultures, and the occasional eagle.

Ohio River country at its best!

The campground has 59 first-class sites. Trail 3 has good local fishing access. You'll also find picnic areas, shelters, and a playground for the little ones.

Jonathan Jennings, first governor of Indiana (1784-1834), is buried in the local cemetery. Archaeologists say a ridge southeast of Charlestown was built as a battlement by a Mound Builder culture, but others say it was built by the Welsh in the twelfth century. According to local legend, after the Prince of Wales died in 1167, one of his sons found his way to the New World with a company of men. This "Madoc's Colony" used the embankment as a natural fort. Scientists dispute this, obviously, but several ethnologists have said that odd things give credence to the story: some Welsh cognate words have been found in Native American languages, Welsh armament has been found locally, and basket designs match Welsh designs. Furthermore, some locals claim that hunters discovered a tombstone with the date 1186. Either way, great stories.

Uncle Sam Was Here

Jeffersonville was the site of the nation's largest U.S. Army Quartermaster Depot, employing nearly a thousand people. Clothing and material for Army and CCC operations were manufactured here and distributed to Indiana, Kentucky, Ohio, West Virginia, Tennessee, Alabama, Louisiana, and Mississippi. In the Civil War it was the base from which all troops and supplies were shipped to points south of Louisville.

From Charlestown take Highway 62 southwest approximately 13 miles to downtown Jeffersonville. As you approach Jeffersonville, the signs that mark the River Road grow fewer and fewer, so that driving in Jeffersonville becomes confusing, but in time you will locate the destinations listed below.

Jeffersonville, seat of Clark County, is one of Indiana's earliest towns, and reportedly even Thomas Jefferson was consulted for its platting; it was named in his honor by William Nery Harrison. It was a major shipbuilding center until it first suffered the decline of its shipyards in the mid-1930s. The town was nearly destroyed in the epic 1937 flood (95 percent of Jeffersonville was under water, and horrified locals watched from bluffs as the town was inundated—national officials claimed no other city had suffered more). But Jeffersonville arose gritty and determined.

It was from here that James Howard launched his Hyperion steamboat in 1834 and what would become the primary local industry. Despite waning a bit, shipping remains crucial to the local economy; one company is a national contender in the business. Jeffersonville isn't the most attractive Indiana river town but it's currently undergoing a rejuvenation. Plenty of historic architecture exists downtown and you can gain a good appreciation of Ohio River history with a walk through the neighborhoods surrounding the city center. Louisville, Kentucky, across the river, does, however, overshadow it a bit. One local tidbit: Jeffersonville was the site of Indiana's first state prison.

For information about Jeffersonville and the surrounding area, stop by the *Southern Indiana Convention and Tourism Bureau Visitor Center,* 315 Southern Indiana Avenue, (812) 280-5566, www.sunnysideoflouisville.org. It's open 9 a.m.–6 p.m. Monday–Saturday, 1–4 p.m. Sunday. Right along the historic river road sits the city's main attraction—the *Howard Steamboat Museum,* 1101 E. Market Street, (812) 283-3728. This wearied but still imposing 22-room 1894 late Victorian mansion was built by later generations of the Howard family, magnates of local shipbuilding, and retains its windows of leaded glass and stained glass. The Howard family shipbuilding business, in continuous operation between 1834 and 1931, turned out some of the highest quality boats on the Ohio River. A huge array of shipbuilding memorabilia, including large pieces of century-old paddlewheels, is on display, along with family furnishings. Guided tours 10 a.m.–4 p.m. Tuesday–Saturday, 1–4 p.m. Sunday. Admission. The town fetes its shipbuilding heritage with *Steamboat Days* in early September.

While driving through town—always keeping your eyes on the road, of course—watch for the *world's second-largest clock* (as if you could miss it) at the Colgate-Palmolive Company. At 40 feet in diameter, it's enormous. But for sports fans like me, the best part of Jeffersonville is baseball. At 1525 Charleston/New Albany Pike is what could become a Mecca for fans of the boys of summer— *Hillerich and Bradsby Company,* (502) 585-5226, makers of the legendary Louisville Slugger bat. That's right, the epic stick of swat. It's a great slice of Americana and it's hard not to get chills watching those wondrous tools being created by artists of the craft. You'll find examples of summertime timber from legends of the game, past and present. Did you know that bats are generally made from 40-plus-inch boards of white ash? Or that only 10 percent make the grade? Or that an average major leaguer can use as many as 100 a year? And as more than one media outlet has pointed out, shouldn't the sticks of summer logically be called Jeffersonville Sluggers since operations have relocated here? Anyway, don't miss it, no matter what it's called or where it's located. Call for tour details or, better, to get directions to the Louisville burial place of the company founder.

From downtown Jeffersonville, head west along Market Street until it turns into West Riverside Drive and drive a short distance to Clarksville. (Keep your eyes peeled because this can be very tricky. If you get lost, backtrack to I-65 and exit at Exit 0, then head west on Riverside Drive.) Along West Riverside Drive in Clarksville is a splendid spot for exploring the Ohio River valley—the *Falls of the Ohio State Park,* 201 W. Riverside Drive, (812) 280-9970. This is the only spot along more than 900 miles of Ohio River where explorers had to portage. The 400-million-year-old Devonian fossil beds here are Indiana's only natural obstacle along the Ohio River. They cover 220 acres, have yielded some 600 fossil species—some of them the largest in the world—(and two-thirds of those are "type specimens," or fossils described for the first time (over 250 species of coral have been identified). Federally protected conservation lands pump up the total to nearly 1,500 acres and create a wonderful combination of geology education and wilderness in proximity to an urban area. More than 265 species of birds have been spotted; fishers will find 125 species of lunkers, including the primeval paddlefish. Even John James Audubon called this one of the places he treasured most in America; he made more than 200 sketches of 14 species here. And Mark Twain and Walt Whitman both wrote rapturously about the area.

An interpretive center (I like its life-size model of a woolly mammoth) has exhibits on the fossil beds. A loop trail traces wildlife west of the center. Numerous trails, from easy to very tough, cover more than 175 acres of the fossil beds. NOTE: If you hear a siren, get to a safe point as the dam will be opening and water levels will be rising. Even boat access is available for top-notch fishing. Late summer and fall are the best seasons to visit, generally August to October.

In 1778 George Rogers Clark established the first permanent English-speaking settlement in the Northwest Territory on Corn Island here. He would later found Clarksville in his name. His home site below the falls is now part of the state park. He died near Corn Island, impoverished. William Clark, his younger brother, set out from here with Meriwether Lewis to explore the Louisiana Purchase.

Clarksville was also the site of some real frontier blood and guts activity. Two members of the Kentucky legislature—Henry Clay and Humphrey Marshall—fought a duel on the west edge of Clarksville in 1808. Clay claimed he had been personally insulted and challenged Marshall to a duel. Not wanting to risk the marshal's wrath, they wisely moved to a site in Indiana. Each man fired one shot, received a wound . . . then called the whole thing off!

Head west out of Clarksville a very short way along Highway 111 to New Albany. (You can hardly tell where one ends and the other begins.) New Albany sits proudly across the Ohio River from Louisville, Kentucky, flanked by the Knobs, a grouping of bluffs some 150 feet high. As you drive these roads you'll be sweeping past impressive ledges and craggy outcroppings and looking at things some 500 feet below; you'll definitely give your engine and brakes a workout. New Albany shipyards rivaled those of neighboring Jeffersonville. Its speed demon steamships were said to be the best on the Ohio River; the most famous was the *Robert E. Lee.* It too was ravaged by the floods of 1937 (see the sidebar "The Ohio River" in Tour 1 for a brief summary of the devastation). Later, New Albany became an important glassmaking center.

For more information, go to the Southern Indiana Convention and Tourism Bureau Visitor Center (see the details in the earlier discussion of Jeffersonville) or the *Southern Indiana Chamber of Commerce,* 4100 Charlestown Road, New

Albany, (812) 945-0266. The town throws the fun *Harvest Homecoming* in the first week of October, one of the state's largest festivals.

Less than three miles from the Falls of the Ohio in New Albany is the grand *Culbertson Mansion State Historic Site,* 914 E. Main Street, (812) 944-9600. Built in 1869 in French Second Empire style, it was the home of local financier and philanthropist William Culbertson. The hand-carved three-story staircase is breathtaking and just one of many opulent details to be admired here. Hours are 9 a.m.–5 p.m. Tuesday–Saturday, 1–5 p.m. Sunday, mid-March to mid-December.

Also in New Albany is the *Carnegie Center for Art and History,* 201 E. Spring Street, (812) 944-7336. This local history museum-cum-contemporary art gallery features revolving exhibits and is the home of an intriguing folk art diorama. Hours are Tuesday–Saturday, 10 a.m.–5:30 p.m.; closed Sundays.

The Scriber House, State and Main Streets, (812) 944-7330, was built by a city founder and today it is filled with art, antiques, and memorabilia of two centuries. It dates from 1814 and is one of the oldest buildings in the city. Open by appointment only.

From New Albany go north on Highway 111 for 8 miles to the small community of St. Joseph. Initially you'll pass those imposing heights of the Knobs; they grow higher with each mile that clicks off after leaving New Albany, eventually rising nearly 500 feet.

At St. Johns Road in St. Joseph, turn left (west) and wind your way for about 7 miles to Louis Smith Road. Along the way, you'll pass through Starlight (population 600). Eventually you'll come to the *Forest Discovery Center,* 533 Louis Smith Road, (812) 923-1590. This award-winning center has an indoor forest, a theater, interactive exhibits, and a forestry product manufacturing tour. Kids love to step through the giant oak tree. Hours are 9 a.m.–5 p.m. Tuesday–Satur-

Misdeeds and Shady Dealings

Jeffersonville and Clarksville were sites of some local treachery involving duels, conspiracy, and even foreign intervention. Aaron Burr, vice president of the United States 1801–05, came to Jeffersonville two years after killing Alexander Hamilton in a duel. Like many good Americans looking to start again, if not flee the past, he went west and ended up in Jeffersonville, where he launched himself into a massive civic project involving building a canal around the Falls of the Ohio. Apparently he really was cooking up a plot to raise huge amounts of money to lead a quasimilitary campaign to annex Mexico. A member of Indiana's General Assembly, Major Davis Floyd, supplied boats and recruits for an "expedition." Most of the fleet was arrested in Jeffersonville as they prepared to leave; the rest made it to Natchez before they, including Burr, were arrested. Major Floyd was found to be unaware of the treasonous acts and was fined $20 and sentenced to an afternoon in jail.

day, from 1 p.m. Sunday. Admission. Also nearby stands a testament to the emigrants from German wine country who established vineyards here in 1843. Follow the signs to the *Huber Orchard and Winery*, (812) 923-9813, 19016 Huber Road, a 600-acre operation that includes one of the state's original vineyards, its award-winning winery, a cheese factory, petting zoo, and more. It is all great fun. Hours are 10 a.m.–6 p.m. weekdays, till 8 p.m. Saturday, till 6 p.m. Sunday, May–December; reduced hours rest of year.

Go north a short way to Dow Knob Road, turn right and go approximately 2 miles to Highway 60. Turn left (northwest) and cruise approximately 15 miles to Salem. This is one of the most historically significant cities in Indiana. It was founded in 1814 mostly by German settlers and named after Salem, North Carolina, birthplace of the wife of the first surveyor of the county. Salem also suffered at the hands of General Morgan's Confederate raiders (see Tour 1)—though they had presciently sent all their money out of town before the brigands arrived. The *Washington County Chamber of Commerce*, (812) 883-4303, www.blueriver.net/wcegp/tourism/, can provide more information.

The town is best known today as the birthplace of John Hay, author, statesman, and diplomat. He began his career as secretary to President Abraham Lincoln, served as ambassador to Great Britain and secretary of state under President Theodore Roosevelt, and was instrumental in maintaining relations with China during the Boxer Rebellion in 1900. He also wrote folk verse and a multivolume biography of Lincoln. Though he reportedly loathed Indiana (and the rest of the region), his hometown loves him. The *John Hay Center*, 307 E. Market Street, (812) 883-6495, is comprised of Hay's restored 1840s home, a historical museum, and a reconstructed pioneer-era village with a jail, general store, barns, and more. Hours are 1–5 p.m. Tuesday–Saturday. Admission. The town is also home to *Old Settlers Days* the second weekend in September, a great hootenanny of pioneer crafts.

From downtown Salem, head north on Highway 135 approximately 8 miles to Rooster Hill Road at Plattsburg. Turn right (east) and drive past Delaney Creek to Delaney Creek Park and Spurgeon Hollow Trailhead. Delaney Creek Park, part of the Jackson-Washington State Forest, is the northern trailhead for the 58-mile

Knobstone Hiking Trail, a splendid hiking experience that offers glimpses of what Indiana does best. The park has rugged hiking and an 89-acre lake. Five trailheads access the trail before it ends at Deam Lake just north of New Albany. In Delaney Creek Park, waterfowl predominates. Ospreys are everywhere. Ruffed grouse and deer are prevalent on the Knobstone Trail itself. This is a real treat.

Return to Salem on Highway 135 and go to Highway 60 on the south edge of town. Turn left (east) on 60, drive a short distance to Highway 160, and turn left. Cruise for about 12.5 miles to Clark State Forest. The trip is a bit monotonous at first, but after ten or so miles the land gets more aggressive and agrarian stretches turn into hills and forest. East of the town of Bunker Hill, you bisect the *Clark State Forest*, (812) 294-4306, Indiana's oldest state forest and originally an experimental station in restoring native Indiana pine. With its backpack area, backcountry camping, and nature preserves it's a prime spot for heading into the wilderness of southern Indiana. The isolated trekking through its 24,000 acres can be for the ambitious, as areas of escarpment rise dramatically over 1,000 feet. In addition, there are seven lakes for boating and fishing, an archery range, backcountry sites, shelters, and lots of hunting.

Continue southeast on Highway 160 for about 5 miles to Highway 31. You will pass through Henryville at the junction with I-65.

Quick Trip Option: For an interesting side trip, take Highway 31 north for less than 6 miles to *Pigeon Roost State Historical Site*, (317) 232-1637, where the last Indian-led massacre of settlers in Indiana occurred. Theories abound as to what led a band of Shawnee and Delaware to attack Pigeon Roost settlement in September 1812. The most accepted are simple local grievances involving white-native disputes; the most grandiose include anger over the Battle of Tippecanoe or even the War of 1812. Whatever the cause, 24 men, women, and children perished; only one expert marksman and his cabin survived. The victims are buried in one simple grave. Open dawn–dusk daily. Free.

From Highway 31, continue southeast on Highway 160 for another 8 miles or so and return to Charlestown.

Tour 3
Some Caves and a Capital

Corydon–Mauckport–Harrison-Crawford State Forest–Leavenworth–Marengo–Milltown–Corydon

Distance: 100.5 miles

Brief in mileage but heavy on political and Civil War history and cool spelunking, this tour could easily take most of a day. Some very, very back roads are thrown in, just for extra road trip fun.

The tour isn't so much a "loop" as it is a "figure 8"—due to the incredible shrinking rustic roads wending through Harrison County. If you're short on time, stick to state highways; otherwise, try some of the options that are mentioned.

History buffs love Corydon, to which the territorial capital was moved in 1816; it's one of the most popular historical sites in southern Indiana. More than 26,000 acres of state forest—one of the largest in the state—sit on the western edge of this tour, chock-full of varied recreation opportunities, including some worthwhile rustic hiking opportunities. Caves lace the bluffs surrounding Corydon, and two of Indiana's favorite attractions are here.

Start this tour in Corydon. Located west of Jeffersonville and just a bit south of I-64, charming and historically important Corydon served as the territorial capital from 1816 to 1825. The town reached the zenith of its political power in that first year as delegates flocked to the city to begin deliberations—to put it politely—to forge what would ultimately be a state constitution. It became known as the place where much of the state's "aristocracy," such as it was, lived. The land was once owned by William Henry Harrison, then a general who later became our ninth president. Someone else, alas, would plat the town. Harrison did get naming rights and called it Corydon after a character in his favorite song. I love this description from an early twentieth-century guidebook: "From its wide, shaded, and precipitously steep residential streets in the north and northeast sections, clean, dignified homes, most of them white frame or mellow old brick, look down on the level little business district with an air of aloofness."

It's all wonderfully preserved. To get pointed in the right direction stop by the *Harrison County Chamber of Commerce,* 310 N. Elm Street, (812) 738-2137 or (888) 738-2137, www.tourindiana.com, 9 a.m.-5 p.m. Monday-Saturday, from 1 p.m. Sunday. Particularly worthwhile are the walking tour maps of local historic sites and architecture. Just hanging out around the

Old Capitol Square is fun and makes one feel transported to a bygone day.

Corydon Capitol State Historic Site, Old Capitol Square on Capitol Avenue, (812) 738-4890, is among the best preserved historic sites in the state, and also one of the most popular. Construction of the original blue limestone building took two years; it was supposed to be the county courthouse, but the relocation of the capital necessitated its use by the legislature and, later, the supreme court. Across the street stands *Governor Hendricks's Home,* built in 1817 to house several local officials. Today it represents life in the region from different time periods, right down to period furnishings. Kids like the *Constitution Elm* outside the original capitol; it was here, shaded from a hot summer sun, that legislators hammered out the original structure of the state's charter. Hours are 9 a.m.-5 p.m. Tuesday-Saturday, and 1-5 p.m. Sunday, mid-March to mid-December; hours vary the rest of the year

An interesting bit of Civil War history can be viewed south of town along Business 135 at the

Corydon and the Civil War

Corydon was also the site of Indiana's only Civil War battle. Oft-mentioned in these parts are General John Hunt Morgan and his Confederate brigands, who descended on southern Indiana in an attempt to pillage and replenish Confederate coffers with northern loot. Under a waning moon on July 8, 1863, these raiders crossed the Ohio River and landed at Mauckport, Indiana. Attacking Corydon the following day, they met resistance from the city's militia; three locals were killed, along with eight of Morgan's men. The rebels held the town for a few hours. Despite the losses, Morgan's men were actually remembered for acting, well, gentlemanly while holding the town and emptying the pockets of local merchants! To save their factories, millers were each required to pay General Morgan $1,000; Morgan even returned $200 to one man who accidentally overpaid. According to one book, "A Confederate veteran, reminiscing years later at a reunion in Louisville, Kentucky, told of the 'enjoyable time' he had in Corydon during the raid. 'As we rode to the northwest corner of the square,' he recalled, 'we met two young ladies who we later learned were Emma Jones and Mary Mitchell. Upon being dared, they mounted behind a couple of boys and we decorated their hair with bolts of ribbon that trailed out behind them as we rode.'"

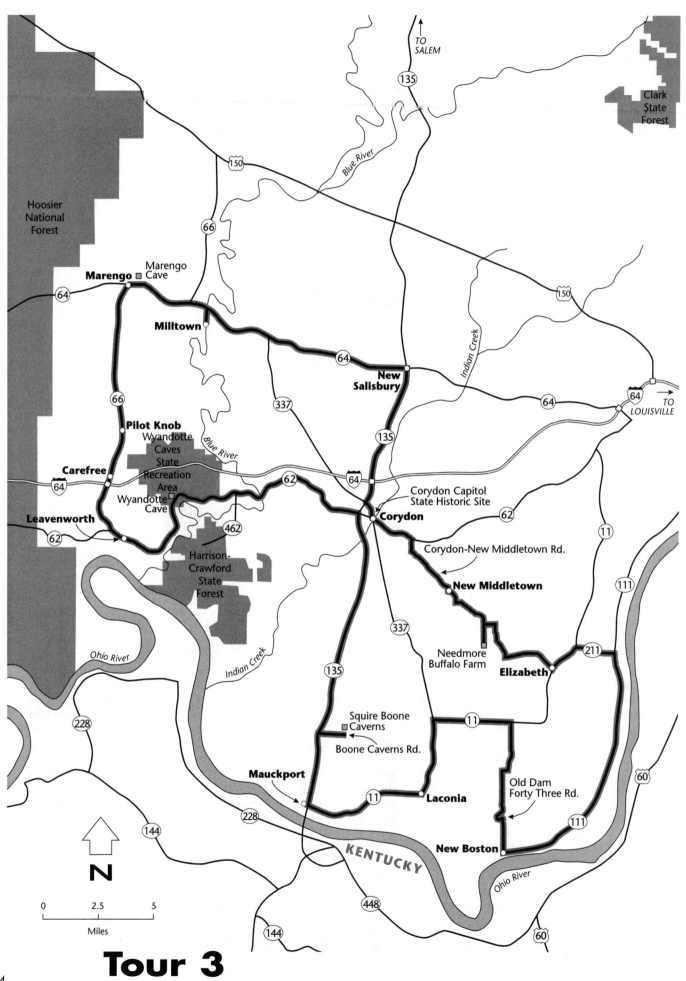

Marengo Cave

Marengo

Hoosier National Forest

Clark State Forest

TO SALEM

Blue River

135

150

66

Milltown

64

New Salisbury

337

Indian Creek

150

64

64

TO LOUISVILLE

66

135

Pilot Knob

Wyandotte Caves State Recreation Area

Blue River

Carefree

64

Wyandotte Cave

62

64

Corydon Capitol State Historic Site

Corydon

62

11

Leavenworth

62

462

Harrison-Crawford State Forest

Corydon-New Middletown Rd.

New Middletown

111

Indian Creek

337

Needmore Buffalo Farm

211

Elizabeth

Ohio River

Squire Boone Caverns

11

228

Boone Caverns Rd.

135

60

Mauckport

Old Dam Forty Three Rd.

144

11

Laconia

111

228

New Boston

KENTUCKY

N

448

Ohio River

60

0   2.5   5

Miles

144

Tour 3

Battle of Corydon Memorial Park. Travelers will find a mock-up of a period cabin, a real cannon from the skirmish, and a nature trail. It feels eerie to wander about the battlefield.

Another wonderful way to get into the countryside is to clamber aboard the *Corydon 1883 Scenic Railroad,* Water and Walnut Streets, (812) 738-8000, which operates narrated 90-minute tours through the surrounding countryside. Tours vary wildly in frequency, May–November, but generally you should figure on 1 p.m. (and sometimes 3 p.m.). The rolling hills, classic Indiana land, are gorgeous in autumn. The railway cars are even air-conditioned for your comfort.

One site that most folks completely overlook is the *Leora Brown School,* 400 E. Summit Avenue, (812) 738-3376, Indiana's oldest African American elementary/secondary school. Dating from 1891, it has been lovingly restored. Today it hosts cultural and community events; it also acts as a research and resource center. It's a unique look at African American life in southern Indiana.

An attraction of a different sort is the *Zimmerman Art Glass Company,* 395 Valley Road NW, (812) 738-2206. A generations-old company performs the painstaking processes of glassblowing, and visitors are welcome to watch artisans at work during business hours, 8 a.m.–4 p.m. Tuesday–Saturday. The family operation produces various glass items—from wind chimes to paperweights, all delicate and lovely.

If you're in town the third weekend in May, you can celebrate a local economic staple at the *Popcorn Festival.* I have always been a fan of county fairs and one of the most enjoyable is the *Harrison County Fair* in July, still going strong after nearly 150 years. *Old Settlers Day* on the Fourth of July takes travelers back to the original days of settlement with living history demonstrations and tons of cheery fun.

From Corydon, go east on Highway 62 a short distance, then turn right (southeast) on Corydon–New Middletown Road. Drive about 5 miles and look for the signs for the Needmore Buffalo Farm. (It may be tricky to see the turn for the farm, so be prepared to backtrack.) Along the way, you'll pass through New Middletown. The *Needmore Buffalo Farm,* 4100 SE Buffalo Lane, (812) 968-3473, is the site of the largest American bison herd in southern Indiana. Tours are

A view of the Ohio River from one of its many aeries.

available by request. A trading post displays bison wares, and at the restaurant you can down a delectable buffalo burger. You can also spend the night with the majestic creatures, as the farm is also a bed and breakfast.

Return to Corydon–New Middletown Road and cruise almost 4 miles to Elizabeth. If you're pressed for time but still want to experience more of the local flavor, head south on Highway 11 in a zigzag southwesterly direction to Highway 135, then continue north back toward Corydon. But if you want the more scenic ride and have time to spare, follow the route below, which parallels the Ohio River for about 12 miles.

At Elizabeth, turn left (east) on Highway 11 and then, after about 2 miles, veer east onto Highway 211; take that for 2 miles until it turns into Highway 111 south. This ribbony highway traces the Ohio River and passes some imposing bluffs towering up to nearly 800 feet. Otherwise, there's no pressing reason for this little excursion, but who needs a reason to take a side trip?

Follow Highway 111 for about 15 miles to New Boston, turn right (north) on Old Dam Forty-three Road, and go about 4.5 miles to Highway 11. Turn left on 11 and follow it west, then south through Laconia, then west again to Mauckport, a distance of about 13 miles. At Mauckport, you can take a break from the winding roads and sit back and again ponder history for a moment. It was here in 1863 that General Morgan and his men disembarked from com-

Southern Indiana—a region with a profusion of gorgeous wildflowers.

mandeered riverboats to lead the raid on Corydon. This is also one of the last glimpses of the Ohio on this tour, so you may want to linger here awhile.

From Mauckport, head north on Highway 135 for about 4 miles to Squire Boone Caverns Road; turn right and go east for approximately 3 miles. There you'll come to the *Squire Boone Caverns,* (812) 732-4381, a series of subterranean chambers discovered by Daniel Boone and his brother Squire in 1790. You can espy stones carved by Squire, see million-year-old stalactites and stalagmites, take the kids through a petting zoo, and see living history demonstrations of candle dipping, soap making, and the like. I was particularly fascinated to learn about rare rimstone dams. Note that a lot of climbing on steep, narrow staircases is required. A short nature trail leads from the cavern entrance; you can take it to Squire Boone's grave. Take a jacket, as those caverns can be chilly. Cavern tours depart every half-hour 10 a.m.– 5 p.m. during summer; at 10 a.m., noon, and 2 and 4 p.m. the rest of the year. Admission.

Return to Highway 135 and continue north for 10 miles; you'll be back just west of Corydon. At the junction with Highway 62, turn left (west). You'll immediately enter the *Harrison-Crawford State Forest,* at 26,000 acres one of the state's largest. Many travelers feel it's one of the most beautiful spots in Indiana and cannot understand why it's so underused. It's also an official state recreation area, so you're sure of finding something of interest. Hikers have nearly a dozen

trails just south of Highway 62 on Highway 462. Most are moderately difficult, but some have names like Adventure Trail that help you imagine what kind of path it's going to be. (The Adventure, by the way, is no picnic; it tops out at 22 miles.) A personal favorite is the Post-Oak Cedar Nature Preserve Trail, as it wends through protected lands along the eastern edge of the property. Gaze at it and recall that once much of Indiana—and the Midwest—looked just like that.

The campsites here are grade A; even a canoe campsite is accessible from Stagestop Campground. At one campground you'll find a nature center and an Olympic-size pool. Anglers love the Blue River for lunkers; the Ohio River isn't bad either. Be careful to get the scoop on fishing regulations; depending on where you are, you may need either an Indiana or Kentucky license. The Blue River, incidentally, is an official state Natural and Scenic River, and lots of hydrophiles come to set out in a canoe. No liveries are in the park, but several are nearby in Leavenworth. Milltown and Frederick are common put-in sites. Lots of hunters search the stands for turkey, deer, and squirrels.

Stop by the ranger office along Old Forest Road SW to pick up maps, especially for the trails. It's generally open 8 a.m.–4:30 p.m. While there, pick up a nifty auto tour map the forest has put out, in case you prefer to see the trees and critters from your car. You can also get information at the Hickory Hollow Nature Center near a funky old anachronistic church. The center has exhibits and informational brochures—this is one very well-stocked and well-informed place.

You probably didn't bring your own horse, but if you did you're in luck; this area has the best bridle trails in the state. Animal peepers and birders could not pick a better spot. Songbirds abound, including hummingbirds right outside the nature center. An overlook along the Ohio River is outstanding for watching hawks soar. Riverine areas will have plenty of ospreys and red-headed woodpeckers. Inland, you can even spot the tough-to-find kinglet. Note that the venomous copperhead is found in the park; it is against the law to bother any snake, not that you'd want to bother one of those! The nature center, again, is a good place to discover all you can about the area's biodiversity. Here I was amazed to learn that the white-tailed deer was actually eliminated from Indiana in the 1940s. A great and obviously successful program brought them back, as you can see driving in any county in the state.

Farther west along Highway 62 is a spelunking adventure—*Wyandotte Caves State Recreation Area,* 315 S. Wyandotte Cave Road, (812) 738-2782. Two caves actually form this natural complex. Used by prehistoric peoples for shelter originally and later by settlers looking for minerals, the caves are famed for several features, among them Monument Mountain—possibly the largest subterranean mountain in the world—and Pillar of the Constitution, a stalagmite larger than the Christmas tree at the White House. Several of these draws have made it into the *Guinness Book of World Records.*

A half-dozen tours are offered, ranging from brief and no sweat to a couple very strenuous all-day exploratory tours that are not for the large-boned, the out-of-shape, or the claustrophobic. The Little Cave Tour is a short, half-miler that takes about 45 minutes to get through a surface cave. It's $4 per adult. The perennially popular Big Cave tour starts just 700 feet north of the little cave and lets you look at the largest underground mountains of any U.S. caves. This 1.5-mile, two-hour tour features well-preserved helictites, which are rare twisted outcroppings. Note that pathways can be steep and in poor condition. The tour costs $5. You can also register for spelunking courses and tours. A three-hour introductory spelunking tour costs $7 per adult and you register in advance. They also have four-hour and eight-hour spelunking tours.

Continue west on Highway 62 to Leavenworth. This village has an interesting river history. Between 1843 and 1893 it was quite possibly the most prominent Ohio River community (at least till the railroads arrived). In 1937, the massive flood that hit the area inundated the village, which was unlucky enough to be at the base of an Ohio River bluff. Waters raged in, then doubled back off the bluff face. The gritty locals lost more than 60 homes and the rest, including those who hadn't lost homes, said that enough was enough and found this new spot, sufficiently elevated that they should never again have to worry about the mighty river vanquishing them.

Leavenworth offers an exceptional view of the river and is famed for the country cooking that goes on at the *Overlook* restaurant, (812) 739-4264. Across the road, at *Stephenson's General Store and Rivertown Museum,* you can get a deli sandwich or excellent ice cream while perusing historical photographs, many having to do with devastating floods that necessitated the entire community moving to higher ground.

Continue west on Highway 62 a short distance to Highway 66; turn right (north) on 66 and drive 12.5 miles to Marengo. Along the way, you pass through a couple of towns with names that are typical of these parts: Carefree and Pilot Knob. Just northeast of Marengo is yet another subterranean delight, a perennial favorite spot for families. *Marengo Cave,* (812) 365-2705, is a U.S. National Landmark and Indiana's number one natural attraction. The cave was originally discovered by intrepid schoolchildren in 1883; speleologists are still exploring its spacious interiors. Two organized tours take visitors either past delicate helictites and totem pole stalagmites or past flowstone formations. A third tour for the brave takes budding spelunkers into sections of the cavern not mapped out for tours. You can espy weird, primeval-looking species of fish gone transparent and blind in the lightless caves. Park areas outside offer canoeing, horseback riding, gemstone mining, a cave simulator, fishing, and more. An outdoor center offers climbing, obstacle courses, and simulated spelunking. The zip line is wildly popular. Hours are 9 a.m.–6 p.m. daily, Memorial Day–Labor Day, till 5 p.m. the rest of the year. Cave tours run every 30 minutes in high season. The park is free. The Crystal Palace tour of the monstrous chamber costs $10.50; remember it's only a third of a mile but it isn't the easiest access. The Dripstone Trail to see totem pole stalagmites costs $11.

Marengo is also a good spot for access to the Blue River, Indiana's original designated wild and scenic river. It's got awesome fishing and superb canoeing. Several outfitters in Marengo offer rentals and trips. If you're around in late October, the town's *Sorghum Festival* is a real hoot. It takes place in the local high school—gotta love that.

From Marengo, go east on Highway 64 for approximately 4 miles to Milltown. Just west of town is an enormous abandoned limestone quarry. Local officials seriously frown on exploration, but the catacomblike chambers, some have reported, are haunting . . . and huge. Explore at your own serious risk.

Continue east on Highway 64 for 12 miles to Highway 135; turn right and continue south to return to Corydon.

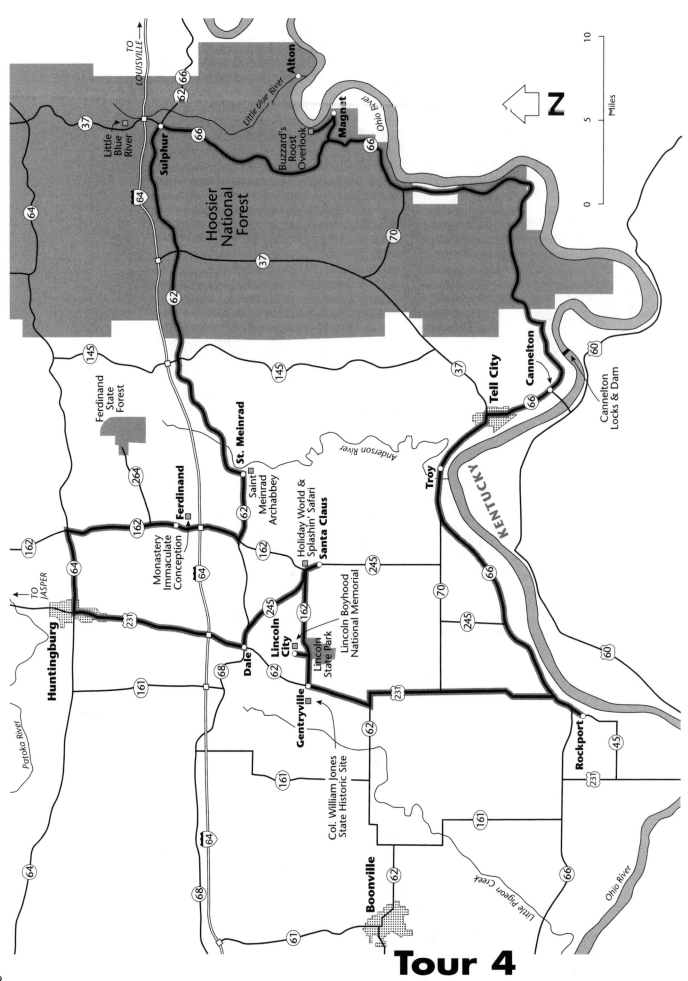

Tour 4

Tour 4
Land of Lincoln . . .
and Santa Claus

Dale–Santa Claus–Lincoln City–Gentryville–Rockport–Troy–Tell City–Cannelton–Sulphur–Saint Meinrad–Ferdinand–Huntingburg–Dale

Distance: 143.5 miles

What a difference a mile makes on this trip. With each click of the odometer a sight of a completely different sort appears—some serious U.S. history, some kitschy fun, some solemn spirituality. Even Jolly Old Saint Nick pops up for an appearance. You're also still near the Ohio River, so you've got a handful of miles of riverine history and natural splendor. And not just the Ohio River, either. We can exit the vehicle and paddle on the state's first Natural and Scenic River, the Little Blue River. The hills positively roll through these parts, and lots of our time is spent just idling away the miles between stops, as a good road trip should do. Add to that a hefty slice of Hoosier National Forest verdancy to meander through, and it adds up to a heck of a slice of Americana.

Start your trip in Dale, just south of exit 57 off I-64. Dale is a cheery little community with one unique draw: *Dr. Ted's Musical Marvels*, Highway 231N, (812) 937-4250. A bit hard to categorize, it is mostly a one-of-a-kind array of vintage mechanical music machines from the early nineteenth century to the mid-twentieth century. Great fun for music buffs. Hours are 10 a.m.–6 p.m. daily, 1-6 p.m. Sunday, Memorial Day–Labor Day; weekends only May and September

Also in Dale near the junction of I-64 and Highway 231 is *Fun Island,* (812) 937-2020, a kid's delight of a playground, to be sure. You'll find a giant maze, putt-putt golf, and a host of other kid-centric events. Mom and Dad better get in line and start unshackling the wallet and purse. Hours are 10 a.m.–10 p.m. daily, Memorial Day–Labor Day; reduced hours spring and fall. Admission.

If you're in town around the second and third weeks of September, visit the *Yellow Banks Craft Fair.* More than 300 craft and flea market booths spring up offering everything under the sun, including old-fashioned craft demonstrations.

From Dale, head east on Highway 62 for about 1 mile, then bear south on Highway 245 for 5 miles to Santa Claus. This diminutive little burg is one of the cheeriest places you'll visit in Indiana, and who wouldn't be cheery, given the name. Travelers from far and wide send their mail here around Christmas just to get it postmarked with the name of jolly ol' Saint Nick. This is the only place in the world where you can get a Santa Claus postmark!

Interestingly, when the town was platted in 1846, the name was purportedly going to be Santa Fe but Indiana already had a Santa Fe (who'da thunk it?). Since it was Christmastime, somebody joked, "How about Santa Claus?" And the rest is ho-ho history. During the Christmas rush, literally millions of cards and letters descend on the tiny post office, whose postmaster must be a saint. Santa Claus Park in town has a smiling statue of Saint Nick, not that you could miss him anywhere. Obviously, the visage and the name of everyone's favorite holiday gift-giver is everywhere. Local shops and restaurants are quaint too; it's a good family stop. For more information on the rotund one, contact the *Spencer County Visitors Bureau,* (888) 444-9252, www.legendaryplaces.org, in the post office building.

If this isn't enough, families can flock to the cacophony of the huge *Holiday World Theme Park and Splashin' Safari Park*, at the junction of Highways 162 and 245, (812) 937-4401. This rollicking place has themed areas featuring Christmas (of course), the Fourth of July, and other holidays. Adrenaline-inducing amusement park rides predominate (the whitewater log flume ride is a personal favorite); the Legend rollercoaster is Indiana's largest, and the Raven has been ranked by mavens as the Midwest's number one wooden coaster. There are other attractions, such as live music shows, a high-dive show, wax museum, and many more. A water park features lots of kid-centric waterslides and pools. Hours are 10 a.m.–dark daily during summer, reduced hours other times. Admission.

From Santa Claus, head west on Highway 162 for about 5 miles to the Lincoln City area. Set among the trees is a site every American could feel drawn to. The *Lincoln Boyhood National Memorial,* Highway 162, (812) 937-4541, marks the homestead of Abraham Lincoln and his family from 1816 to 1830. Here he lived until age 21, when, with a glorious future ahead of him that he could not have imagined, the family decamped for Illinois. His sister is buried in a local Baptist church. When the family arrived from Kentucky, Lincoln's father planned to clear 160 acres, but in the end he cleared far fewer. The elder Lincoln did odd jobs for locals and eventually returned to Kentucky and married the woman he had courted many years earlier. They returned to Indiana and Abraham took to her well. She ran an organized household and encouraged education. Abe wasn't good at math and attended school for only about a year of his life, but he took an interest in his new mother's library, which ranged from the Bible to *Pilgrim's Progress* and *Robinson Crusoe*. He would later borrow copies of Indiana law books, and we all know the rest of that story.

The *Memorial Visitor Center* has excellent exhibits on the Lincoln family and the life they hewed out of the wilderness. Many fascinating displays focus on young Abe's personal life. A half-hour film offers an excellent glimpse of the man as a boy.

Surrounding the center are 80 acres of the original homestead; these are still worked as a living history museum, complete with log cabin, privies, split-rail fences, and chickens. One interesting local tidbit: it appears Abe was well liked and did just enough work to have people like him, as if rumors of his work ethic have been greatly exaggerated. Nearby is the original family log cabin site. Two miles of trails snake through the woods. It was a pretty grim existence, to be sure. The family slept together on a dirt floor and hygiene was absolutely horrible, even when spruced up nearly two centuries later. Lincoln's mother, Nancy, died of a horrible illness called "milk sick" in 1818. Her own foster parents had died of it a week earlier, and it killed many locals in the region. She was buried in what is now *Lincoln State Park*, across the street from the visitor center, and it's a haunting walk to her gravesite along a quiet path.

The Lincoln Boyhood National Memorial is open 8 a.m.–5 p.m. daily, May–September. Admission. The Memorial Center is open 8 a.m.–5 p.m. daily. Admission. Combined tickets are possible.

Also in Lincoln State Park is the *Lincoln Amphitheater*, site of *Young Abe Lincoln*, a wildly popular outdoor musical drama tracing the life and times of Lincoln the adolescent. Other musicals are

Young Abe

An incident occurred near Troy, Indiana, that, according to anecdotal evidence, sparked Abe Lincoln's interest in the legal world. Young Abe worked for a nearby merchant and also constructed his own boat to ferry passengers across the Ohio River. This activity landed him in court, as a competing Kentucky ferryman complained that Lincoln had been operating sans license. Lincoln shrewdly argued that he had taken passengers only to midstream, where he off-loaded them onto passing boats, which didn't constitute crossing the river; thus, no ferry activity had taken place and no license was necessary. Impressed, the judge looked over the statutes governing high and low tides, which determined state boundaries, and, determining that Lincoln had already perused them carefully, found him not guilty.

presented throughout the summer as well. Great fun!

Continue west on Highway 162 for 2 miles to Gentryville and turn left (south) on Highway 231. In town, watch for signs for the *Colonel William Jones State Historic Site,* which is on Boone Street, a mile west of Highway 231, (812) 937-2802. This Federal-style mansion was the home of jack-of-all-trades Colonel William Jones, a merchant/farmer/politician/soldier who lived here and befriended Abraham Lincoln (young Abe did odd jobs in the Jones general store), to whom he remained close throughout his life before falling in battle in Atlanta in 1864. Lincoln stayed in the house in 1844 while campaigning for Henry Clay. The site also includes a walking trail, gardens, 100 acres of forest, and an original rough-log barn. Hours are 9 a.m.–5 p.m. Wednesday–Saturday, 1–5 p.m. Sunday, mid-March to mid-December. Free.

Return to Highway 231 and continue south for 16 miles to Rockport. This gritty little river town seems to offer little, but it has another connection to our most famous president. Right downtown in Rockport City Park is *Lincoln Pioneer Village and Museum,* (812) 649-2615. The buildings are not originals but reconstructions faithful down to the last detail of period dwellings. Lots of artifacts pertaining to local history are displayed here. Among the most intriguing is a hutch made by Abe Lincoln's father and a 1598 Bible. I also enjoyed the perhaps-apocryphal stories of how pirates lurked locally in limestone quarries, waiting to rob passing flatboats.

From Rockport, go north on Highway 231, then east on Highway 66 for 16 miles to Troy. There isn't a lot of eye-catching scenery along the way, but after a while you start to see signs of city life again, where the Ohio River bends precipitously to the south. In Troy you can trace the path of Father Joseph Kundek, a Catholic priest who founded numerous parishes in southern Indiana in the 1830s and 1840s. The statue *Christ of the Ohio* stands 75 feet above the roadway. Commemorating the good father, it was created during World War II by a German sculptor who was a prisoner of war at the time.

Continue southeast on Highway 66 for 4.5 miles to Tell City. This riverside town was named for legendary William Tell, of apple-on-the-head fame. Founded by Swiss Germans, the town was originally planned for a population of nearly 100,000, a goal that was never reached, not even close. One thing you do notice is that the streets are wide and incredibly long. Tell City is known throughout Indiana for its pretzels—seriously! You can get luscious, hand-twisted pretzels, following time-honored Swiss tradition. People actually buy them by the bucketful. Then head downtown

Tell City's statue of forefather William Tell (try the pretzels).

along Main Street to get a gander at the bust of William Tell before a fountain opposite the county courthouse. Stop by the *Perry County Convention and Visitors Bureau*, (812) 547-7933, www.perrycountyindiana.org, for the lowdown on the William Tell connection.

Two fun festivals locally are the *Dogwood Festival*, the last weekend in April, and the *Hoosier Heritage Fall Tour*, weekends in October, when different counties are highlighted. Great auto tour guides of the area are also available.

Continue east on Highway 66 for 4 miles to Cannelton. Here you'll find one of southern Indiana's most imposing historic landmarks. The small town has an impressive assortment of historic structures; detailed walking tour brochures are available. The grand dame here is the enormous *Cannelton Cotton Mill*. For more than a century before it closed in the 1950s, this mill was one of Indiana's economic linchpins. Once a gleaming jewel of state industry—for a time it was the most advanced factory in Indiana and the largest industrial building west of the Alleghenies—it now sits, a forlorn, monstrous hulk. The five-story building is dwarfed by 100-foot twin towers, which still are used as navigational aids along the Ohio River.

Continue east on Highway 66 a short distance. After a few minutes of twists and turns, you'll come to the *Cannelton Locks and Dam,* a U.S. Army Corps of Engineers project. There's a parking area and overlook of this impressive project. Glance up at the sheer cliff faces. You may notice water sprinkling down. This water provided sustenance to no less than the Lincoln family, who landed here on their way north. Marquis de Lafayette, the French hero of the American Revolution, was forced to camp here when his steamboat ran into rocks. No one drowned but Lafayette lost everything, including about $8,000 in gold.

Continue on Highway 66 for about 40 zigzag miles until you see the sign for the town of Magnet. There's not a lot here other than twisty, serpentining roads between the lush greenery of the Hoosier National Forest and the Ohio River. For a quick diversion, pull into any of the roads leading into this wonderful—and enormous—national treasure. Keep your hands on the wheel and your eyes peeled for deer. You'll have plenty of ups and downs and even pass a couple turnoffs for wildlife viewing.

At the road to Magnet, turn right and drive east for about 1 mile. Turn left (north) on County Road 27 and go about 3 miles, following the signs to the *Buzzard's Roost Overlook*. This U.S. Forest Service lookout, (812) 547-7051, provides lovely vistas of Kentucky and the Ohio River. Best time to come is in fall. Hawks are absolutely everywhere. You can explore the 80 acres surrounding the overlook and go birding.

Return to Highway 66 the same way you came and continue north about 10 miles to Sulphur. As you approach Sulphur, you pass through Sulphur Springs, which was once a popular health resort; today it lies decayed in the weeds.

Quick Trip Option: One mile north of Sulphur is the access to the gorgeous Little Blue River, one of the state's most precious resources. One especially scenic stretch runs south 14 miles to the town of Alton (which also has access) along the Ohio River. Along the route you can see ducks and herons, as well as Carolina wrens. The dense shoreline verdancy is extraordinarily lovely. For information, contact the local Sulphur office of the U.S. Forest Service, (812) 547-7051. (If you want to access from Alton, travel north from Alton—it's tiny—to a crossroads; go right about a mile.)

At the junction of Highway 66 and Highway 62 in Sulphur, head west on 62 for about 21 miles to Saint Meinrad. You'll roll through some of southern Indiana's loveliest roads. The road alternately zips between alleys of trees and then past entire meadows of wildflowers. It's tiny, it's two-lane, it's winding, it's grand. Enjoy!

In Meinrad, you'll learn that the *Saint Meinrad Archabbey,* Highway 62, (812) 357-6585, was founded in 1854 by Swiss and German immigrants as a retreat and learning center for Benedictine monks. The magnificent abbey is one of only seven like it in the world. It's hard to miss its soaring, almost hopeful, twin spires as you come around a bend and behold the hillside upon which the abbey sits. Travelers are often surprised to wander the grounds and discover that neither are the monks silent nor is the place heavy hearted. Monks may speak (observing strict rules regarding time and place, so please be sensitive), and in fact enjoy company, and the abbey maintains lively business activities—even a pizzeria! Wandering the grounds—which includes a college and theological seminary—inspires reflection and makes for an excellent, inspirational break.

Continue west on Highway 62 for 4 miles to Highway 162; turn right (north) and go for 4 miles to Ferdinand. If you are interested in more monastic life, be sure to visit the *Monastery Immaculate Conception,* 802 E. Tenth Street, (812) 367-1411. It is among the largest monasteries for Benedictine women anywhere (so large that locally it's known as the Castle on the Hill), and people often visit just to take in the magnificent Romanesque architecture. The 190-acre complex includes an inspiring domed church, grotto, outdoor stations of the cross, retreat center, and girls boarding school. The pews were hand carved in Oberammergau. The stained glass windows are particularly lovely. Tours are available and an information office has historical displays and exhibits on the facilities.

While you're in the area, consider a side trip (go north another mile or so, then east on Highway 264) to the *Ferdinand State Forest,* (812) 367-1524. Established in 1934 as a Civilian Conservation Corps camp, the 7,650 acres of forest and lakes have boat launches, cultural arts programs, fishing, hunting, hiking trails, and rentals of canoes and rowboats.

From Ferdinand, go 6 miles north on Highway 162 to Highway 64; turn left (west) and drive 5 miles to Highway 231 in Huntingburg. Huntingburg is picturesque and has a nicely restored downtown. These days it's known as Little Hollywood or Hollywood of the Midwest because Huntingburg's League Stadium was used to film the movies *A League of Their Own* and *Soul of the Game,* while the Fourth Street Shopping District was used to film *Hard Rain.*

Head south on Highway 231 for 10 miles to return to Dale.

Tour 5
Communes and Steamboats in Indiana's "Pocket"

Evansville–Newburgh–New Harmony–Owensville–Princeton–Evansville

Distance: 107.5 miles

There's more wonderful diversity in store for you in this drive through the far southwestern slice of Indiana, known as the Pocket. With a pair of the state's most perfectly preserved steamboat communities along the Ohio River and an almost breathtaking example of communal development, this tour certainly brings together disparate elements for an engaging tour. Don't forget that you're still along the Ohio River, so you've got lots of options for exploring great riverine stretches of beauty. If there were one tour that offers the most Indiana history, this may be it.

Start your tour in downtown Evansville. This city of about 125,000 residents is one of Indiana's great old riverboat enclaves and one of the best examples of the genre that we'll be seeing on our tours. Located halfway between the Falls of the Ohio and the river's mouth, it was strategically located and is blessed with one of the best natural harbors for U.S. river traffic. This beneficial geography and topography allowed it to rise in prominence as steamboat traffic rose in importance to U.S. commerce in the nineteenth century; it would become Indiana's fifth-largest city, though it rarely feels *that* big. The old 1940s-era WPA guidebook on Indiana precisely described it as "a link between the unhurried Old South and the bustling, industrial North." It's a not-inappropriate description today. It was devastated in the epic 1937 flood, and this after a 1913 deluge flooded the city. On January 30, 1937, floodwaters raged to levels above 54 feet. Nearly half of the city was covered with fetid floodwater and over 10,000 homes were destroyed, causing some $30 million in damage, certainly a princely sum for 1937. Several relief workers died from flood-related sickness. An enormous levee was constructed to protect against future floods.

The city does spread a long way through its western suburbs, but the downtown is quite compact. Loads of nineteenth- and twentieth-century structures line the streets bordered by the Lloyd Expressway (Highway 66), Riverside Drive, Mulberry Street, and Eighth Street. In fact, 63 buildings are architecturally significant, ranging from the 1848 Greek Revival Carpenter House at 405 Carpenter Street (it now houses public radio and TV stations) to the 1938 Art Deco Greyhound bus ter-

minal. The city *Visitor Center,* 401 SE Riverside Drive, (812) 421-2200 or (800) 433-3025, www.evansvillecvb.org, has a fantastic guidebook for a walking tour. Hours here are 9 a.m.–5 p.m. daily.

Ask at the office about the *Pigeon Creek Greenway Passage,* Evansville's 2-mile segment of a 42-mile greenway/bikeway being constructed in the county, connecting to the American Discovery Trail. If you're here in the last weekend of June and July 4, show up for the *Evansville Thunder Festival,* with a range of events packaged around hydroplane races on the river. Also, the third weekend in May and second weekend in September there are huge crafts fairs in town, with more than 400 booths at two locations. It's huge!

First stop for many architecture aficionados is the *Reitz Home Museum,* 224 S.E. First Street, (812) 426-1871, the only Victorian you'll actually be able to step inside of. Built in 1871 by a wealthy lumberman, this French Second Empire structure features ornate furnishings and decorations—ornate even by most Victorian standards, down to the magnificent, intricate parquet floors (perhaps not unexpected in a mansion built by someone known as the lumber baron). Hours are 11 a.m.–3:30 p.m. Tuesday–Saturday, from 1 p.m Sunday. Admission.

Near the visitor center is the second stop for most folks, the *Evansville Museum of Arts and Science,* 411 S.E. Riverside Drive, (812) 426-2406, which has a permanent collection of fine arts specializing in still life, landscape, genre, and figurative and allegorical works. Two other chambers offer changing exhibits. Excellent is *Rivertown USA,* a re-creation of a nineteenth-century river village. Newest to the museum is the Transportation Center, detailing the history of transportation in southern Indiana since the early 1800s. Families will find lots of hands-on activities for kids. Hours are 10 a.m.–5 p.m. Tuesday–Saturday, from noon Sunday. A planetarium has weekend shows at 1 and 3 p.m. Admission to the museum is free; planetarium shows charge admission.

Families also like *Mesker Park Zoo and Botanic Gardens,* 2421 Bement Avenue, (812) 435-6143. Over 70 acres of rolling hills are a children's zoo, walk-through exhibits (butterfly and train exhibits are popular), paddleboats, and an

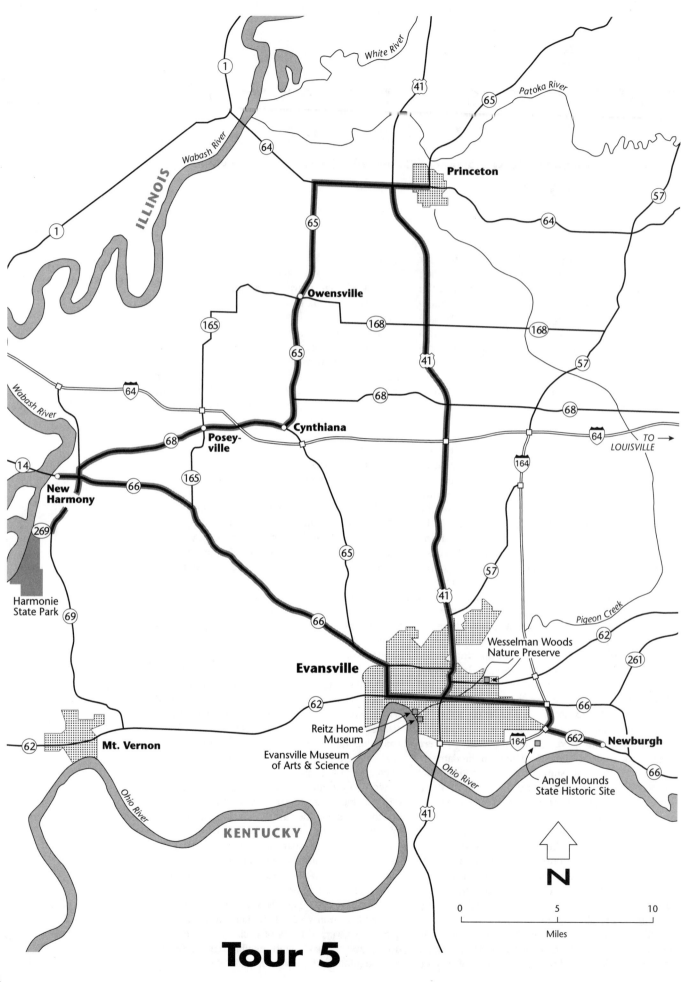

ILLINOIS

White River

① 1

Wabash River

④ 64

⑥ 41

Patoka River

⑥ 65

Princeton

⑤ 57

⑥ 64

⑥ 65

Owensville

⑥ 168

⑥ 168

⑥ 165

⑥ 65

⑥ 41

⑤ 57

Wabash River

□ 64

⑥ 68

⑥ 68

⑥ 68

⑥ 64

TO → LOUISVILLE

⑥ 68

Posey-ville

Cynthiana

① 14

⑥ 66

⑥ 165

New Harmony

⑥ 164

⑥ 269

⑥ 65

Harmonie State Park

⑥ 69

⑥ 66

⑤ 57

⑥ 41

Pigeon Creek

Wesselman Woods Nature Preserve

⑥ 62

Evansville

⑥ 261

⑥ 62

⑥ 66

Reitz Home Museum

⑥ 164

⑥ 662

Newburgh

⑥ 62

Mt. Vernon

Evansville Museum of Arts & Science

Ohio River

Angel Mounds State Historic Site

⑥ 66

⑥ 41

Ohio River

KENTUCKY

N

0   5   10

Miles

Tour 5

24

excellent Discovery Center that educates visitors on the crucial nature of ecosystems. More than 700 animals are found on site, including some that are quite rare. Hours are 9 a.m.–4 p.m. daily, with extended weekend and holiday hours. Admission.

More nature awaits at the *Wesselman Woods Nature Preserve*, (812) 479-0771, 551 N. Boeke Road, which has a lovely 200-acre spread of virgin bottomland hardwood with marked nature trails and an adjacent park—perfect for a family picnic. It's also good for a secluded walk. Birders will find hordes of songbirds (over 130 species are found within the park's acreage) and the wildflowers explode in spring. The site in its entirety is designed to resemble the Midwest before settlement. Stop by the nature center for an up-close education on birding and other wildlife on site. Small animals abound; you may even see coyotes and deer. Hours are 6 a.m.–7 p.m. Tuesday–Sunday in summer, 8 a.m.–4 p.m. at other times.

The oldest public library in Indiana, the *Willard Library*, 21 First Avenue, (812) 425-4309, has outstanding genealogical collections, with over 60,000 volumes. Hours are 9 a.m.–8 p.m. Monday-Tuesday, 9 a.m.–5:30 p.m. Wednesday-Friday, 9 a.m.–5 p.m. Saturday, 1–5 p.m. Sunday.

Standing solemnly on the banks of the Ohio River is *Angel Mounds State Historic Site*, 8215 Pollack Avenue, (812) 853-3956. One of North America's best-preserved prehistoric Native American settlements, it dates from approximately A.D. 900 to 1200, when up to 3,000 people occupied the settlement. The 103 acres include 11 earthen mounds (used as elevated structures, not for burial). At its zenith, the complex was the epicenter of Mississippian culture for a 50-mile radius.

Downtown Evansville isn't particularly attractive, but it's sprucing itself up nicely. If it's a gentrified Ohio River town you're looking for, head east.

From downtown Evansville, go east on Highway 62 a short distance to its junction with Highways 66 and 41. Continue east on Highway 66 for 5 miles to I-164. Head south on I-164 for 1.5 miles to Highway 662. Turn east and go 2.5 miles into the town of Newburgh. This community is one of those little road trip gems, a visual delight usually seen only in imagination or on postcard images that rarely match reality. Settled in 1803, Newburgh was originally called Sprinklesburg (great name, no?). One intriguing note is that it was actually taken over by Confederates during the Civil War, one of the few places north of the Ohio River to experience battle. It underwent the usual boom-bust cycles of river towns, but today a tiny, carefully gentrified section of downtown boasts restaurants, shops, and another opportunity for perusing historic structures. The areas bordered by Jennings, Water, and State Streets are most popular for architectural strolling (most buildings bear self-explanatory plaques); stop by the *Visitor Center*, 9 W. Jennings Street, (812) 853-2815 or (800) 636-9489, for a free walking tour brochure. It's an ambitious and friendly operation. A more recent U.S. Army Corps of Engineers lock and dam system is also nearby, with viewing platforms overlooking Ohio River traffic. The entire river walkway is a personal favorite in Indiana.

From Newburgh, go west on Highway 662 and backtrack to Highway 66. Turn left (west) on Highway 66 and proceed through, then past Evansville for 28 miles to New Harmony. At first the landscape seems unimpressive, unchallenging. Perfect, because it understates what's about to come. You've left behind the Ohio River country and are about to enter another, wholly different country—the Wabash River region, the southern terminus of the Indiana Wabash River Heritage Corridor, which stretches north and northeast to Fort Wayne and beyond. This "Avenue of the Midwest" rivaled the Ohio and Mississippi Rivers as one of the most crucial to U.S. expansion. (See the sidebar on the river in Tour 6.) Along this route you can find some extraordinary riverine scenery and some of Indiana's most important architecture.

Thirty miles west of Evansville you come upon the small, beautiful, and subdued town of New Harmony. It's been dubbed "Athens of the West" because for nearly two centuries it's been a place to rejuvenate oneself spiritually and mentally. Early guidebooks noted its lovely "gate" trees, imported from China and Korea early in the century. For anyone who has spent a great deal of time in China—and even for those who haven't—these are gorgeous things to behold in the Midwest.

In 1814 a religious communal group from Germany under the leadership of George Rapp purchased 20,000 acres along the Wabash River. (Early books called his beliefs "Christian communism"— not a bad way to describe it.) An experiment in community planning, it was designed to perfect social reform. The community was a world leader in an effort to support equal rights for women and ethnic minorities and education for all. The Rappites cleared forests, platted a town and outlying farms, and established a trading center. This was no mean feat: the swamps and spinneys of forests in the area were some of the most formidable in the Midwest; somehow they persevered. A decade later the community, then called Harmonie, was purchased in its entirety by Scottish philanthropist Robert Owen. Leading scientists, artists, intellectuals, explorers, and various other cultural experts came in droves to study this experiment in utopian social planning. The community had profound effects. Some claim that Robert Owen was the first nineteenth-century critic of capitalism and that Karl Marx and Friedrich Engels learned from the community's ultimate failure to find perfection. An apt quote from Engels: "Every social movement, every real advance in England on behalf of the workers, links itself on to the name of Robert Owen."

These were lofty goals indeed, especially given the rough land surrounding the perfect little community. The eclectic populace that had descended on the town wasn't quite sure what to expect, or what was expected of them. Instead of a new moral order two years later, a bit of disorder reigned, and the little utopia that could foundered. However, it didn't blow away. Owen's sons stayed on and were in part responsible for an ember of cultural and intellectual activity that continued on. The community and its members did succeed in making grand contributions to social equality, women's suffrage, and higher education. (For example, Owen's son founded and led the U.S. Geological Survey from here.) Alas, even his sons had to admit in an editorial in a local paper that the grand experiment had failed. Still, it did influence—and even spawn—other communal experiments in the U.S.

The most logical place to start a visit to New Harmony is at the *Atheneum*, two blocks north of Highway 66 on Arthur and North Streets, (812) 682-4474, www.newharmony.evansville.net or www.newharmony.org. This sleek, chic white edifice rises from the plain on the western edge of town. Its ultra-modern design reflects the progressive spirit of the two communities. Acting as the visitor center, the Atheneum offers short films and

Feeding the animals in rural Indiana.

biographical exhibits giving an overview of the planned communities. You can even get an up-close look at a large replica of the town as it looked in the 1820s. Docent-led tours depart from here throughout the day; ranging from one to three hours, they are highly recommended. They begin with a video presentation at the Atheneum and proceed to local historical structures. They are generally offered 9 a.m.–5 p.m. daily, April–October, shorter hours the rest of the year.

The *roofless church,* North and Main Streets, (812) 682-4431, a nonsectarian open-air worship site designed by Philip Johnson, has a wonderful cedar shake dome and understated landscaping. The Jacques Lipchitz sculpture *Descent of the Spirit* is a focal point. Designed in 1960, it's a remarkably modern place but one that retains a palpable sense of the long-ago community that inspired it. It's open 24 hours daily and is highly recommended.

The *New Harmony Gallery of Art,* 506 Main Street, (812) 682-3156, has rotating exhibits of modern art. Hours are generally 9 a.m.–5 p.m., Tuesday–Saturday.

Another intriguing few hours could be spent exploring the *Labyrinth,* a restored maze of hedges on the southern end of town that symbolically reflect the turns we confront in our lives.

The *Workingmen's Institute,* 407 W. Tavern Street, (812) 682-4806, is housed in what was one of the first free public libraries in the United States. Today it houses artifacts and manuscripts from the two utopian communities. Also on the premises are an art gallery with revolving exhibits, natural science displays, a library, and archives. It's open 10 a.m.–noon Tuesday–Saturday and 1–4 p.m. Sunday. Admission.

The *New Harmony Theatre* downtown has summer-stock drama and musical productions in summer that are great fun.

Drive south on Highway 69 for 4 miles to Highway 269; turn west. Here you'll find *Harmonie State Park,* (812) 682-4821, a 3,500-acre spread of prime riverfront land with good camp-ing, three miles of bike trails, eight miles of hiking, and an Olympic-size swimming pool. No campsites can be reserved, so get here early. The park does have family cabins. The open grasslands here are rife with white-tailed deer; you're probably best off looking for waterfowl here. Located next to the Wabash River, the park has excellent opportunities for wildlife viewing. The six trails aren't a strenuous challenge but they reward you with nice vistas. A personal favorite is Trail 5 as it passes wildlife areas. As is often the case in southern Indiana, there are bridle trails. Interpretive services are seasonal but can be quite informational. The park office is usually open 8:30 a.m.–4 p.m. daily throughout the year.

Return to New Harmony. Go east on Highway 66 for about a mile, then bear left onto Highway 68 and follow it for about 16 miles to Cynthiana, passing through Poseyville on the way. The drive is in a generally northeast direction, but it's sometimes hard to tell because of all the tight turns you'll encounter. Enjoy the ride!

From Cynthiana, turn left (north) on Highway 65 and cruise for about 5.5 miles into Owensville. This community is a somnolent little town with a pretty little old-fashioned town square.

Continue north, then east on 65 for 12.5 miles to Princeton. Princeton was founded in 1814 and named for Captain William Prince, who later became a member of U.S. Congress. Princeton is proud that Abe Lincoln once lugged wool to its wool-carding mill. The *Gibson County Courthouse* on the town square is the model for the miniature courthouse featured in the Dept. 56 line of collectibles.

To return to Evansville, where this tour started, go to Highway 41 on the west edge of Princeton, turn left (south) on 41, and drive 30 miles to Evansville.

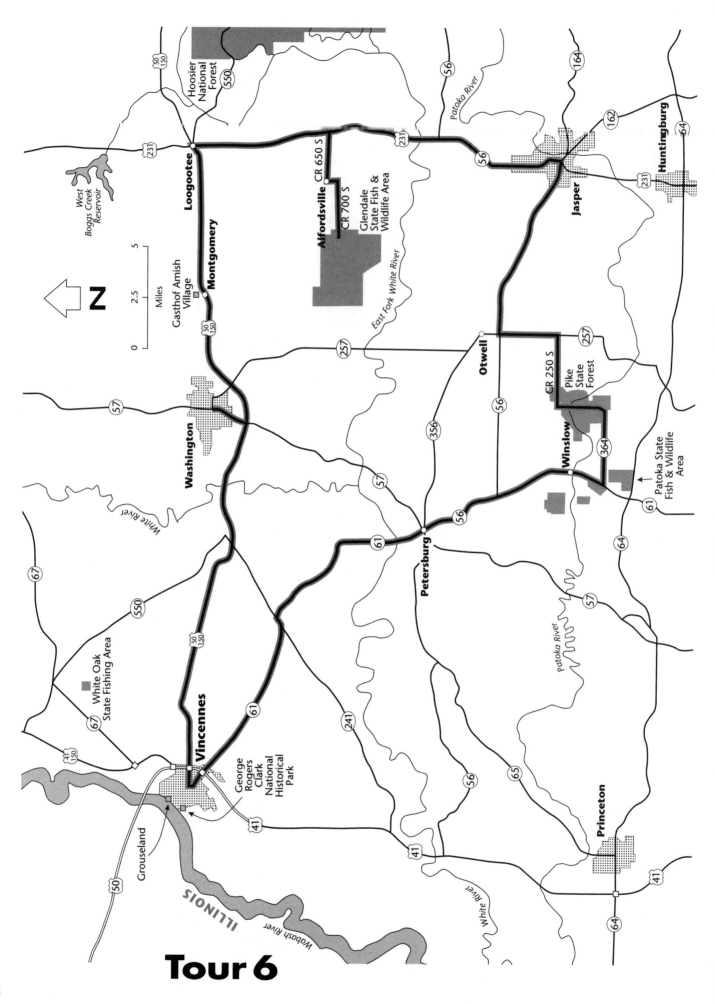

Tour 6

Tour 6
Old Indiana and
Old Order Indiana

Vincennes–Winslow–Jasper–Loogootee–Montgomery–Washington–Vincennes

Distance: 126.5 miles

What a tour! We start in Vincennes, Indiana's oldest town and one that deserves more attention than it gets. This old fort town has oodles of great sights to take in; the place virtually drips with history. Then we traipse into some of Indiana's most isolated wooded areas to do a little hiking or wildlife watching. We head into the Quiet Country, a region of Amish culture second only to northern Indiana's enclave of the Old Order. Along the way we meet historic Swiss communities, experience some great festivals (we indulge in copious heartland fare, but that's what travel is all about!), and even learn something about woodworking.

Start your tour in downtown Vincennes. The best place from which to begin your tour is the *Vincennes/Knox County Convention and Visitors Bureau,* 102 N. Third Street, (812) 886-0400 or (800) 886-6443, www.accessknoxcounty.com, where you can pick up all the maps and brochures

you may need. Hours here are 8 a.m.–5 p.m. weekdays and the staff are wonderful. If you come the first weekend in August, you can enjoy the *Knox County Watermelon Festival* downtown. You'll find plenty of arts and crafts, basketball tournaments, pageants, big-name national music acts, and, best of all, free watermelon! The *Spirit of Vincennes* over Memorial Day weekend has living history demonstrations and battle reenactments.

As Indiana's oldest city, Vincennes has a wealth of historic sites. The town's beginnings were humble. A French fur trading outpost was roughly assembled here way back in 1732, one of many links in a chain of "forts" intended to impede British expansion. (Traders had been coming through since the 1680s.) The area fell to the British during the 1760s but they lost it in the American Revolution. In 1778 25-year-old George Rogers Clark and seven companies of men arrived under orders from the government of Virginia to

A barn in Amish country.

secure all lands north of the Ohio River for that state. The troops seized Fort Sackville from the British but it almost immediately returned to British hands. Undaunted, Clark attacked again the following year, routed the British, and ultimately opened up the entire Northwest Territory. Virginia in 1784 made the entire region public domain and the town sprouted from that original trading post. Vincennes served as the capital of Indiana Territory in the years 1800–1813. The city was one of the few in Indiana to be under French influence, though later migrations brought Germans and Yankees.

At the visitor center, get directions to the *Oubache Trails* along the Wabash River. More than four miles of trails wend through a lovely 254-acre park. There's even a river-fishing trail and modern campground. Raccoons are pervasive here. Bald eagles are a majestic sight; songbirds feature such

The Wabash Rolls Along

The mighty Mississippi and the meandering Ohio Rivers have been granted legendary status in the annals of American exploration and expansion, and for good reasons. As a consequence, however, other "little" rivers (diminutive only in historical awareness, not size or importance, to be sure) are seriously underappreciated: the Fox in Wisconsin and the Rock in Illinois, among others. Few people outside of Indiana seem to know of the Wabash River. It certainly was one of the most crucial waterways in the Northwest Territory and was absolutely essential to the westward expansion of the frontier. It is truly the "Avenue of the Midwest."

In Indiana the Wabash stretches approximately 475 miles from Jay County in east central Indiana to Posey County in the southwest. The Miami people called it *waapaahsiki siipiiwi* ("bright, white river"). The first well-known westerner to exploit the region was the explorer Robert de La Salle, who arrived in 1679 as the French were intensifying their so-called Beaver Wars. The highlight of Miami culture, an indigenous tribe that held sway over much of the region (along with the Potawatomi, Delaware, and Shawnee), came with the great leader Little Turtle, who opposed Europeans at every turn and died in the War of 1812.

Westward expansion necessitated waterways and eventually canals. A canal between the Wabash River and the Erie Canal could ultimately link the Great Lakes with the Gulf of Mexico. Treaties granting land to the Miami were ignored and construction started in the 1830s. The 1840s were the halcyon days of the canal; many of the towns along it flourished. Details of these early communities are found in the many tours in this book. One of the last surviving locks of the old canal is Kerr Lock in Lagro, a personal favorite. I also like to walk the towpath in Cass County's France Park.

Geological formations along the Wabash are amazing in Huntington and Miami Counties in northeast Indiana; exposed limestone is superb in Wabash County sandwiched between the two. The epic stands of hardwoods have long since been cleared away, but some prime stands still can be found in Allen, Cass, and Wabash Counties. All along the river are signs of Native American and U.S. heritage, as well as great recreation.

species as Indigo bunting. Wildflowers explode in spring, a wonderful time to visit.

Clark's exploits are recounted at the *George Rogers Clark National Historic Park,* located just south of the Lincoln Memorial Bridge that spans the Wabash, (812) 882-1776. On this site Clark and his men skirmished twice with the British. A memorial building commemorates the battles, while a visitor center has exhibits and a short film. The park is open 9 a.m.–5 p.m. daily. Admission.

Close by, on Church Street, stands the *Old Cathedral* (better known as Saint Francis Xavier Church), 205 Church Street, (812) 882-5638. It was founded not long after that first fur trader raised a cabin and thus is Indiana's oldest place of worship. Across the courtyard is the state's oldest library, with volumes dating from the *twelfth century!* It was founded in 1794, contains more than 10,000 volumes, and is regarded by some as one of the best collections in the state. The original bell hangs in the steeple. Access is usually available 7 a.m.–4 p.m. unless services are underway. Admission.

It would take more than a day to cover the Vincennes State Historic Sites, a group of attractions that reflect significant developments in Indiana history. Happily, most of them are in the downtown area within walking distance of one another.

Following Vincennes's designation as the capital of Indiana Territory, William Henry Harrison became governor (and later the ninth president of the United States). *Grouseland,* 3 W. Scott Street, (812) 882-2096, was his residence. This mansion, purportedly the first brick building in the town, was built over the course of two years; Harrison would live in it until 1812. Much of the house's interiors are original, but the history may be more fascinating. In this house Harrison negotiated—some say rammed home—treaties with Native American leaders, including Tecumseh following the Battle of Tippecanoe, which broke the spirit of Native fighters east of the Mississippi. Hours are 9 a.m.–5 p.m. daily, March–December; reduced hours the rest of the year. Admission.

Opposite Grouseland sit the *Indiana Territory Capitol,* the *Elihu Print Shop,* and the *Maurice Thompson Birthplace.* Though the legislature originally had to move from place to place, it eventually settled on this building as the capitol, also known as the Red House. It is considered to be the oldest major government building in the Midwest. Next to the capitol is the building where the laws of the territory and also the *Indiana Gazette,* the first newspaper in Indiana, were printed. The original wooden printing press is on display. The birthplace of Maurice Thompson honors the man who penned the famed novel *Alice of Vincennes,* set during the Revolutionary War. Hours here are 9 a.m.–5 p.m. Wednesday–Saturday, 1–5 p.m. Sunday, mid-March to mid-December.

West of here a few blocks is the *Old State Bank,* 114 N. Second Street, (812) 882-7472, a smashing example of Greek Revival and one of the oldest bank branches in the state. Hours are 1 p.m.–4 p.m. Wednesday–Sunday, mid-March to November 1.

A couple of miles to the north, overlooking a bluff on the Wabash River, is *Fort Knox II,* (812) 882-7422, one of three forts built and garrisoned by the U.S. Army to protect settlers and control the strategic Wabash River valley. This fort was the staging area for the bloody Battle of Tippecanoe. You can guide your own tour here 9 a.m.–5 p.m. daily.

And this being southern Indiana, there's no way you can escape without a reminder of Abraham Lincoln. At the western edge of town, spanning the Wabash River into Illinois, the *Lincoln Memorial Bridge* marks the spot where the future president crossed the river on a ferry in 1830. This spot, incidentally, was also where hundreds of buffalo would ford on the great Buffalo Trace stretching from the Great Plains to Indiana and ending in Kentucky. Note the figures on the east end of the bridge: Tecumseh and his brother the Prophet, those vanquished Miami leaders, now guard the entrance to the bridge.

From downtown Vincennes, head southeast on Highway 61 for 20 miles to Petersburg. Continue through Petersburg on 61 for another 10 miles to Highway 364, passing through Winslow. Turn left (east) on 364 and go about 3 miles. Here is your gateway to more southern Indiana bucolic loveliness, courtesy of the *Pike State Forest and Patoka State Fish and Wildlife Area,* (812) 367-1524. The 2,914 acres of the state forest have rustic campsites, lots of hiking trails, hunting, and fishing. It's isolated and relatively untrampled, so you won't have too much company while you're poking around looking for critters or songbirds. Fishing is good for bluegills and crappies. You can also view abundant deer, dove, turkeys, and more.

Continue east on Highway 364 to County Road 650E; turn left (north) and go 2.5 miles to County Road 250S. Turn right and drive 3 miles to Highway 257. Turn left (north) and cruise 5 miles to Highway 56 at Otwell. Turn right and proceed for 9.5 miles to Jasper. This quintessential Indiana town is known as the Nation's Woodworking Capital though the reason isn't readily apparent—perhaps because its mills led in the manufacture of desks for most of the century. Of course, Abe Lincoln and his family lived here as well. One anecdote tells of Abe's father trading a handmade desk for some ground meal. Stop by the *Dubois County Tourism Commission,* 610 Main Street, (812) 482-9115 or (800) 968-4578, www.duboiscounty.org.

Jasper is well known for its Germanic heritage. Early guidebooks spoke of a peculiar colloquial mishmash of English and German called Jasper Dutch. Even if German is your first language,

you'll be baffled (and this is a trained linguist speaking). German heritage is feted annually in August at *Strassenfest.* You'll find music, parades, games, rides, and tons and tons of German cuisine. Don't eat before you arrive! During Prohibition Jasper was famous for its moonshine; known as Jasper corn, it was one of the most popular corn mashes put out by the rumrunners.

A wonderful sight is Jasper's *Saint Joseph Church,* Thirteenth and Newton Streets, (the cornerstone was laid in 1868) Old World–style church listed on the National Register of Historic Places. Teutonic imagery and craftsmanship are obvious in the stained glass windows, marble statues, and Austrian mosaics. Its tile roof is supported by four enormous trees; the congregation scoured southern Indiana's Hoosier National Forest to make sure they got the biggest and best. The result: graceful 90-foot columns. The chimes in the 205-foot steeple weigh 12 tons. Hours are 8 a.m.–9 p.m. daily. But wait, we're not done with churches yet. Along Highway 162 on Jasper's southeast side, the *Holy Family Church* contains the nation's second-largest stained-glass window, this one detailing the life of Christ; the church also has the longest unsupported wood beam in a church ceiling. Hours are daily until 8 p.m.

Finally, something for baseball fans to cheer about. The *Indiana Baseball Hall of Fame,* Highway 162 and College Avenue (at the Ruxter Student Center, Vincennes University–Jasper), (812) 482-2262, recognizes all high school and college players, coaches, and managers, along with any player or coach in the majors or minors with Indiana ties. You'd be surprised how many boys of summer the land of *Hoosiers* has produced. Hours are 9 a.m.–4 p.m. daily.

Leave Jasper on Highway 231 and go north 13 miles to County Road 162. Turn left (west) and go 2.5 miles to Alfordsville. (County Road 162 becomes County Road 650S as you cross into Daviess County.) Turn left on County Road 1200E and go a short distance to County Road 700S; turn right and drive 5 miles west to the *Glendale Fish and Wildlife Area.* This massive 8,061-acre spread, (812) 644-7711, is highlighted by 1,400-acre Dogwood Lake and its many ponds. Fishers will find bluegill, catfish, crappie, bass, and redear. You can espy deer, dove, turkey, waterfowl, and lots of upland game. The open areas attract a plethora of songbirds; also look for red-tailed hawks especially. Waterfowl are abundant. Pheasant hunters love the place. In fact,

Amish Country

When traveling in Amish country, respect and caution are paramount. In particular, take care with your camera. Amish take seriously the sin of pride, and self-imagery fits that bill. Always politely ask permission to take photos. More important is caution when driving. Slow down and always anticipate the possibility of a buggy over the next rise or around the next bend. Understand that it's very possible to spook a horse as you go roaring by.

Buggies, buggies everywhere in Amish country.

note that this a public hunting area, so in season you'll hear booms from hunters. Dress appropriately. The modern campground has nearly 120 campsites.

Return to Highway 231 and head north 8 miles to Loogootee; at Highway 50, turn left (west) and drive 7.5 miles west to Montgomery. Here you'll see *Gasthof Amish Village,* a collection of shops, woodworkers, a market, and an excellent restaurant in a hand-hewn wood barn. The Amish flea market here is amazing; don't miss it. Just seeing all the buggies lined up alongside tour buses will be a highlight. *Dillon Tours,* (812) 486-3491, offers horse-drawn carriage tours of the area. They stop at Amish shops, crafters places, antique dealers, and more. Incidentally, the founder of the University of Notre Dame once considered Montgomery as the site for a Catholic university.

All along the way, you'll pass through the heart of another of Indiana's Amish regions. You'll see the influence of Old Order Amish everywhere. Old Order Amish first began to settle here in the 1850s, coming from Pennsylvania. Today approximately 500 families are spread throughout the area. (See "The Gentle People" sidebar for Tour 18.) The road is also a primer of southwestern Indiana geology. Highway 50 crosses miles and miles of bedrock hills dating from the middle Mississippian period.

You can see glacial outwash of the East Fork White River. Keep an eye out for sandstones and shales interspersed with lots of coal seams.

Quick Trip Option: West of Loogootee you could opt to take County Road 900E north to Odon. There's not a whole lot to see but Odon is the site where George Rogers Clark and his men camped while buffalo hunting. A plaque gives details. The town used to host one of the largest picnics in the state.

From Montgomery, continue west on Highway 50 for another 8 miles to Highway 57; turn right (north) and drive a short distance to Washington. The *Daviess County Historical Society,* housed in a historic elementary school, is worth a visit. You can see exhibits detailing the life of these quiet people, along with general county history. The *Amish Community of Daviess County Visitor Center*, Depot Street, (812) 254-5262, www.daviess.net, is in a restored train depot right downtown. They can provide information and brochures or even arrange a tour for you.

Return to Highway 50 and continue west for 18 miles back to downtown Vincennes.

Tour 7
Limestone, Astronauts, and Basketball

Bedford–Mitchell–Orleans–Paoli–West Baden Springs–French Lick–Hoosier National Forest–Shoals–Williams–Bedford

Distance: 104 miles

This engaging tour takes you through places that make southern Indiana one-of-a-kind—start with a hometown industry, travel through the backyard of a famous local-boy-done-good, wind through resplendent avenues of gorgeous trees, tour one of the most jaw-droppingly beautiful pieces of construction in the state, and make a pilgrimage to the hometown of an American legend. Oh, and beyond that, you've got plenty of lovely Hoosier National Forest greenery to gaze at and a couple of choice parks to hop out and stretch the legs with some recreation. All this in a fairly brief loop trip. What else could one ask for?

Start your tour in Bedford. This town, smack dab in the middle of Lawrence County about 25 miles south of Bloomington, is quite literally a city of limestone. Perhaps Bedford is not particularly romantic but it's historically relevant. Limestone quarrying began in earnest in the 1850s, and by its zenith some 32 quarries operated constantly, supplying work for 39 stone cut mills and some 5,000 laborers. Indiana limestone built this country, earning Bedford the moniker Stone City. Here's a very short list of famous architecture built with local stone: Washington Cathedral, Pentagon, Departments of Commerce/Labor/Justice, IRS Building, Department of Interior, Lincoln Memorial (all in Washington, D.C.); Tribune Tower (Chicago); Empire State Building, Saks Fifth Avenue, Cathedral of Saint John, Chase National Bank, Rockefeller Center (New York City); most post offices, banks, and universities throughout the country. There are many other structures too numerous to mention.

Stop by the *Bedford Area Chamber of Commerce,* 1116 Sixteenth Street, (812) 275-4493, for lots of friendly advice and fistfuls of free walking tour brochures. An excellent place to witness Bedford's stone artisan work is at the *Land of Limestone,* an Indiana Heritage Exhibition at the Bedford campus of Oakland City University, 405 I Street, (800) 798-0769. Maps, photographs, sketches, and news accounts paint the picture of this region's most crucial economic foundation. If that's closed, here's a great option: *Greenhill Cemetery* off Eighteenth Street, where the work of local stone carvers can truly be appreciated. Or stop by the *Lawrence County Historical and Genaological Museum,* (812) 275-4141, at the county courthouse. You'll find exhibits of limestone here as well, in addition to military items dating from the Civil War and assorted county memorabilia. Hours vary.

Bedford has other sights for travelers. Near the intersection of Highway 450 and Highway 37 in the Stone City Mall, you'll find more than a hundred race and antique cars at the *Antique Auto and Race Car Museum,* (812) 275-0556, featuring many cars driven by veterans and winners of the Indianapolis 500. Southwest of town along Highway 50 is the *Bluespring Caverns Myst'ry River Voyage,* (812) 279-9471. Discovered in the 1940s when a farm pond was swallowed up by a sinkhole, these underground caverns—the longest in Indiana—can be explored on foot or by boat on one of the longest underground rivers in the country. Look for albino crayfish and the like and, as always in caves, bring a jacket. Hours are generally 9 a.m.–5 p.m., Memorial Day–Labor Day; reduced times rest of season (it generally closes up around Halloween and reopens April 1).

From downtown Bedford, drive south on Highway 37 for 10 miles to Mitchell. The first thing visitors to Mitchell become aware of is local-boy-done-good Virgil "Gus" Grissom, one of the original Mercury astronauts. At 407 S. Sixth Street you can find one of two memorials to the native son; the other is in Spring Mill State Park (see below). Mitchell also has a lovingly restored 1906 *Opera House,* Seventh and Brook Streets, downtown, (812) 849-2337, that offers a wide variety of musical and theatrical performances. The town was settled as early as 1813 (around a mill) but not founded until much later, with the arrival of the railroad—in fact, two railroads, which really allowed the town to grow. Stop by the *Greater Mitchell Chamber of Commerce,* 602 W. Main Street, (812) 849-4441 or (800) 580-1985, for more information.

Just south of Mitchell, take Highway 60 east 2.5 miles to *Spring Mill State Park.* Visitors will find camping, hiking trails through lovely oak stands of a nature preserve, and various other recreational opportunities. The big draws, however, are another memorial to Gus Grissom (this one has a visitor center with space capsule and other rem-

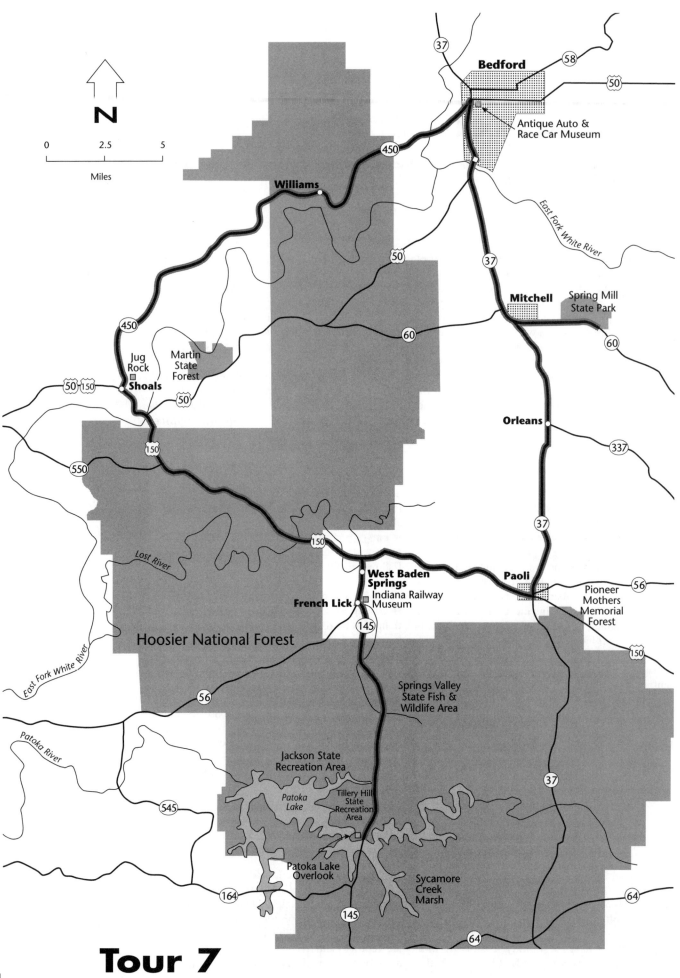

N

0   2.5   5

Miles

37

58

Bedford

50

450

Antique Auto &
Race Car Museum

Williams

50

37

60

Mitchell

Spring Mill
State Park

East Fork White River

450

Jug
Rock

Martin
State
Forest

60

50 150

Shoals

50

150

Orleans

337

550

Lost River

150

150

37

West Baden
Springs

Paoli

56

Indiana Railway
Museum

Pioneer
Mothers
Memorial
Forest

French Lick

145

150

Hoosier National Forest

Springs Valley
State Fish &
Wildlife Area

East Fork White River

56

Jackson State
Recreation Area

37

Patoka River

Patoka
Lake

Tillery Hill
State
Recreation
Area

545

Patoka Lake
Overlook

Sycamore
Creek
Marsh

164

64

145

64

Tour 7

nants of the space race) and *Spring Mill Village*, a reconstructed nineteenth-century village. Buildings on site include a gristmill, an old kiln, an original sawmill, a reconstructed trading post, and a half-dozen other structures. The water powered gristmill is probably the park's most popular attraction. You can even purchase corn ground from the mill at the park shop. It's another of those living history places that are so educational.

Caves can be explored on foot or by boat. Boat rides can be arranged into the caves as well into Twin Caves; get there very early in the day and on the day you wish to enter the cave. You can explore Donaldson Cave on your own, however. Take the right side, which is usually not submerged but can be very muddy and difficult. To visit other caves you must register at the visitor center.

Park facilities include over 200 camp sites (reservations are available), cultural arts programs, fishing, an inn, a nature center with educational activities, a saddle barn, and a big old swimming pool for the urchins. Wildlife viewing here is superb; there are ample opportunities to wander through virgin hardwood spreads that surround spring-fed streams.

To get a great look at some original Indiana forest, take Trail 3; it's excellent. Its first section traces a route to the locally famous Donaldson Cave and a bunch of limestone sinkholes. Eventually it leads to the Donaldson Woods Nature Preserve—great to espy wildlife and nature as it existed over a century ago. Trail 4 also leads to Donaldson Cave; its other sections are a bit rugged. If you don't have much time, try Trail 5, a mile-long

easy trail around manmade Spring Mill Lake. Fishers can land bluegill, trout, and other species.

Return to Mitchell and turn left (south) on Highway 37; cruise about 4.5 miles to Orleans. Orleans is known as the Dogwood Capital of Indiana and the citizenry cheerily participate in dogwood planting; in spring the town can be awash in dogwoods. Best bet for viewing color is a springtime jaunt around the quaint town square. A personal favorite is the local *Orleans Dogwood Festival* the first week of May. In addition to viewing resplendent dogwoods in bloom, you can enjoy carnival rides and entertainment, sample arts and crafts, and wander about a community yard sale.

Continue south on Highway 37 for 7.5 miles to Paoli. The stretch of highway here can be downright gorgeous with dogwood color. Like Orleans, Paoli has its own attractive Greek Revival courthouse on the town square. Just southeast of town via Highway 37 is the *Pioneer Mothers Memorial Forest,* a tract of old-growth forest that contains some of the best stands of black walnut trees in the United States. Also just outside of town is one of southern Indiana's best options for snow lovers—*Ski Paoli Peaks,* (812) 723-4696, with 15 slopes, 8 lifts, a vertical drop of 300 feet (longest run is 3,300 feet); you'll also find a ski school, restaurant, and plenty of activities for everyone in the family. Hours are 10 a.m.–9.30 p.m. Monday–Thursday, till 10 p.m. Friday, 24 hours a day on weekends during the winter months. Call ahead for ski conditions.

The hard-to-miss West Baden Springs Hotel, a National Historic Landmark.

Paoli also has a great *Indian Summer Festival* the third weekend in September. Carnival rides are the draw but I prefer the great pancake feed on Saturday. The *Lotus Dickey Hometown Festival* the third weekend in June features great acoustic music.

From Paoli go west on Highway 150 for 7.5 twisting miles to Highway 56 at West Baden Springs; turn left (south). In the heart of artesian springs country, West Baden, known as one of the hilliest towns in southern Indiana, had the original monster resort-cum-casino. Now a National Historic Landmark, the magnificent *West Baden Springs Hotel,* Highway 56, (812) 936-4034, was built in 1902 after fire razed the 1851 original. Before the stock market crash of 1929 put the damper on well-heeled hedonists, this was the place to see and be seen among celebrities and the well-to-do. Later it became a Jesuit seminary and private college. This splendid building—easy to see from afar with its distinctive architecture and spacious grounds—is famed for its elegant six-story domed atrium, larger than Saint Peter's Cathedral in the Vatican. Upon completion, it was dubbed the Eighth Wonder of the World. The interior must be seen to be believed.

Continue south on Highway 56 to French Lick. Like West Baden, French Lick has numerous artesian springs (you can still fill your own bottle) in the vicinity; unlike West Baden's resort, the *French Lick Springs Resort,* (812) 936-9300, fared well and is one of the most impressive lodgings in Indiana. French Lick is on the map for another reason. To basketball fanatics, the tiny town is the birthplace and hometown of Larry Bird, one of the greatest basketball players of his generation and for many years a star with the Boston Celtics—and an American icon. Die-hard fans make pilgrimages to French Lick, and the downtown is peppered with number 33 (his Celtic jersey number) and Celtic

Healing Water

The region around Paoli and west toward West Baden and French Lick was a popular resort area in the early twentieth century. What drew visitors were mineral spas that dotted the Lost River Valley of the Hoosier National Forest. Long before humans discovered the springs, animals were drawn to "lick" the springs (hence the name French Lick. A snake oil salesman was purportedly the first to notice the beneficial nature of the springs and opened the first hotel in West Baden in 1851. The artesian wells, often bubbling at 100 gallons per minute, became famous throughout the Midwest for their salubrious properties. The area soon became known as the "Carlsbad of America," a reference to the mineral springs in Czechoslovakia that Europeans had been visiting for centuries. One similarity between the two was the extensive casino gambling and assorted hedonism that went on in the evenings.

green. Get your photo snapped at the downtown sign proudly proclaiming itself the hometown of Larry Bird.

Railroad aficionados flock to French Lick and its *Indiana Railway Museum,* 1 Monon Street, (812) 936-2405, where they hop aboard the French Lick, West Baden & Southern train for a 90-minute ride through 20 miles of Hoosier National Forest, limestone rock cuts, and the 2,200-foot Burton Tunnel, one of the longest tunnels in the state. Lots of railroad mementos are inside and outside the depot, including several diesel and steam locomotives, a rare railway post office car, and a 1951 dining car. For a long time, the Springs Valley Electric Trolley has been the shortest trolley line in the world and carries passengers between French Lick and West Baden.

From French Lick, take Highway 145 south into the Hoosier National Forest. This could be considered as an optional side trip, but you really should make it part of your required itinerary. Endless touring opportunities exist here; the roads twist and turn and rise and fall, and they're a joy to drive. Just a few moments south of town you'll come to the *Springs Valley State Fish and Wildlife Area,* one of the state's newest, with access to excellent wildlife viewing at Youngs Creek and not one but two state recreation areas.

And be sure not to miss the *Patoka Lake State Reservoir,* (812) 685-2464, a gloriously lush tract of over 25,000 acres that includes an 8,800-acre lake, the state's second largest with a lovely craggy shoreline. You'll see houseboats galore on this lake, one of its trademarks. Over 140 miles of trails wend through the area in the Hoosier National Forest. You'll also find an archery range, nearly 500 campsites (reservations), cross-country skiing, fishing, cultural arts programs, hiking and biking trails, a beach, and a whole lot more.

One of the best and most convenient ways of experiencing the Patoka Lake area is along Highway 145, about 10 miles south of French Lick, at the *Patoka Lake Overlook.* This is probably one of southern Indiana's best wildlife viewing sites. Here you are guaranteed a beautiful vista and virtually assured of seeing bald eagles; others have seen ospreys and blue herons.

Quick Trip Option: If you're really up for wildlife viewing, continue south on Highway 145 to Highway 64, then head east and follow the signs out of Taswell to the *Sycamore Creek Marsh* (the signs say Little Patoka Boat Ramp). Here you'll find a very narrow edge of the huge reservoir to the north. Waterfowl dominate the scene here; it's amazing how many mallards you can see. Herons and egrets are also in abundance. Red-tailed hawks soar all over the place. Numerous amphibious animals like muskrats are common.

Backtrack on Highway 145 to West Baden Springs. Turn left (west) on Highway 150 and

Anachronistic railroading in French Lick.

go about 13 miles to Shoals. For most of the trip, you'll cruise through more of the Hoosier National Forest. At the tiny community of Shoals, once home to rumrunners and bootleggers, you'll see *Jug Rock,* a natural cliff formation 60 feet high and 15 feet wide resembling an enormous jug. It's tough to find so you may need to ask for directions.

Head north on Highway 150 a short distance out of Shoals to Highway 450. Turn right (north) and drive about 13 miles to Williams. If you haven't gotten your fill of the Hoosier National Forest just yet, this stretch of road should satisfy your appetite. And there's a covered bridge to look forward to. Just west of Williams, you'll find a turnoff (Williams-Huron Road) to the largest covered bridge in Indiana still open for traffic.

Return to Highway 450 and head east for about 10 miles back to Bedford.

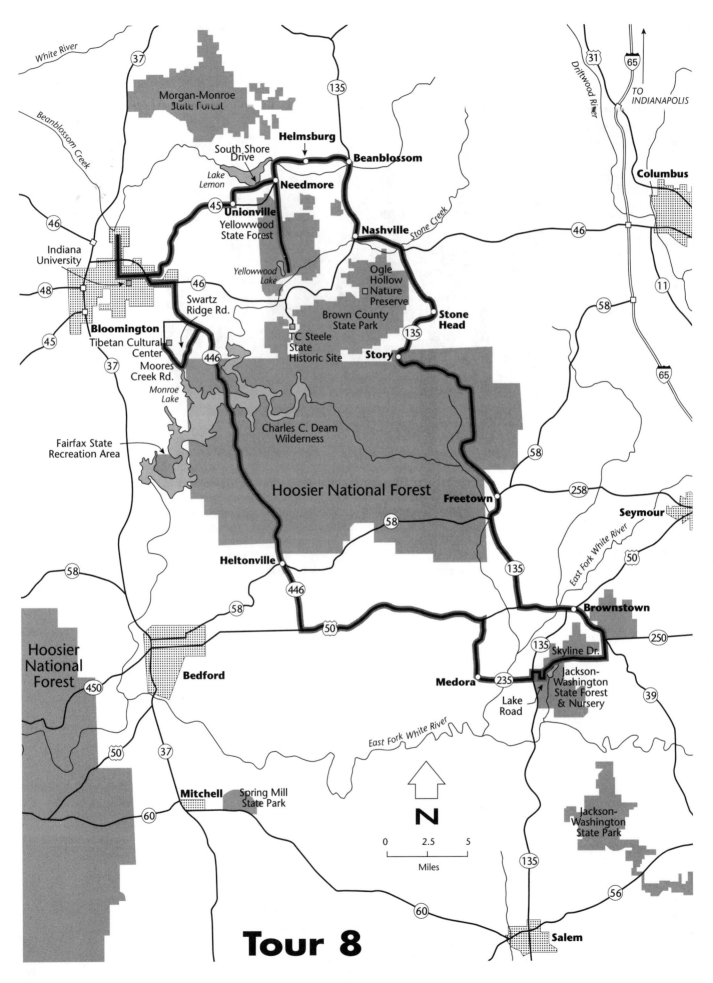

Tour 8

Tour 8
Lakes, Ridges, Galleries, and . . . Tibet

Bloomington–Nashville–Brown County State Park–Brownstown–Medora–Hoosier National Forest–Bloomington

Distance: 133.5 miles

Brown County, one of the most popular destinations in Indiana, is the heart of south central Indiana tourism, with its bucolic back roads, antique-shop-lined streets of quaint Nashville, and a state park unparalleled for outdoor splendor. To enhance this thoroughly satisfying tour, we'll roll and twist through the largest (and best) swath of the Hoosier National Forest, whose spiny ridges and fish-stuffed lakes offer outstanding opportunities for hikers, fishers, canoeists, birders, and anyone else interested in the great outdoors. Top it all off with the easy diversity of Bloomington, a refreshing midwestern-hip university town with loads of attractions.

Start your tour in Bloomington. The first order of business is to check out the *Bloomington Convention and Visitors Bureau,* north of the downtown area at 2855 N. Walnut Street (Business 37), (812) 334-8900 or (800) 800-0037, www.visitbloomington.com. Here you can arm yourself with tidbits of chatty advice, brochures, or maps. (They sure are friendly at this office!) Hordes of road trippers roaring and rumbling toward south central Indiana's crown jewels, the ribbony byways of anachronistic Brown County, often wholly (and unfairly) blow past Bloomington, a Big Ten university town with all the superlatives that entails: relaxed and sociable, with an eclectic charm and bohemian-chic style, due in large part to the youth of the populace (tens of thousands of college students lower the median age more than a bit). Hungry travelers can find a chipped-mug-and-three-egg-omelette joint next door to a Nepali-Tibetan vegetarian café . . . and their clienteles are similar.

Bloomington usually rates in the top five in surveys of "best places to live" in oodles of national media—as much for its lovely green spaces as its great restaurants, healthful lifestyle, or simple down-home charm. With all that, it definitely warrants a visit.

Drive north on N. Walnut Street (Business Highway 37) until you come to Old State Road 37; turn left and drive a few blocks to Cascades Park. In the heart of this lush green is one of the most unusual sights you'll experience anywhere in Indiana—*Dagom Gaden Tensung Ling Monastery,* 102 Clubhouse Drive, (812) 339-0857. This is an authentic Tibetan monastery, the first one ever established in the United States. Visitors interested in temples (this one is an interesting combination of old and new) or in Buddhism in general are welcome. You may see monks making a sand prayer mural (the sand represents impermanence, an essential tenet to all strands of Buddhism—even things of sublime beauty blow away eventually); you can gaze at precious *thangka,* sacred representational scroll paintings; if you're lucky, one of the monks will be available for a chat. Buddhism is an all-embracing belief system; combine this with the extraordinary friendliness and gentleness of Tibetans, and you could be in for a memorable experience. (The trip around the grounds from the visitor center might make a short but ambitious walk, so inquire before you set off.) Hours are not set for visiting, so it's a good idea to call first and see if anyone will be around to let you in or if any special programs are upcoming.

Return to Business 37 and turn right (south). The highway soon splits off into College Avenue. Go south on College to the parking area between Sixth and Seventh Streets in downtown Bloomington. Park your car and forget about it for a while. An aside: though this book may be designed for road trippers, even the most hardcore of us mileage pile-uppers occasionally need to stretch the legs. Bloomington, with its compact, gridlike setup, makes it perfect for walking the following route. But be forewarned: it is a lengthy jaunt, even for the halest of travelers, so driving it is an option and parking generally isn't impossible to find. And it's cheap. Even more out of this world: we once found a friendly note on our car, cheerfully filling us "outstate friends" in on the omnipresence of parking enforcement, thus saving us a ticket we surely would have gone home with. Wow.

On Sixth Street, walk two blocks east to Washington Street. At the corner of Sixth and Washington, you'll spy the *Monroe County Historical Society Museum,* 202 E. Sixth Street, (812) 322-2517. The larger-than-most-county-museums complex is housed in a historic library (built from local limestone, of course) that has three exhibit galleries with rotating displays. Of greatest interest are the displays on the local stone industries, but you could easily spend a couple of hours poking through an old log cabin and myriad objects from the past 150 years of county history. Hours are 10 a.m.–4 p.m., Tuesday–Saturday, from 1 p.m. Sunday.

Walk south on Washington to Kirkwood Avenue, then head east for four blocks to Indiana Avenue. Carmichael Center, at the corner of Kirkwood and Indiana, houses the *Indiana University Visitors Center,* (812) 855-0850 or (800) 937-3448. Here's a good place to pick up a detailed map of the university. You'll need it; this is one of the best campuses to stroll around and take in the sights—though with all that is mentioned here it ain't a picnic for some people, so take it slow. (It even has its own *forest,* Dunn's Woods, right on campus—you'll see students jogging or, likely, lounging and debating whether or not they really, really want to go to that afternoon history lecture.) By the way, if the campus looks familiar, it should. Used as a location for filming of that tender coming-of-age film *Breaking Away*—especially its legendary Little 500 bike race in which local boys take on the arrogant university boys and win (natch)—it's burned into the memories of many Americans. Across the street from the information center is *Kirkwood Observatory,* built in 1900 and named after a prominent professor of math and avid astronomer. The 12-inch refractor is available for viewing on clear Wednesday nights when classes are in session.

Go south on Indiana Avenue to Third Street. Turn east and walk 5 to 10 minutes. *Jordan Hall,* 1001 E. Third Street, (812) 855-7717, houses the botany department. A modest but impressive facility houses exhibits of flora organized into tropical and desert plants from around the world, along with more traditional garden displays. You can generally pop in during business hours.

Continue east on Third Street for one block, cross Hawthorne Street, and bear left on a path past Memorial Hall. After a few minutes, turn right at Goodbody Hall to Morrison Hall. Most folks don't know about this diminutive but fun little museum, in room 006. The *Hoagy Carmichael Room,* (812) 855-4679, is dedicated to this local boy who graduated from IU with a law degree (of all things) in 1926 but never could shake the music bug. It was in a local gin joint that Hoagy finally worked out "Stardust,"—and the rest, as they say, is history. You'll find loads of memorabilia to the songster, a piano, a jukebox, and lots of LPs. By the way, Morrison Hall houses one of the country's greatest repositories of sound recordings, from music to ethnography. Great fun! Closed weekends. Carmichael is buried in a local cemetery.

Walk due north to the Lilly Library. Located at the base of Showalter Fountain, the *Lilly Library,* (812) 855-2452, houses an internationally renowned rare book library containing nearly half a million books, 6 million manuscripts, and 150,000 pieces of sheet music and compositions. If for no other reason come to see a Gutenberg Bible, which dates to 1456. There's something for everyone here—serious historical works, literature (Shakespeare to Sylvia Plath), pop culture icons. It's all tremendously fascinating. Open weekdays and until 1 p.m. Saturdays. Tours are given Fridays at 2 p.m.

Continue on to the north end of Fine Arts Plaza. The *Indiana University Art Museum,* (812) 855-5445, is an eye-catching building designed by I. M. Pei. Ranked among the best university art museums (for its astonishing and extensive collections), it has something for all tastes in its permanent collections—Andy Warhol to pre-Columbian sculpture. This one stop could take up your whole afternoon. Open 10 a.m.–5 p.m. Tuesday–Saturday, noon–5 p.m. Sunday.

Walk west along Eighth Street to Fess Avenue. You haven't finished your museum tour just yet. (Didn't we say this place was an awesome spot to wander?) The *Mathers Museum,* 416 N. Indiana Avenue, (812) 855-6873, has changing anthropological exhibits. Indiana University has a strong anthropology department (hey, they didn't call him Indiana Jones for nothing!), and the scope of the exhibits here is impressive. Folklore exhibits seem to draw the most interest. Open 9 a.m.–4:30 p.m. Tuesday–Friday, from 1 p.m. weekends.

Walk one block north on Fess Avenue. Last stop on the museum express is the *Glenn A. Black Laboratory of Archaeology,* Ninth and Fess Streets (weekends you can enter via the lobby of the Mathers Museum), (812) 855-9544. Hoosier archaeology in all its glory is examined through exhibits of Native American life throughout the Great Lakes and Ohio Valley, dating back to the first proto-historical settlers. Hours are the same as the Mathers Museum.

Quick Trip Option: By this time you may just want to return directly downtown and avail yourself of one of Bloomington's numerous ethnic eateries and/or cozy pubs. If you've still got gas left in your tank (as it were), consider a healthy walk north to take in some sports-related sights (hey, this is the Big 10 after all!). Or you may want to retrieve your vehicle and drive to these places.

Head north on Indiana Avenue for nine blocks to Seventeenth Street. Here you can behold *Memorial Stadium,* built in 1960 and home to the IU football team. Let's face it, the team has been on an up-and-down ride for the past decade, but it's still the Big Ten, and the stadium and facilities are worth a look-see. Check in with the receptionist at the football office complex under the east stands, 8 a.m.–5 p.m. weekdays.

Brown County State Park just after sunrise.

But let's be honest. The main reason most people traipse up to this part of campus is to experience one inescapable facet of Hoosierdom: basketball. East of the football stadium is *Assembly Hall,* (800) 447-4648, one of the country's most recognizable basketball arenas and home to powerhouse men's basketball since 1971 (though it seems to their Big Ten victims that the facility has been around *forever*). Just gaping at the 20,000-seat capacity is enough (it incites goosebumps, it really does, if you have even a modicum of sports fan in you), but there's also a nifty trophy area (most Big Ten programs would kill to have a fraction of the hardware they've accumulated) and Athletic Hall of Fame (a veritable Who's Who of American sports). Definitely recommended.

Go south on Indiana Avenue to Kirkwood Avenue and to wherever you parked your car. Drive south on College Avenue, turn left (east) on Second Street, and continue for three blocks. Our last stop is the *Wylie House,* 317 E. Second Street, (812) 855-6224, the home of Andrew Wylie, first president of Indiana University. Dating from 1835, this stately mansion is now listed on the National Register of Historic Places and is a period museum re-creating the family home. It's a fine way to glimpse the way of life at the time.

Continue east on Second Street to Highway 45/46. Take Highway 45 east, then northeast

for approximately 10 miles to Unionville. Turn left on N. Suffle Creek Road and go to South Shore Drive. Turn right. *Lake Lemon* is a 1,650-acre lake surrounded by challenging ridge and ravine topography that's completely overlooked by most travelers. It's a pity, really, since it offers one of the state's most productive fisheries and even a nice mile-long wildlife viewing trail through the Little Africa Wildlife and Goose Hollow Areas: excellent spots for birders (eagles are common!).

Take South Shore Drive approximately 8 miles east to Highway 45 and the town of Needmore. Turn right (south) on 45 and follow the signs to Yellowwood Lake. The road passes through the northern reaches of the *Yellowwood State Forest.* At Yellowwood Lake Road, head south for a quick jaunt into the maw of the 20,000 acres of hardwood and pine. At the northern end of Yellowwood Lake you'll find an excellent wildlife-viewing site set out in a 20-acre wetland. High probabilities exist to espy woodland songbirds year-round; migrating waterfowl stop off on their seasonal migrations and grand herons stand out prominently spring through fall. Deer are abundant, particularly in the morning and evening. Check out more information at a visitor center farther south along Yellowwood Lake Road.

Return to Highway 45, turn right, and continue east through Needmore, Trevlac, and

Helmsburg. At Beanblossom, turn south on Highway 135. As you drive south, keep your eyes peeled for signs indicating where to turn west on an unmarked road that leads to the Beanblossom Bridge, yet another of Indiana's treasured covered bridges. Wander about the bushes and take some photos, then it's back to the highway.

Also near Beanblossom on Highway 135 is the *Bill Monroe Memorial Music Park,* (812) 988-6422, a huge and well-kept campground and "historical music show park" on 55 acres. Bill Monroe was the father of bluegrass and this is the site of the longest running bluegrass festival in the world—the Beanblossom Bluegrass Festival (festivals actually take place throughout the year). You can visit the cabin where Bill Monroe spent his teen years; also of interest is the Bluegrass Hall of Fame, heavy on Monroe memorabilia but not limited to that granddaddy of the genre.

Continue into Nashville. Flyspeck Nashville sure has some big britches to fill as the unofficial gateway to Brown County, arguably the largest tourist (and certainly road-tripper) getaway in southcentral Indiana. This vibrant community is an anachronistic little gem, filled with tourists but nevertheless keeping its small town charm. The streets are loaded with antique and bric-a-brac shops, and you'll likely be muscled out of the way by bus tour grandmothers in quest of Stuff. But it's all great fun.

As far back as the 1930s guidebooks were mentioning Nashville's spot on the tourist map. The mother of all guidebooks—the Depression-era Works Progress Administration guide to the 48 contiguous states—politely mentions that the town "is a mecca for painters, photographers, and tourists who mingle on the streets with the permanent residents. The latter are not unmindful of their opportunities, and living costs for tourists are higher here than in many Indiana cities." The 1940s and already people were complaining about tourists ruining places. In all, the town today boasts more than 350 shops of one sort or another and on weekends a tourist invasion rivaling D-Day. It truly can be a mesmerizing experience, wandering the warrens of studios (you can get close-ups of many artists at work), chi-chi boutiques, upper-crust cafes, and even the odd hardware store or two. The town has not one, not two, but three anachronistic carriage ride operators, and more sybaritic inns and B&Bs than you'd imagine.

Park the car (if the belching buses or hordes of weekend day-trippers leave you any space) right downtown at the *Brown County Convention and Visitors Bureau,* (812) 988-7303 or (800) 753-3255, www.browncounty.com, and avail yourself of their solicitous help and encyclopedic knowledge.

Along Museum Lane is the *Brown County Historical Museum,* (812) 988-4153, a grouping of buildings that include an 1850s pioneer cabin, an 1879 log jail, an 1897 doctor's office, a blacksmith shop, and a loom set-up with original spinning and weaving equipment. It's open 1–5 p.m. weekends, May–October.

West of town via Highway 46 is the *T. C. Steele State Historic Site,* (812) 988-2785, home of a noted Indiana landscape artist. Inspired by the gorgeous natural beauty of the county, Steele, a native-born Hoosier, relocated here in 1907 after studying in Chicago and Munich. His impressionist paintings are considered state treasures. The site has guided tours, hiking trails, and a nature preserve. On a dewy morning or crisp autumn evening, it's not hard at all to see what moved Steele so much. Open 9 a.m.–5 p.m. Tuesday–Saturday, 1–5 p.m. Sunday.

Besides the shopping and historical attractions, live entertainment is a local specialty. The *Brown County Playhouse,* (812) 988-2123, is the state's longest-running professional summer stock theater company and presents four well-received productions (many affiliated with the Indiana University drama department) June–October. Not to be outdone, five other performance venues offer everything from vaudeville to follies extravaganzas to musical theater. For a town of its size, this is quite impressive.

If you get tired of walking, consider the *Nashville Express Train Tours,* (812) 988-2355, leaving from the corner of Franklin and Van Buren Streets. This simulated steam locomotive train has 2.5-mile tours through the town (it stops at most hotels and motels).

Head east on Highway 46 a short distance to Brown County State Park. Watch for several entrances to this, the Hoosier State's largest state park, (812) 988-6406. This massive park, which could warrant a trip all by itself, has absolutely everything one could want. It's so enormous that many travelers never even disembark from their vehicles. They simply take the scenic—and it is scenic, to be sure—route along the park's hollows and ridges, then leave.

The park is extremely well managed and therefore popular. Established in 1929, it was the site of one of the Civilian Conservation Corps' most ambitious efforts; today you can appreciate the herculean planting project, soothing erosion with enormous tracts of black locust, black walnut, spruces, and a hell of a lot of pines. The best way to appreciate the natural beauty is at the Ogle Hollow Nature Preserve, doubtless the park's number-one attraction. You'll find a mile-long (slightly less, actually) nature trail that starts near the paved road north of Rally Campground. It rolls through yellow-wood stands (watch for pileated woodpeckers) and hooks up with another trail that leads through upland trail to eponymous Ogle Lake.

If you'd rather leave the wilderness to the wild turkeys (and deer—its most famous resident, with a mind-boggling number in the park's herds—nuthatches, junco, and assorted other critters) then head immediately for the nature center, which has a snake exhibit, bird-watching room, and a number of other displays on the natural history of the area,

The entrance to Brown County State Park, one of the best in the state.

not to mention loquacious naturalists who can answer absolutely any question (dim or not) that you can think up. Pick up a highly useful self-guided auto tour guide.

This is also prime horseback riding country, and up to 75 miles of bridle trails are available; two stables (replete with pony and hay rides) are found in the park. For campers, there are approximately one gajillion campsites (and yes, they're oft booked out); for more creature comforts, you'll find the Abe Martin Lodge and 24 sleeping cabins.

Return to Highway 46 and head east to Highway 135; turn right (south) and go about 5 miles to Stone Head. Along the way you'll pass by the covered Ramp Creek Bridge before the road gets ambitious (not to mention considerably narrower). With every twist and turn the trees seem to encroach more and more; if a deer jumps out, you think, you're done for. The community of Stone Head is named for a famous white-stone carving. See if you can spot it.

Continue on Highway 135 for another 5 miles to Story. The dot-sized community of Story (don't blink or you *will* miss it) is a grouping of gracefully aging buildings that include the legendary *Story Inn,* (800) 881-1183, an old general store gentrified into a luxurious B&B but even more famous for its epicurean (and pricey) feasts. For all the throngs in Nashville and Brown County State Park, this place oddly always seems tranquil and hushed and makes for a great retreat. The surrounding countryside is peppered with sharp peaks, which naturally makes for some great snooping (there's even a bike trail to the west).

Continue south on Highway 135 through Freetown until you come to Highway 50. Take

your time. The surrounding scenery is subtle but sublime, alternating between exposed limestone holes and thick spinneys of pine. Near Spurgeons Corner you find a turnoff to Maines Pond, a wildlife viewing area—high on the list are meadowlarks and quail and many deer. The meadows here are particularly riotous in color.

Turn left (east) on 50 and drive through Brownstown to Highway 250 on the southeast side of town. Continue on 250 until you come to Skyline Drive and the entrance to the *Jackson-Washington State Forest*. Turn right on Skyline and follow it to Starve Hollow; turn right. The drive provides a scenic tour through the southern portion of the forest that offers five pullouts and scenic vistas. Camping is available in the northern section just east of Brownstown; in the south you'll find great lake recreation, a bike trail, and more camping around Starve Hollow Lake. The Oak Leaf Trail is actually a handful of trails (easy to rugged) departing from the lake's campground. Wild turkeys are ubiquitous throughout the year, along with ruffed grouse and a variety of other critters.

Continue on Starve Hollow to Lake Road; turn right, then take a quick left at County Road 350 S to Highway 135; turn left (south), then right onto Highway 235. Drive west, then north, on 235 through Medora to Highway 50. Along the way, you'll pass through picturesque little Medora Bridge over the east fork of the White River. Well, not so little: at over 458 feet it's the longest three-span covered bridge in the United States. Continuing west you'll go through pretty village of Medora, after which the road bends sharply to the north, edging along county forestland.

At Highway 50, turn west and continue for about 10 miles to Highway 446. Turn right (north) on Highway 446 and head into the largest section of the *Hoosier National Forest.*

Quick Trip Option: If you're up for a hike, turn east on Highway 58 just east of Heltonville and travel to Norman Station. Just east of that town, a road leads north into Lawrence County to the Hickory Ridge Trails, a set of backcountry primitive trails stretching throughout the region.

Back on Highway 446, continue north. Cruising through the stands of reforested pines, you'll eventually come to the *Charles C. Deam Wilderness,* likely the most convenient part of the 78,000 acres of the Hoosier National Forest, with excellent hiking (and bridle) trails throughout the challenging ravine and ridge topography (and a home to bald eagles). Keep an eye out on the right for Tower Ridge Road and follow it for three miles past a campground and unpaved roads leading to primitive backcountry campsites. At the end of the road is a grand fire watcher's tower; scramble up for commanding vistas of the region. Hiking trails spiderweb through the ridges from here—it's outstanding for hikers.

Farther north, you'll cross a portion of *Lake Monroe,* Indiana's largest lake (10,750 acres) and one of its best spots for outdoor recreation. It's an outstanding place to land crappie, and Crappie USA, a dedicated crappie-fishing organization, holds its annual tournament here in April and May. For information about the area, stop north of the lake at the Paynetown Visitors Center; you'll also find plenty of established camping.

Continue north on Highway 446 to Swartz Ridge Road. Turn left (west) and go to Moores Creek Road and turn right (north) onto Snoddy Road. We finish as we began—a visit to the quiet contemplation of Tibetan culture. The *Tibetan Cultural Center,* 3655 Snoddy Road, (812) 334-7046, is unique among Buddhist cultural sites in the United States. Most prominent here is the country's only *chorten,* a multi-tiered Tibetan monument, usually containing sacred relics. The 35-foot-tall copper-topped cornerstone is a memorial to Tibetan culture as it slowly dissipates under Chinese rule; it contains many sacred Tibetan Buddhist items. If nothing else, it makes for a special spot to reflect on the world. The grounds are open noon–4 p.m. Wednesday, 10 a.m.–4 p.m. Saturday–Sunday. A visitor center is open 1–3 p.m. Sunday.

Retrace your route back to Highway 446. Turn left (north) and drive back to Bloomington.

Tour 9
Magnificent Architecture and Some Greenspace

Columbus–Hope–Greensburg–Westport–Vernon–Seymour–Columbus

Distance: 120 miles

Here are places most midwesterners have never heard of, and yet they may be the loveliest spots in the entire region. Our tour starts out in Columbus, famed for its astonishing architecture—you could literally spend days wandering about, gaping at the complex and challenging building designs. We pay homage to that oh-so-American ideal of road tripping and classic cars, then roll through classic Indiana limestone country to Decatur County and Greensburg, another classic friendly small town. The eye-candy architecture behind us, we find refuge and history together at Muscatatuck National Wildlife Refuge and Park, with numerous trails, historical structures, and opportunities to espy wildlife.

Start your tour in downtown Columbus at the *Columbus Area Visitors Center,* 506 Fifth Street (at the corner of Franklin Street), (812) 378-2622 or (800) 468-6564, www.columbus.in.us. The center offers an audiovisual display and a variety of exhibits on the history and aesthetic vision of the city's architecture; you can also organize a guided tour here—highly recommended even for building mavens. They depart the visitors center at 10 a.m. weekdays, at 10 a.m. and 2 p.m. Saturday, and at 11 a.m. Sunday, March–November. Tours last two hours (though guides can whip you through in one) and cost $9.50 (various discounts available).

Columbus otherwise is made for walking. Pick a direction, any direction, and stroll; you'll be passing by some of the nation's finest architecture. There are other diversions, however, in case you begin to suffer the occupational hazard of a stiff neck from looking up at buildings all the time. The Commons Mall between Third and Fourth Streets at Brown Street is the site of the *Indianapolis Museum of Art—Columbus Gallery,* (812) 376-2597, the only satellite gallery of the famed IMA. You'll find five major exhibitions annually of works from the main museum and other traveling collections. Open 10 a.m.–5 p.m. Tuesday-Saturday, till 8 p.m. Friday, noon–4 p.m. Sunday.

East of the visitors center along Fifth Street you'll find the local library. Adjacent are the lovely *Irwin Gardens,* part of a private residence open to the public on weekends mid-April to mid-October. These sunken gardens are on the estate of the late William G. Irwin; you'll find formal flower, shrub,

One of Columbus's many famed church steeples.

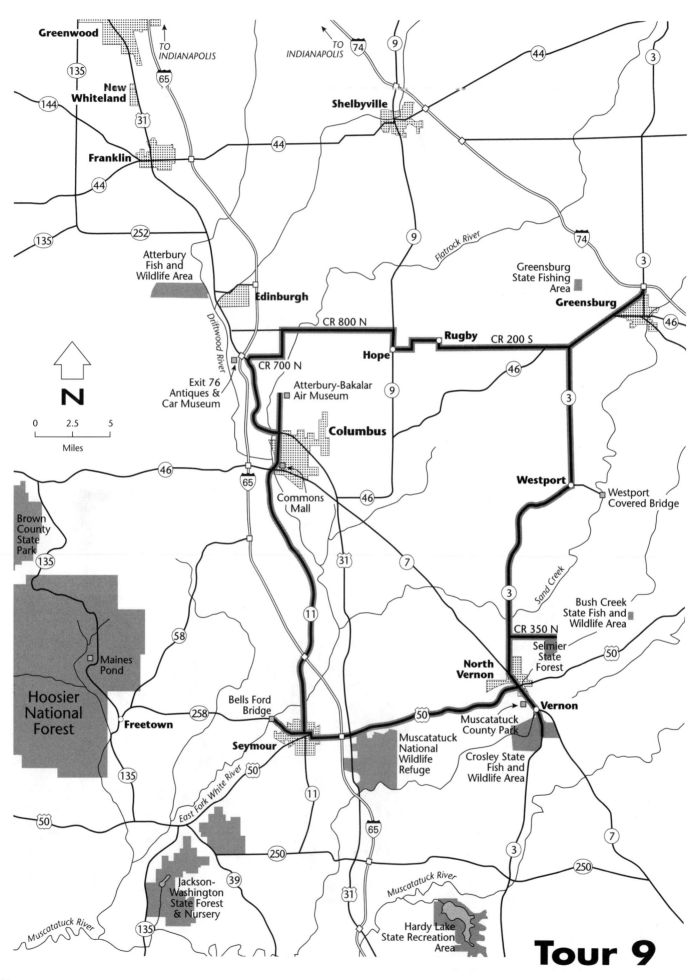

Greenwood

TO
INDIANAPOLIS

TO
INDIANAPOLIS

135

144

New
Whiteland

31

Franklin

44

135

252

44

65

74

9

Shelbyville

44

3

Atterbury
Fish and
Wildlife Area

Edinburgh

Flatrock River

Greensburg
State Fishing
Area

74

3

Greensburg

46

CR 800 N

Rugby

CR 200 S

N

Hope

CR 700 N

9

46

0   2.5   5

Miles

Exit 76
Antiques &
Car Museum

Atterbury-Bakalar
Air Museum

3

Columbus

46

65

Brown
County
State
Park

135

Commons
Mall

46

Westport

Westport
Covered Bridge

7

Sand Creek

31

Bush Creek
State Fish and
Wildlife Area

50

11

CR 350 N

Selmier
State Forest

58

3

Maines
Pond

North
Vernon

Hoosier
National
Forest

258

Bells Ford
Bridge

Vernon

Freetown

50

Muscatatuck
County Park

135

Seymour

East Fork White River

50

11

Muscatatuck
National
Wildlife
Refuge

Crosley State
Fish and
Wildlife Area

65

50

250

7

Jackson-
Washington
State Forest
& Nursery

39

3

250

135

31

Muscatatuck River

Muscatatuck River

Hardy Lake
State Recreation
Area

Tour 9

Columbus's jail, believe it or not.

Columbus's Crown Jewels

How on earth can a small town (some 37,000 cheery souls) in southern Indiana come to possess some of the planet's most highly respected examples of civic architecture? In a word: philanthropy; well, two words—philanthropy and vision.

As far back as 1942 Eliel Saarinen, of the famed Finnish family, designed the First Christian Church. This city-block–sized church at once gave the city a majestic—and unique—architectural linchpin, and set some city leaders and bigwigs to thinking. In the 1950s, the Cummins Engine Foundation, a local philanthropic trust, began to offer payment of architectural fees for the construction of public buildings. Voila! In the ensuing five decades, a veritable who's who of international architects came to be represented here, from I. M. Pei to Robert Trent Jones. Prominent architects have designed more than 50 buildings, and the American Institute of Architects has ranked the city sixth in innovation and design. The only other cities with such a concentration of buildings are Boston, Washington, Chicago, and San Francisco.

Prominent structures abound. Businesses, factories, fire stations, schools, churches, even jails and city parks. The Commons Mall between Third and Fourth Streets and Brown Street, anchors the downtown. It has a public hall, indoor park and playground, performing arts center, and an enormous moving sculpture. Most eye-catching to some are the churches. In addition to the 166-foot steeple of the First Christian Church (stop by the church office for visitation details), which dominated the skyline for decades, is the copper-clad 186-foot steeple of Saint Peter's Lutheran Church, built in 1988. Eliel Saarinen's son Eero designed the distinctive North Christian Church and gave it an imposing 192-foot spire, now the most commanding presence downtown. If you're just going to the visitors center, that too is of note. The 1864 Victorian underwent a $2 million renovation, which more than doubled its size; the new elements faithfully reproduce the older wing, thanks to a successful search for the same brick and roofing materials. Even the local Bartholomew County Jail stands out just southeast of the visitors center, with its distinctive white meshlike dome, looking for all the world like an observatory.

One thing most people don't realize at first is that all of the city's structures were designed with aesthetics of another kind—concealed parking. Most parking lots were "hidden," allowing the perimeters of buildings to be ensconced by trees. What a wonderful idea.

and herb gardens, gurgling fountains, and leafy trees. Interesting to note that some of the coping work for the rock wall was found in an Italian city buried by lava.

South of here at 524 Third Street is the *Bartholomew County Historical Society,* (812) 372-3541, housed in an elegantly restored Italianate mansion. Five galleries display furniture and art from the Victorian days along with a variety of regional historical detritus. One nice thing is a hands-on area for kids. Open 9 a.m.–4 p.m. Tuesday–Friday.

If you're a festival goer, from November to January 1, the city lights up downtown Mill Race Park brilliantly with over two million lights of all sorts, 300 displays, electric rides, and more—looking at it you're pretty sure the space shuttle could see this baby from space. The third weekend in September brings folks by the hordes to the *Chautauqua of the Arts,* the state's favorite two-day arts and crafts festival.

Drive east to Central Street and turn north, following the signs to the Columbus Municipal Airport at the edge of town. Adjacent to the airport is the *Atterbury-Bakalar Air Museum,* 4742 Ray Boll Boulevard, (812) 372-4356, a fun little museum paying homage to the fliers who have served the nation from World War II through Vietnam. You'll find scale models of vintage aircraft, uniforms, and assorted other memorabilia. It's open 10 a.m.–4 p.m. Saturday.

Return to Central Street and go south to Highway 31 (National Road). Turn right on 31 and drive about 9 miles to the intersection with I-65 (exit 76). Here, you'll find the unique *Exit 76 Antiques and Car Museum,* a 20,000-square-foot museum housing '55, '56, and '57 Chevys and other classic vehicles, all dating from the glory days of American design and automaking (and, some say, civilization in general). There's also a nice hodgepodge of antique farm vehicles, military trucks, and patriotic artwork. This is one of those labors of love that pop up on the road occasionally and represent the personal passions of their creators. For a hearty slice of Americana, this can't be beat. Open 9 a.m.–7 p.m. Monday–Saturday, noon–5 p.m. Sunday. Admission; net proceeds are donated to world missions.

From the intersection of Highway 31 and I-65, go east a short distance on County Road 700N to County Road 200W. Turn left and go to County Road 800N. Turn right (east) and go about 10 miles to Highway 9. Along the way you could opt for a visit at the *Historic Henry Breeding Mill,* (812) 372-3541, operated by the Bartholomew County Historical

Society. This collection of Federal-style farm buildings dates from 1860 and is a fine example of period rural architecture. There are also antique farm implement displays and seasonal herb and flower gardens. The home is open for tours by appointment only.

Go south on Highway 9 for 2 miles to Hope. This fascinating little community was founded in 1830 by Moravians, the oldest mainstream Protestant denomination. Here you'll find a *Moravian church,* one of the nation's oldest. Its God's Acre cemetery—tread lightly, please—is filled with a wondrous array of headstones arranged in a system known as a choir. Tours of the church are available 9 a.m.–1 p.m. weekdays. Call (812) 546-4641 for more information. In Hope you'll also find the *Simmons School,* a newly restored 1890s one-room schoolhouse. Tours are available 9–11 a.m. and 1–3 p.m. Stop by the superintendent's office in the Hope Elementary School for information or call (812) 546-4922 weekdays, (812) 546-4877 weekends. Also right along Highway 9 is the *Yellow Trail Museum,* a small but worthy museum giving an overview on Moravia, the church that took its name, and the journey to Indiana and the community it founded.

From Hope, head east via County Road 200S for about 8 miles to Highway 46. Proceed on 46 (which is soon joined by Highway 3) for another 8 miles to Greensburg. Finding Highway 46 can be a bit tricky, so keep your eyes peeled. You may get lost; you may have to cobble together a route from various back roads, but isn't that the fun of touring? This friendly little community, seat of Decatur County, is famous for one thing: trees. But not where you'd expect them. Rather than in the parks or along the avenues—oh, they've got them there too—people have come to know of the trees that have grown for more than a century out of the roof of the county courthouse tower. Thus, the city's proud new moniker is Tower Tree City. They even whoop up the honor with a fun September festival.

If you have some extra time in the area, stop by the local chamber of commerce office, 325 W. Main Street, (800) 210-2832, 8 a.m.–4 p.m. Monday–Friday (closed noon–1 p.m.). Here you can pick up brochures and (much-needed) local expertise on the hour-long county tours that offer road trippers unparalleled views of covered bridges, the eskers and kames of a million years of geology, dormant townships, old mills, earth-sheltered homes, and even Glacier Terminus, the highest point in the county. You'll need explicit directions for each of the four tours, which are definitely worthwhile.

With all the attention paid to the tree on the tower, the city has rededicated itself to planting trees and there's a walking tour to appreciate them. It's a nice touch. Along the way stop off at the *Decatur County Historical Society,* 222 N.

Covered Bridges

Covered bridges were also known as kissing bridges. When young folks were courting and their buggy entered the tunnel, the young man could expect a kiss from his girl—no doubt due to the inherent secrecy. The bridges also served double duty as the site of large community gatherings—like weddings.

The Hardy Trees of Greensburg

The first tree sprouted from the courthouse tower roof in 1869. Not surprisingly, it was removed as a pest. When another one took hold, however, locals knew powers far stronger than botany were at work and left it there. The second tree died in 1929 (you can check out the details at the local county museum), and lo and behold not one but two trees later took root. In 1958 one tree was removed and yet another tree was soon discovered. Finally, one tree was removed, leaving a sole representative, 110 feet up. This large-toothed aspen somehow manages to hold on where it shouldn't and, if nothing else, give a warm sort of local pride, kind of a respectable stick-to-it-iveness that befits a community of hardworking midwesterners. Businesses all use it as a trademark, and even local schools name their athletic teams after it—not exactly ferocious, but at least highly relevant historically.

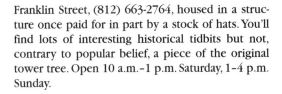

Greensburg's weird and wonderfully hardy courthouse tree.

Franklin Street, (812) 663-2764, housed in a structure once paid for in part by a stock of hats. You'll find lots of interesting historical tidbits but not, contrary to popular belief, a piece of the original tower tree. Open 10 a.m.–1 p.m. Saturday, 1–4 p.m. Sunday.

From Greensburg go west on Highway 46/3 to the junction of 46 and 3. Turn left (south) on Highway 3 and proceed 11 miles to Westport. Follow the signs to the downtown. Now start asking for directions on how to get to the *Westport Covered Bridge;* believe me, though it's only three or so miles east of town, it can be tricky (hopefully, signs will be posted by the time you read this). This gem of a bridge was built in 1880 of skew-type stone abutments cut from a nearby quarry. The bridge spans Sand Creek and is over

130 feet long, with a clear span of 11 feet 6 inches, and is on the National Register of Historic Places.

Return to Highway 3 and continue south about 12 miles. At County Road 350N head east for 3 miles. You'll find a little patch of verdancy here, the southern lobe of the Selmier State Forest, (812) 346-2286. Altogether there are 355 scenic wooded acres for fishing along the Muscatatuck River or small ponds (decent bass fishing). No public rest rooms or campgrounds are here but you'll find nicely secluded trails.

Return to Highway 3 (which is soon joined by Highway 7) and head south through North Vernon to Vernon. Equidistant between these neighboring communities is *Muscatatuck County Park,* (812) 346-2953. What was once an Indiana state park (the fourth, originally called Vinegar Mills State Park) is now a quaint little county park. One national wildlife refuge, two state wildlife refuges, and a state forest are all within 15 minutes of the park, too. On site is the Walnut Grove one-room schoolhouse, redone in period detail with garbed docents doling out information on area history. A popular Civil War reenactment and a bluegrass festival take place in summer. Five short but pleasant hiking trails snake throughout the wooded acres. The River Trail is a particularly nice 2.5-miler with falls, oxbow bends, canyons, overlooks, and a lot of wildlife. The county and state are planning to extend this trail through Vernon and into the Crosely State Fish and Wildlife Area. When this happens, it will be an absolutely lovely hike. You start and end with splendorous natural beauty and loads of wildlife. In between you'll have a chance to stop off in anachronistic *Vernon,* easily one of the state's most picturesque towns. The National Register has high praise for the examples of nineteenth-century Indiana architecture found in its gem of a historic district.

Return to Highway 3/7 and go north a short distance to Highway 50. Turn left (west) and proceed approximately 12 miles to the entrance of the *Muscatatuck National Wildlife Refuge.* The refuge, (812) 522-4352, contains nearly 8,000 acres spread out throughout the area just east of Seymour and I-65. With 12 miles of hiking trails—not to mention a great guided auto tour—with lots of overlook and observation points, opportunities for espying wildlife abound. Stop first at the visitor center, which has a mini-museum on the natural history of the area. Excellent brochures detail interpretive trails that wend through the marshlands and soggy bottoms. Even the berry picking is great here. The optional auto tour is a good idea. At four miles, it's not too long

and the highlights are well marked and very informative. Best spots for wildlife viewing are an overlook at North Endicott Marsh and Richart Lake, not far from the visitor center.

Continue west on Highway 50 to Seymour. This charming town warrants a mention as the purported site of the nation's first armed robbery of a train. It also produced medicinal artesian salt water for area bathhouses in the nineteenth century. If you need to stretch your legs, visit the downtown library, which has an excellent display of Hoosier artwork.

In downtown Seymour, turn right (north) onto Highway 258 (S. Broadway Street) and follow it for about 3 miles. You'll come to a fork of the White River and *Bells Ford Bridge,* the only remaining post-truss covered bridge in the world. (Post-truss is an engineering design that combines wood with iron and is known as a transitional bridge between all-wood and all-steel bridges.)

Return to Seymour and turn left (north) on Highway 11. Drive about 20 miles back to Columbus. This road traces the sheer Knobstone Escarpment, which stretches all the way from Indianapolis into Kentucky. The roadway passes through a wondrous geological melange of glacial after-effects—moraines and eskers are readily apparent—and exposed ancient bedrock.

Quick Trip Option: Instead of returning to Seymour and Highway 11, you could continue west on Highway 258 to Freetown and the edge of the Hoosier National Forest. Continue north on Highway 135, past excellent wildlife viewing at *Maines Pond,* and ultimately bringing you to Brown County State Park (see Tour 8) west of Columbus.

Critters of the Marsh

Of all the creepers and crawlers of the Muscatatuck National Wildlife Refuge, a couple are of note. First, look for members of what arguably may be the cutest of all species—the otter. Twenty-five river otters were transplanted here from Louisiana in 1995; the fish-eating species has thrived. Keep your eyes peeled for the frisky critters.

Second, keep a lookout for the copperbelly water snake. This nonpoisonous water snake has a lethal-sounding name but is harmless . . . unless you're a frog, that is. It is so rare that it is being considered for placement on the federal list of threatened species. It is particularly vulnerable to vehicular traffic when it uses roads to travel between bogs. Please pay attention and give these little guys the right-of-way. (By the way, no poisonous snakes have been found at the refuge, so relax!)

Tour 10
Steeples, Canals, and the National Road

Richmond–Centerville–Cambridge City–Knightstown–Rushville–Connersville–Oldenburg–Metamora–Brookville–Liberty–Richmond

Distance: 146.5 miles

What better place to begin a tour than at a node on the National Road, the first interstate "highway" built in America? In this land of the automobile culture, where the ribbony roadways are revered in a quasi-religious sense, it's perfectly fitting. But Richmond isn't simply the road—there are miles of antique shops, Underground Railroad stations, and more. The retreat into transportation history really heats up, but for reasons of an entirely different nature in Metamora, which is a must-see for its historic canal district. Before the advent of roadways, canals were crucial transport links between waterways. Metamora's district draws history buffs, road trippers, and a heck of a lot of antique/craft fans as well. We'll descend—quite literally—gently into Oldenburg, famed for its steepled skyline, quite definitely the best spot for a photo-op on this tour. To return to Richmond, we patch together a network of Blue Highway-quality back roads, where you'll be digging out the detailed atlas because the state freebie maps can't hope to keep up with the spiderweb network. The route passes along rivers and streams and through modest stands of pine.

Start your tour east of Richmond at the junction of Highway 40 (the National Road) and I-70/35. There you'll find one of the best-stocked (and irrepressibly cheery) visitor centers you'll ever see, the *Richmond/Wayne County Convention and Visitors Bureau,* 5701 Highway 40, (765) 935-8687 or (800) 828-8414, www.visitrichmond.org. The accommodating staff can give you all the information you need on local spots and will load you down with bags full of maps and brochures. And there are loads of sights to see.

Begin your trip by driving west on Highway 40 about 2 miles to Elks Road. Turn right and drive about a mile to the *Hayes Regional Arboretum.* This 355-acre nature preserve, (765) 962-3745, is devoted to plants native to the region (over 175 woody plants are found within the landscape). In addition to nature trails, there's a bird sanctuary, an 1833 barn retrofitted with all the accoutrements of a first-class nature center. If you're short on time, no problem—there's a three-mile auto tour through the grounds. Open 9 a.m.- 5 p.m. Tuesday-Saturday, 1-5 p.m. Sunday; auto

tour has admission charge, grounds are free.

Just to the east of the arboretum, *Glen Miller Park* is one of Richmond's innumerable swaths of green space, all a veritable necklace of parkland. Within the park is the *Madonna of the Trail,* a monument to the National Road (one of 12 across the country) depicting a pioneer woman and her two children. Even more of a draw is the *E. G. Hill Memorial Rose Garden and German Friendship Garden.* Centered on a fountain, the garden has more than 1,600 roses and hundreds of perennials, with a gazebo thrown in for restful contemplation; much of it was done in partnership with sister city Zweibrücken.

Nearby is the entrance to *Whitewater Gorge Park,* a huge chasm formed by retreating glaciers. You'll find a spectacular array of hiking trails through the heart of the channel; the highlight is the grouping of Thistlewaite Falls. A four-mile trail is marked with geological and historical attractions.

Go back south to Highway 40 and turn right (west). Proceed to downtown Richmond. Founded on the banks of the powerful Whitewater River in 1806, Richmond had a population that was predominantly German intermingled with a sizable Quaker presence from North Carolina. In addition to building Earlham College, the Friends (as Quakers are known) added a voice of social conscience prior to the Civil War. In a debate in Richmond in 1842, presidential candidate Henry Clay was challenged by a Quaker protestor to denounce slavery (and free his slaves). Clay proceeded to put his foot in his mouth by refusing to free his slaves and saying that they were better off sans emancipation. Many believe this pronouncement opened the door for the election of James Polk in the 1844. Richmond, owing much to its access to hydropower, rose to become one of Indiana's industrial leaders, with up to five dozen factories at work at the onset of World War II.

The better part of a morning or afternoon could be spent in downtown Richmond, which has one of the largest concentrations of historic architecture in Indiana. The granddaddy, the *Old Richmond Historic District,* spreads over 250 acres and has 213 structures of historic significance, most of these being Federal and Greek Revival

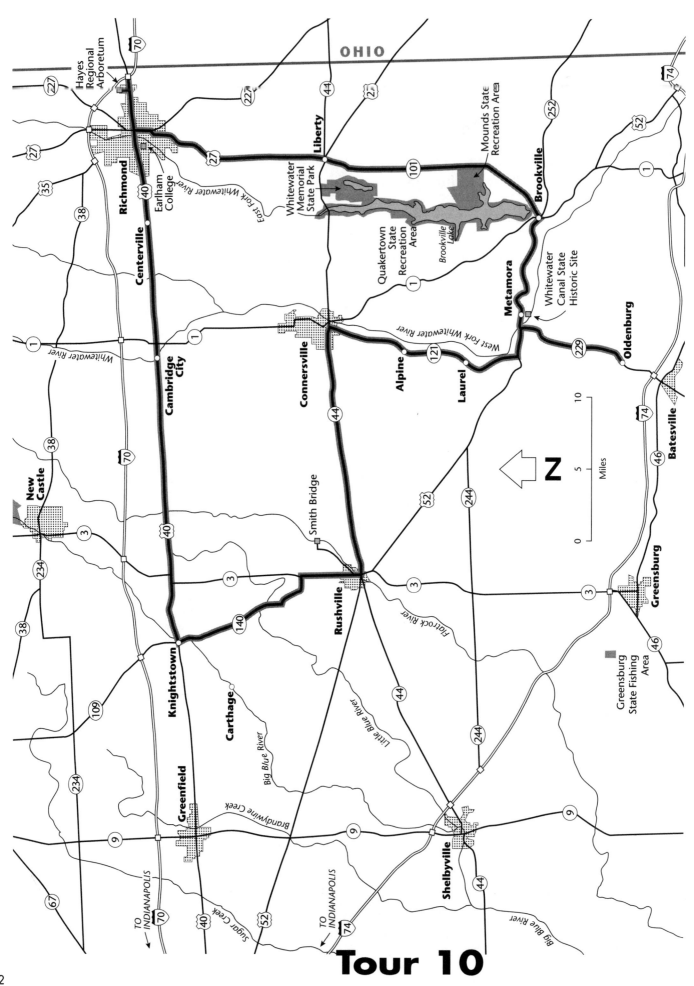

OHIO

Hayes Regional Arboretum

Richmond
Centerville
Cambridge City
Earlham College
East Fork Whitewater River
Whitewater River

Liberty

Whitewater Memorial State Park
Quakertown State Recreation Area
Brookville Lake
Mounds State Recreation Area

Brookville

Metamora
Whitewater Canal State Historic Site
West Fork Whitewater River
Oldenburg
Batesville

Connersville
Alpine
Laurel

New Castle

Smith Bridge

Rushville

Greensburg

Greensburg State Fishing Area

Knightstown

Carthage

Flatrock River
Little Blue River

Greenfield

Shelbyville

Big Blue River
Brandywine Creek
Sugar Creek

TO INDIANAPOLIS
TO INDIANAPOLIS

N
Miles
10
5
0

Tour 10

52

townhouses and cottages. You can walk this district; the visitor center has brochures. It's bounded by South A and E Streets north to south, and South Fifth to Third Streets east to west.

Another historic district is the *Starr District* to the north, the Midwest's best example of Victorian architecture. Its dozens of structures include an original railroad depot and the Scott House at 126 North Tenth St., an imposing piece of Italianate eye-candy open for tours ($1); call (765) 962-5756 for details. This district lies between North A and North E Streets and South Tenth and South Sixteenth Streets.

But Richmond isn't only a collection of wide tree-lined avenues with stately mansions. For a peek at the history of local industry and the presence of the Quakers, head for the *Wayne County Historical Museum,* 1150 North A Street, (765) 962-5756, the site of a former Quaker meetinghouse. Local oddities include exhibits on Richmond's fledgling auto industry; who knew that 13 autos were built here (six are on site)? You'll also see airplanes built by local factories, local inventions, and a set of Egyptian mummies. Open 9 a.m.–4 p.m. Tuesday–Friday, 1-4 p.m. weekends, mid-February to mid-December. Admission.

Four blocks from here, at 815 North A Street, you'll find a museum of an entirely different sort. The *Indiana Football Hall of Fame,* (765) 966-2235, gives an incredibly detailed overview of Hoosier-connected football, with a hefty dose of high school football. Richmond's own Lamar Lundy, who played at Purdue University and for the Los Angeles Rams, sometimes serves as a guide. Open 10 a.m.–5 p.m. weekdays, weekends by appointment, May–September, reduced times rest of year.

Drive a few blocks west from the downtown area on Highway 40; soon after it crosses the Whitewater River and jogs left, you'll come to Hub Etchison Parkway. Turn left. You'll come upon the *Richmond Art Museum,* (765) 966-0256, the only public art museum in the United States housed in a functional high school. You'll find both Hoosier artworks and traveling exhibits on a wide range of disciplines. Open 10 a.m.–5 p.m. Tuesday–Friday, 1-4 p.m. weekends.

A few blocks west of the museum is Earlham College, a fine liberal arts school. If you're interested in Quakers and their practices, you'll find artifacts, documents, art, and historical items at the Friends Collection in the *Lilly Library* at Earlham College, (765) 983-1511. Hours are 9 a.m.–noon, 1-4 p.m., and 7-9 p.m. Monday–Thursday; 9 a.m.–noon and 1-4 p.m. Friday; 1-4 p.m. weekends. Also at Earlham College is the *Joseph Moore Museum* (765) 983-1303, with an impressive natural history collection, ranging from an Egyptian mummy to a 15,000-year-old mastodon skeleton. Open 1-4 p.m. Monday, Wednesday, and Friday, till 5 p.m. Sunday, September–April; Sundays only, May–August.

The legendary steeples of Oldenburg.

Return north to Highway 40 and go 6 miles west to Centerville. Centerville's endless strings of row houses—all in remarkably pristine condition—owe their existence to the National Road. This was once a primary stopping point, with up to 200 wagons per day passing through. The clapboard hotels, blacksmith shops, and general stores have been re-created into one of the Midwest's—if not the country's—largest conglomerations of antique and craft shops anywhere: some 500 antique booths over two acres—wow! In fact, Centerville is called the linchpin to "Antique Alley"—a stretch of the National Road from Richmond to Knightstown. If you've got the will to unshackle the calfskin (and have had a big breakfast of energy-inducing carbs), there is no better place to go than here.

As you tool around the small town, you might see what appears to be a somewhat decrepit little log cabin–looking thing. Well, that's exactly what it is, and it's the only log cabin courthouse of the Northwest Territory still in existence (though not in use).

Continue west on Highway 40 approximately 12 miles to Cambridge City. Here the *Huddleston Farmhouse Inn Museum,* (765) 478-3172, dates from 1839 as one of the original lodging spots for weary travelers (and workers) along the National Road. All the original buildings—including the smokehouse, farmhouse, springhouse, and barn—have been lovingly restored. The interiors use original finishings and furniture to re-create a typical day of life on the road. Open 10 a.m.–4 p.m. Tuesday–Saturday, February–December, also 1–4 p.m. Sunday in summer. Admission.

Also in Cambridge City is a look at decades of pottery work at the *Museum of Overbeck Art Pottery,* 33 West Main Street, (765) 478-3335. A cornerstone to regional artwork in the first half of the twentieth century, Overbeck Pottery was run by six sisters until 1955. Hours are 10 a.m.–noon and 2-5 p.m. Monday–Saturday; tours by appointment.

Proceed west on Highway 40 from Cambridge City for about 20 miles to Knightstown. This is one of the most historic National Road "pike towns." You can get an up-close look at historic architecture, a mixture of Federal and Victorian styles. The gentrified downtown is an eye-catching treat. Most visitors come here to hop aboard the *Carthage, Knightstown, and Shirley Railroad,* (765) 345-5561, an anachronistic railroad with vintage cars and coaches. The route follows a lovely 10-mile track over the Big Blue River to Carthage and back; it takes about one hour one-way. The track was once part of the Cleveland, Cincinnati, Chicago, and Saint Louis Railroad. Carthage has some antique railroad equipment on display. Trains depart from the Knightstown depot, 112 W. Carey Street, (765) 345-5561, at 11 a.m. and 1 and 3 p.m. Saturday, Sunday, and holidays, 11 a.m. Friday, May–October.

A nostalgia-drenched, only-in-Indiana attraction is the *Knightstown Hoosier Gym,* 335 N. Washington Street, (765) 345-2244. Located in the old Knightstown Academy, this gym was used to film the movie *Hoosiers.* For the basketball-mad, this could be considered a pilgrimage. Note that it's open only by appointment. Another site for the nostalgia lovers is *Trump's Texaco Museum,* 39 N. Washington Street, (765) 345-7135, a tribute of sorts to the open road. Created by an aficionado of, well, Texaco memorabilia, it's kind of cool to get the feel of a classic old gas station, with some stuff dating back to the 1920s.

At Knightstown turn south onto Highway 140 (aka County Road 360W) and proceed about 15 miles to Highway 3. Turn right (south) and go to Highway 44 in Rushville. Turn left (east) on Highway 44 and continue for 15 miles to Connersville.

For aficionados of old-fashioned train travel, you've come to the right place—Connersville. This gem of a town is the terminus of the *Whitewater Valley Railroad,* (765) 825-2054, which offers scenic 16-mile, 1.5-hour long (one-way) journeys between Connersville and Metamora along the towpath of the Whitewater Canal; for the round-trip ticket you get a layover in Metamora (do some shopping). Fall color season is the best time to come, though be forewarned: hordes of people will

The National Road—the Original Interstate

The National Road was established as the country's first interstate road by an act of Congress in 1806. It had originally been proposed by George Washington and Albert Gallatin in 1784. It slowly expanded westward—the original segment begun in 1811 stretched 677 miles from Cumberland, Maryland, to Wheeling, West Virginia—reaching Indiana by 1829 as it tried to find its way to Saint Louis. Originally it consisted of rough ruts of dirt (a quagmire in spring), then gravel by 1818. Indiana gave the road its own twist: it leased its section to a private company, which paved it with planks and made it a toll road. Construction lasted from 1827 to 1839, when it finally reached Terre Haute. The road would start in Richmond and ultimately became Indianapolis's first real street (you can still see the memorial marker outside the statehouse in Indianapolis). The government never really improved the road west of Indianapolis and the state ultimately took control of it in 1839. All along the route "pike towns" arose, usually one every 10 miles or so; they served the needs of travelers but also gave isolated farmers more outside contact.

Like the Lincoln Highway (see Tour 13), the National Road represented not so much a simple road as a change in American culture. This original road represents metaphorically the manifest destiny of the American vision; much of how our culture evolved took place and is taking place along our routes of transportation (strip mall hell zones, anyone?). The billboard's dastardly genesis—this author is firmly of the opinion that billboards are nothing more than

litter on sticks—came directly from transcontinental highways' development. "Gypsy camps" set up by vagabond auto tourers led the way to civic camps; the historic inns transmogrified into open court motels. Much like today's mind-numbing but thoroughly necessary and oh-so-American interstates, these nation-spanning avenues contain their own culture; they are stretched out cities themselves if you think about it. The transcontinental highways are just more fun—you're slower, you're experiencing the communities directly. Although railroads and interstates reduced the need for roads like Highway 40 (I-70 finally eclipsed the highway in the 1960s), a modern revival of bicycling and back-to-the-roots travel has brought new life to these roadways.

The route is now established as an Official State Scenic Drive. It's fun to experience the individual communities' take on the whole thing: to some it's a source of pride, to others, just a road. Seven National Register Historic Districts line the route across Indiana. The stretch between Dunrieth and Knightstown, an original segment, is a great way to experience it; other "pike towns" like Pennville and Dublin still have that feel of the great American open road. Centerville's Federal-style buildings show a distinct mid-Atlantic influence, reflecting the effect of a migration westward. Note the interesting nomenclature: National Road, National Pike, National Avenue, even Cumberland Street or Avenue. Visitor centers and chambers of commerce all along the route have brochures on the heritage and history of the route.

be riding the rails with you. Trips are on weekends and holidays, from the first Saturday in May until the last Sunday in October (also Thanksgiving weekend's Saturday and Sunday). Trains depart at noon and return by 5:30 p.m. Special trips, such as a dinner train, are also offered throughout the operating season; call for details.

Optional Side Trip: Between Rushville and Connersville, you can take in some great covered bridges. Northeast out of Rushville, take Fort Wayne Road to County Road 150N; here you'll find the *Smith Bridge,* which dates from 1877. It's 121 feet long, with a vertical clearance of 14 feet. If you go back to Fort Wayne Road and continue north to County Road 300N, then go east, you'll come to the last covered bridge constructed in the county—and the only one constructed by this company in the twentieth century still standing. From here it's easiest to return to Fort Wayne Road and backtrack to Highway 44.

From Highway 44 in Connersville, turn right (south) at Highway 121 and proceed south through Alpine and Laurel for about 16 miles to Highway 52 just west of Metamora. Turn left (east) and go about 2 miles to Highway 229. Turn right (south) and head for about 10 miles to Oldenburg. This is one of the loveliest drives in the area. The road winds through forest land and over glacial moraines and other topographical residue. Tiny Oldenburg is legendary among road trippers as having the most scenic skyline in the state, and it truly is inspiring as you come over the final rise and see the steeple-specked sky. The collection of spires is impressive for a town of its size. Its Germanic heritage is in full swing; on a recent visit I noticed that even the local priests were wearing lederhosen for some reason.

Backtrack on Highway 229 to Highway 52; turn right, and proceed to Metamora. More old-fashioned anachronism is found in Metamora, a time-locked town where the heyday of canal transportation is revisited daily. The village dates to 1838 and was once a major player on the canal scene, with the waterways also allowing hydro-powered gristmills. You can see horse-drawn barges slowly being towed past an original gristmill where original stone still grinds wheat. In fact, the entire village is considered a historic district—more than two dozen buildings are listed on the National Register of Historic Buildings. Shops, shops, and more shops, that pretty much sums up the pursuits of most travelers. The Metamora merchants' association, (765) 647-2109, www.metamora.com, has brochures and maps of the area.

An official state of Indiana historic site, the *Whitewater Canal Historic Site,* (765) 647-6512, offers horse-pulled canal boat rides. At the terminus a gristmill grinds wheat into flour and more. Of interest is the nation's only working covered aqueduct. The site is open 24 hours. Hours for the mill

The Whitewater Canal at Metamora.

and canal rides are 9 a.m.–5 p.m. Tuesday–Saturday, 1–5 p.m. Sunday, mid-March to mid-December; boat rides ($1) noon–4 p.m. Monday–Friday, 11 a.m.–4 p.m. weekends, May 1–October 1.

Loads of festivals and events take place throughout the year; the merchants' association has lists. Thousands of aquaphiles come for *Canal Days and Traders Rendezvous* the first weekend in October.

From Metamora, drive east on Highway 52 about 8 miles to Brookville. The road is wide and forgiving but it rolls and twists along the river valley of the West Fork of the Whitewater River through loads of county forest land. (An alternate route is to head east to Brookville through the network of tiny roads east of Peppertown, but it's hopelessly complicated to explain; if you don't mind getting lost, whip out the atlas and have a go.)

Brookville sits at the south end of the third-largest body of water in Indiana (sixteen miles top to bottom)—*Brookville Lake*—and a great source of hydrophilic recreation. Brookville also has a modest historic site—the *Hermitage,* 650 E. Eighth Street, (765) 647-5182, once home to two famous Indiana painters: J. Otis Adams and T. C. Steele. Tours are by appointment only.

For lake-oriented recreation, throw a stick and you'll hit one of the area's many marinas or canoe-rental places. Park the car and rent a canoe, boat, or tube.

Just north of Brookville, get on Highway 101 and drive north for 18 miles to Liberty. You'll pass by rustic camping sites and the reservoir project office. Along the way you'll find a whole slew of turnoffs for scenic views, boat launching, picnicking, water skiing, and even a nice little nature preserve. At *Whitewater Memorial State Park,* just south of Liberty, you'll find camping and hiking trails. The entrance fee for out-of-state cars is $5.

From Liberty, go north on Highway 27 for about 15 miles to return to Richmond.

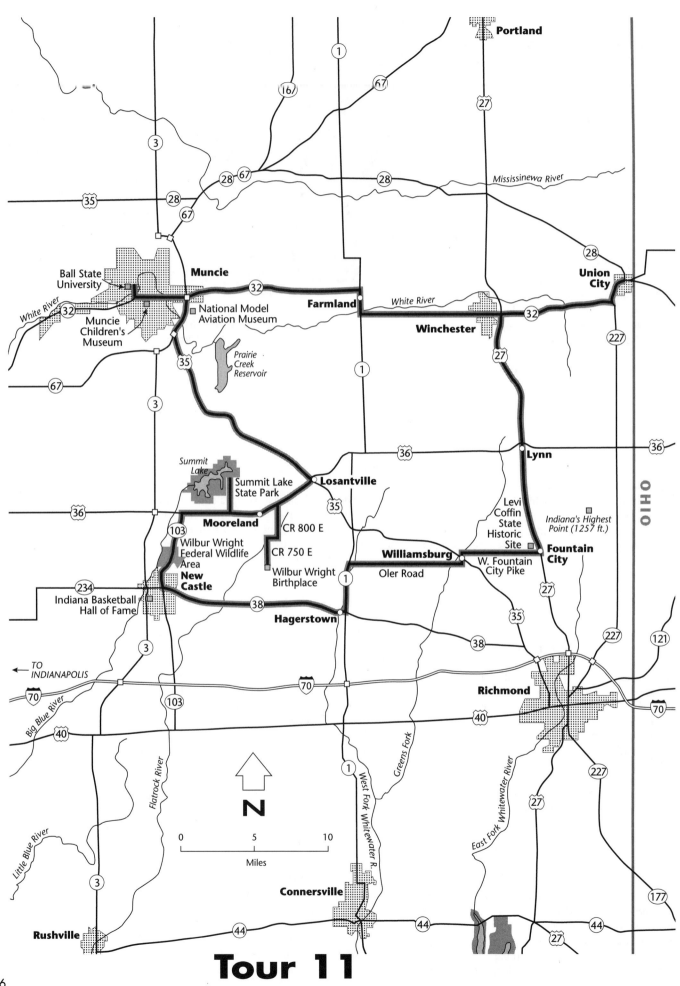

Portland

16/

1

67

27

3

28 67

28

28

35

28

67

Union
City

Muncie

32

Farmland

White River

28

227

Ball State
University

White River

32

National Model
Aviation Museum

Winchester

32

Muncie
Children's
Museum

_Prairie
Creek
Reservoir_

1

27

35

67

3

36

Lynn

36

_Summit
Lake_

Summit Lake
State Park

Losantville

_Indiana's Highest
Point (1257 ft.)_

36

35

Levi
Coffin
State
Historic
Site

103

Mooreland

CR 800 E

Wilbur Wright
Federal Wildlife
Area

CR 750 E

Williamsburg

Fountain
City

234

New
Castle

Wilbur Wright
Birthplace

1

Oler Road

W. Fountain
City Pike

27

Indiana Basketball
Hall of Fame

38

35

Hagerstown

38

3

227

121

TO
INDIANAPOLIS

70

Big Blue River

103

Richmond

70

40

40

Flatrock River

Little Blue River

3

↑

N

1

West Fork Whitewater R.

Greens Fork

East Fork Whitewater River

27

227

0   5   10

Miles

Connersville

177

OHIO

Rushville

44

44

44

27

Tour 11

Tour 11
Heartland Heritage

Muncie–Mooreland–New Castle–Hagerstown–Fountain City–Lynn–Winchester–Union City–Muncie

Distance: 112 miles

"Heartland Heritage" indeed. We start in a town famed for its normalcy (in a state and region already well known for having its collective head on straight, that's a pretty large accomplishment). We stop off for wildlife viewing and getting in touch with our natural side before—surprise, surprise—getting into Hoosier aviation history in the birthplace of Wilbur Wright. The highlight for many on this tour is a visit to New Castle, home of the Indiana Basketball Hall of Fame; you can pretty much guess what's king here. We experience some more natural history—a rare bog is a highlight—and finally arrive at Indiana's most important sites for Underground Railroad history. All this at a little more than 100 miles.

The tour starts in downtown Muncie in High Street Square. Before going to the Muncie Visitors Bureau, a little Muncie history is in order. Located on a plain on lands once occupied by the Munsee Indians, Muncie grew around a railhead to become a thoroughly midwestern, hard-working city. So thoroughly midwestern in fact that in many ways Muncie could be called the most average city in America. Starting in 1924, two well-known sociological studies were undertaken in the city, having been chosen for its, well, averageness—in a good way. (In fact, one of its tourism slogans is: "within a day's drive of 60% of the nation's population.") Small city draws like friendliness and superlatives in quality of life make it a nice city to visit. And, as did those sociological studies, they still call themselves Middletown, as in the Middle of the Nation.

Muncie is known for canning. One of the many local industries was Ball Corporation, maker of the ubiquitous jars that many midwesterners have dealt with during autumn canning season. They aren't made here anymore but the corporation has a cool display in the Minnetrista Cultural Center (see page 58). And for an interesting look at the heritage of canning, *Robinson's Jars,* Wheeling Avenue at West Cowling Drive, (765) 282-9707, is a small private museum with a huge collection of fruit jars; call for a tour. The city is anchored by the eponymous Ball State University, created mainly through the largesse of the Ball family.

First, go to the convenient *Muncie Visitors Bureau,* 425 N. High Street, downtown in High Street Square, (765) 289-2700 or (800) 568-6862, www.muncie visitorsbureau.org. You can do the usual look-see and make sure everything's open. Pick up their invaluable walking-tour brochure. This is quite honestly the best one I've ever seen: not only is it oversized and incredibly detailed but also it includes an overview of the town's general architectural styles and terms, complete with graphics. It really helps. The architectural highlights can be found in an eight-block-by-six-block swath of downtown starting a few blocks southeast of the visitors center.

The best place to start would be the 1850 house containing the *Moore-Youse Home Museum,* 120 E. Washington Street, (765) 282-1550. It contains the original furnishings and stylings of the family that lived in the home for three generations and acts as a living museum. Open Wednesday, March–November.

It's a bit of a walk, but approximately seven blocks south and west is the *Muncie Children's Museum,* 515 S. High Street, (765) 286-1660. If you've got screaming kids looking for something to do on a rainy day, this is the place. Their attention will immediately be drawn to the central theme of the hands-on arena—that lovable loaf of a cat Garfield. Kids can dress up and act out a dozen careers, and there's an excellent outdoor learning area with educational displays on subjects such as limestone, farming, and even tree houses. Tons of other activities make it a worthy family stop. Open 10 a.m.–5 p.m. Tuesday–Saturday, from 1 p.m. Sunday.

Drive north on High Street across the White River and follow the signs to Ball State University on the west side of town. In the Fine Arts Building along Riverside Avenue is a fine collection of the *Ball State University Museum of Art,* (765) 285-5242, including famous masters like Rembrandt and Degas. The permanent decorative arts exhibit is also noteworthy. Hours are 9 a.m.–4:30 p.m. Monday–Friday, weekends from 1:30 p.m. Just to the west you'll find *Christy Woods,* a 17-acre tract with an arboretum, gardens, greenhouses, and excellent botanical collections for viewing. The greenhouse is legendary for its orchid collection. The campus also has a planetarium and observatory open sporadically for viewing.

Hometown pride on display for Ball State University.

Take Riverside Avenue on the Ball State campus east to Wheeling Avenue. Turn left and go a short distance to Minnetrista Boulevard and turn right. The road quickly becomes Minnetrista Parkway. Here just north of downtown are two adjacent and lovely attractions spread over a wooded, riverine 35-acre site of one of the Ball family estates. *Minnetrista Cultural Center and Oakhurst Gardens,* 600 W. Minnetrista Parkway, (765) 282-4848, is a necklace of gardens along the White River. Strolling here makes for a great afternoon. Walking from west to east, you can start at the White River overlook, pass by an estate cottage, and a bit farther along come to a visitor center with slide presentations and tour arrangements. No fewer than five other historic structures are found on the grounds; within are a handful of galleries with revolving and challenging anthropological, archaeological, art, and scientific displays on Indiana, the United States, and international topics. Free concerts outdoors are often given here. Hours are 10 a.m.–5:30 p.m. Tuesday–Saturday, from 11 a.m. Sunday (also till 8 p.m. Saturday). Admission.

From Minnetrista Parkway, continue north to Centennial Avenue. Turn right (east) and continue to Highway 35/3/67. Turn right (south) and go to Memorial Drive. Turn left. The *National Model Aviation Museum,* 5151 E. Memorial Drive, (765) 289-4236, is a fascinating center with a model airplanes of all kinds. From simple free-flight models to ultratechnological radio-control planes, you'll see every conceivable variety. It's a good place to rediscover the love of model making that many of us lost sometime between our youth and, well, nonyouth. Hours are 8 a.m.–4:30 p.m. Monday–Friday, 10 a.m.–4 p.m. weekends, reduced schedule between Thanksgiving and Easter. Admission.

Return to Highway 35/3/67 and turn left (south). After a little more than a mile, bear left on Highway 35 and continue for about 10 miles to Highway 36 at Losantville. Turn right (west) on 36 and proceed about 2.5 miles to County Road 800E. Turn left and go less than 2 miles to County Road 300N; turn right and go about 1.5 miles to County Road 750E. Turn left (south) and drive 1.5 miles. Dayton, Ohio, and Kitty Hawk, North Carolina, may squabble over who should claim the rights to aviation heritage (the Wright Brothers were raised in Dayton and, well, you know what happened in North Carolina), but this tiny town of Mooreland can legitimately add its voice to the list: Orville's older brother Wilbur was born here. The very rustic frontier home has been restored into the *Wilbur Wright Birthplace and Museum,* (765) 332-2495, and contains many of the original items. A replica of the Wright Flyer is also here. Even the original county chapel is here—and it's often used for weddings. Hours are 10 a.m.–5 p.m. Monday–Saturday, from 1 p.m. Sunday, April–October.

Return to Highway 36 and go west for approximately 2.5 miles. At N. Messick Road turn right, following the signs to *Summit Lake State Park.* This 2,550-acre park, (765) 766-5873, is dominated by its 660-acre eponymous lake. Surrounding it are mostly swales and open meadow. Three trails offer excellent birding and wildlife viewing (more than 110 songbird species have been spotted here); the Beach Trail is a self-guided nature trail (pick up a brochure at the visitor center). The northeast corner of the lake is good for birders.

Return to Highway 36, turn right, go less than 3 miles, and turn left (south) onto Highway 103. Continue south 3 to 4 miles into the *Wilbur Wright Federal Wildlife Area.* There are no established wildlife viewing areas but a few unmarked pulloffs exist on little side roads (and there is a boat launch to the east on County Road 200N). This area is used mostly for hunting.

Continue south on Highway 103 into New Castle, where it becomes S. Eighteenth Street. Turn right (west) on Indiana Avenue and go a couple of blocks to S. Fourteenth Street. Turn left and drive to the 600 block of S. Fourteenth. The *Henry County Historical Society Museum/Grose Mansion,* 606 S. Fourteenth Street, (765) 529-4028, is an 1870 Italianate-style Victorian and the erstwhile home of Civil War general William Grose. You'll find memorabilia on Wilbur Wright—natch—but also a wide range of curios of local interest: a sculpture by artist Frances Goodwin, folk craft coverlets woven on the courthouse lawn, and an amazing desk inlaid with over 50,000 pieces—it took more than 40 years for the architect of the house to finish it. Open 1–4:30 p.m. Monday–Saturday. Admission.

Head west one block to S. Main Street, then jog quickly right on Bundy Avenue. Continue to the junction with Highway 3. Here you'll

The Ohio River on an autumn day.

Mount Baldy, a 125-foot-high sand dune, is one of the main attractions at the Indiana Dunes State Park on the shores of Lake Michigan.

Amish horse-and-buggies are a way of life and a common sight in many Indiana communities.

Down-home and friendly people are the essence of the Indiana experience.

An explosion of color awaits travelers to Indiana's parks and other recreational areas.

Southern Indiana is home to some wonderful places for rock hounds, cave explorers, and everyday tourists looking for something a bit different.

The buggy is the primary means of transportation for the Amish.

Covered bridges in Parke County are plentiful, but getting to some of them can
be a bit tricky because of narrow roads and lack of signs—but, hey, that's half the fun.

Parke County, in the western part of the state, boasts tons of covered bridges that draw tourists from all over, especially during the fall.

There's no surer sign that you're in Indiana than a red barn.

The Carmelite Shrines in Munster provide a chance to get away from it all and a glimpse of the contemplative life.

There's nothing quite as serene and peaceful as a sunset over one of Indiana's many state parks and nature preserves.

The gorgeous Golden Dome is the centerpiece of the lovely University of Notre Dame campus in South Bend.

The mill in Metamora is one of the town's two dozen buildings listed on the National Register of Historic Buildings.

find the *Henry County Visitors Bureau,* 2020 Memorial Drive, (765) 593-0764. Hours are 8 a.m.-4 p.m. weekdays. You may need more specific directions to get to the following attraction; lots of people seem to get lost.

From the junction of Bundy Avenue and Highway 3, drive south to Trojan Lane, then turn left and go three blocks to reach one of Indiana's most popular sites. This is the local attraction that makes one pity the fine county historical museum mentioned earlier—everybody overlooks it because they're all coming here, to the shrine of Hoosier hoops, the place where it all means something, where even old geezers get another chance at their glory days. The wildly popular *Indiana Basketball Hall of Fame,* 408 Trojan Lane, (765) 529-1891, is billed as the home of the Magic of Hoosier Hysteria, and it definitely lives up to the hype; even nonhoops fans can't help but get a bit of a chill gazing at the displays and exhibits honoring over 1,000 different high schools, from the jocks to the managers. All Indiana legends and pros are profiled—and that's saying something. Even better are the participatory areas: getting a pep talk from legendary UCLA coach John Wooden and, two personal faves, going one-on-one with Hoosier Oscar Robertson (this author grew up worshipping the then–Milwaukee Bucks player) and the Game Winning Shot exhibit—it seems as if you never miss. Fun stuff aside, it is a wondrous examination of not just a sport but quite possibly the very ethos of a state. Highly recommended. Just east of here you'll find the world's largest high school field house—with its grand, swept-back design, its 9,200-seat capacity sure seems bigger than some NBA arenas. Open 10 a.m.-5 p.m. Tuesday–Saturday, from 1 p.m. Sunday. Admission.

Drive east on Trojan Lane, which becomes Parkside Drive, then Q Avenue, to Fourteenth Street/Highway 103. Turn left (north) on 103 and go to Highway 38. Turn right on Highway 38 and drive 10 miles east to Hagerstown. Another cutie-pie little blip-on-the-radar town, Hagerstown has one worthy attraction—the *Nettle Creek Valley Museum,* 961 East Main Street, (765) 489-4005. Inside an attractive 1880 public hall, the ambitious little museum-that-could has well-done displays on local Native American culture and, especially interesting, the birth of an early canal town. Most intriguing are the frescoes done by local artist Charles L. Newcomb in 1913. Hours are 4-8 p.m. Thursday-Friday, from 2 p.m. weekends, February 1–December 30. Admission.

Continue on Highway 38 to Highway 1 just east of Hagerstown. Turn left (north) on 1 and go about 2.5 miles to W. E. Oler Road (careful, it's easy to miss). Turn right and drive east for about 7.5 miles to Williamsburg, then jog left on N. Centerville Road. Very soon afterward, at W. Fountain City Pike, turn right (east) and head to Fountain City.

This is one of the fun parts of this trip—just trying to find those classic Blue Highways and not spin yourself into a dither. It's easy to get lost, but remember, for true road warriors, this is part of the reason we're here, right? In Fountain City, there is a hot spot for history buffs, especially those looking for info on the Underground Railroad. They're coming for the *Levi Coffin House,* Highway 27N, (765) 847-2432, an unassuming 1839 Federal-style brick house that had more than its share of history. (See the accompanying sidebar.) Hours are 1-4 p.m. Tuesday–Saturday, June 1–August 31; 1-4 p.m. Saturday, September1–October 31. Admission.

From Fountain City, drive north on Highway 27 about 6 miles to Lynn. Lynn is almost a sneeze-and-you-miss it kind of village, but it has the

Local Hero
The town of New Castle boasts one of the state's all-time bests. Local boy-makes-good Steven Alford was a high school hoops star who went on to lead Indiana University to an NCAA championship before striking gold with Team USA (this was all before that Dream Team stuff) in 1984. Indiana folks even seem to forgive him for coaching Big Ten rival Iowa. You can see memorabilia from his career at the Steve Alford All-American Inn south of New Castle.

Union Literary Institute, 8525 S. Arba Parkway, (765) 874-2267, the first school in Indiana to accept freed slaves as students; it was administered by the Quaker church. One original building remains; it can be toured by appointment only.

Continue north on Highway 27 for 7.5 miles to Winchester. The local tourism office, 111 S. Main Street, (800) 905-0514, has information on Retter, Bales, and Schwere round barns that dot the nearby countryside; many can be seen from the road. Round barns were once pervasive throughout the Midwest and are one of the most endangered folk crafts in the country. More heartland heritage can be found at the *Randolph County Historical Museum,* 416 S. Meridian Street, (765) 584-1334, a nineteenth-century home filled with period household furnishings, military uniforms, local and regional art, and a doctor's office. Hours are 10 a.m.-4 p.m. Monday-Friday.

From Winchester, drive east on Highway 32 about 8 miles to Union City. Union City abuts the Ohio state line and in fact lies partly in Ohio. It was also on a route used by Quakers as they resettled westward; like Fountain City to the south, its 25 or 30 Quaker families were active in sheltering escaped slaves, though Union City gets less credit. Locals claim that one John Lambert of Union City actually built the first functional automobile; apparently he was such a good friend of Kokomo's Elwood Haynes that he let his friend take the credit. Hmm. Here's a lighthearted historical tidbit:

Union City produced the McCoys, who in the 1960s penned and recorded that seminal heavy-sound pop song *Hang on Sloopy.*

It's easy to overlook Union City's small *Union City Railroad Museum,* N. Columbia Street, (765) 964-5409, which has a large array of historical railroad artifacts as well as memorabilia on the rail industry. Hours are 9 a.m.–4 p.m. Monday-Tuesday and Thursday-Friday, till noon Wednesday.

Return west on Highway 32 to Muncie, heading back through Winchester, a total of about 28 miles. One noteworthy spot along the route is on Highway 1, south of Farmland. The *Holaday Upland Peat Bog* is the only one in the Midwest and one of few in the United States—it contains 222 species of vegetation found nowhere else in the region. You cannot visit it, since prior traffic—foot traffic, not wheels—has destroyed parts of it.

Follow the North Star

The Underground Railroad is probably the most misunderstood aspect of the antislavery movement. Beyond the fact that some people believe it actually was a railroad (tourist arrives at purported "station" and asks, "So where are the rails?"), it has become equal parts mythology and truth. It seems every time a new homeowner discovers a door to a root cellar, the presumption is it was used for the Underground Railroad; some claim that one or more of their ancestors led the movement or at least that they were deeply involved. This violates the heroic truth of the many, many brave people, white and black, who anonymously decayed in prison or gave their lives in opposition to evil in its purest form.

Every book says it, and every book is right: it was neither underground (in the physical, subway sense) nor was it a railroad. Metaphorically, it was a system (very loosely organized, for the participants' and escaped slaves' sake) of "conductors" (those whites and blacks willing to assist blacks fleeing the chains of slavery), "stations" (safe houses, barns, or whatever was handy), and "passengers."

The goal was "north"—follow the north star (though another misconception is that once slaves crossed the Ohio River they were safe—they weren't). It's impossible to say with any certainty how many slaves were aided; estimates range from 125,000 to more than a million—remember that technically any slave who ever lit out for the north could be considered a passenger.

Southern Indiana's main transport points were from Cincinnati, Madison, and Jeffersonville to Fountain City. That this little town would figure in the movement isn't surprising, as it was founded by Quakers. Fountain City's Levi Coffin House reportedly was a refuge for more than 2,000 slaves between 1827 and 1848; this disputes the supposed age of the home, but no matter. Another likely apocryphal addendum to the Underground Railroad's chronicles is that the name Underground Railroad derives from a remark to Levi Coffin by a frustrated Kentucky slave hunter, who purportedly said, "They must have an underground railroad around here, and Levi Coffin must be the president of it."

Tour 12
Vice Presidents, a Teen Idol . . . and the Old Order

Marion–Gas City–Fairmount–Dunkirk–Portland–Geneva–Berne–Bluffton–Huntington–Wabash–Marion

Distance: 161 miles

One tour could possibly be more jam-packed with visuals . . . but it isn't likely! Our lengthy but worthy roll through this part of northeast Indiana has a lovely balance of city and rural, highway and byway, along with a fascinating mix of history, nature, politics, religion, and even a teen idol. The tour starts in pleasant Marion—birthplace of James Dean, brooding movie idol of the 1950s—and takes in a historic battlefield, site of a conflict between early settlers and local Miami Indians, before James Dean reappears, or at least the town he grew up in. Shifting gears somewhat, we come upon another lovely Indiana covered bridge (can't have a tour in Indiana without at least one historic old bridge—it's like a rule of road tripping here). A fascinating museum offers a look at the important regional industry of glassmaking. As we move north we encounter the Amish in a close-up and personal way. Shifting gears, we visit the home of former U.S. Vice President J. Danforth Quayle (he of "pota-toe" fame, among other verbal gaffes). We return to Marion via Wabash, the first town lit by electricity and the birthplace of country music star Crystal Gayle. Top that for a diverse tour!

Start your tour in downtown Marion. Marion, seat of Grant County, was once known as the Queen City of the gas belt; other Hoosier towns also claim the moniker. Following its inception in 1831, it was strong in farm trade but the discovery of natural gas in 1887 transformed it virtually overnight. Lured by cheap fuel, factories—mostly glassmaking "houses"—relocated here and a boom was on. The gas ran out but *voilà!*, oil was subsequently found. The oil didn't hold out, but sleepy Marion still had its base of agriculture to fall back on. Today, the town is an energetic center of industry and agriculture.

A question that's often heard around these parts is "Where can I find James Dean's birthplace?" But Marion is also a base for visiting nearby Native American memorials and a battlefield. But before you roar off, see the attractions that the town offers. The best place to start your trip is at the *Marion/Grant County Convention and Visitors Bureau,* 217 S. Adams Street, (765) 668-5435 or (800) 662-9474, where you can get an informative and detailed fold-out brochure on the county.

The Angry Young Man, James Dean, immortalized in Fairmount, his hometown.

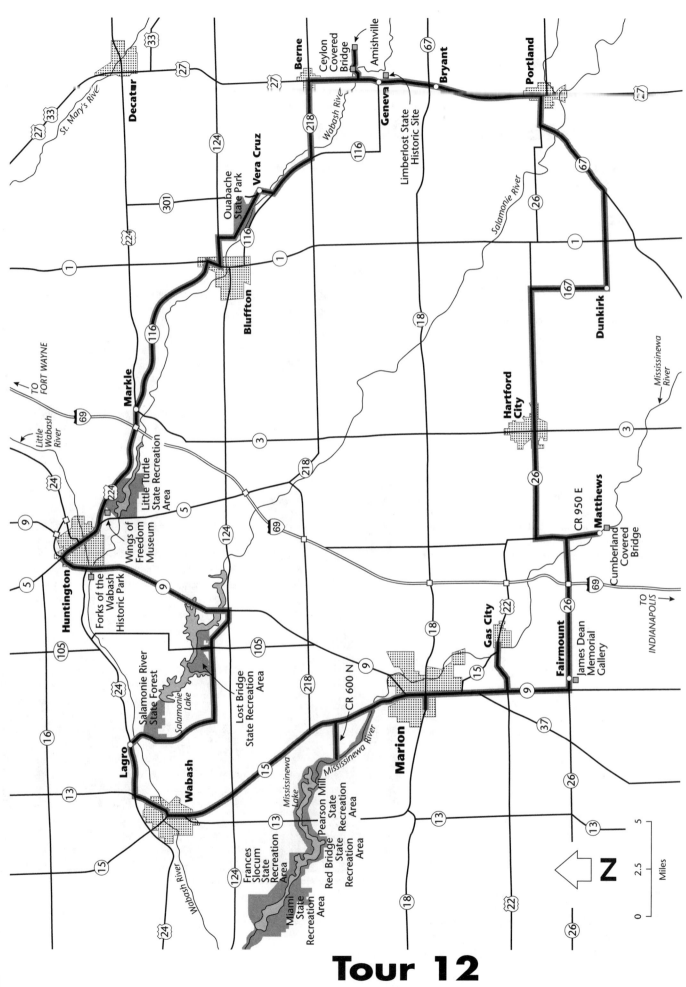

Tour 12

What everyone wants to see, of course, is the birthplace of James Dean. You, too, can find it at the corner of Fourth and McClure Streets, where a plaque tells you that he was born at 2 a.m. on February 8, 1931 (wow, you say, was it *really* that long ago?). The house, known locally as the Seven Gables, is a private residence and there are no visits.

Downtown again at the *Marion Public Library,* 600 S. Washington Street, (765) 668-2900, is a small but engaging museum, anchored by a 1952 Crosley Super Sports automobile, in addition to county displays. A glass and bottle collection reflects the influx of glass factories after gas was discovered in Marion. There's also a small art gallery. Call for hours.

Quick Trip Option: About five miles northwest of town is the Mississinewa Lake Project. Although we'll spend time here on the way back from the rest of the tour, you may want to visit it before you set out. See the end of this tour for the details.

From downtown Marion, go west a short distance to Highway 9 and turn left (south). Drive for 5.5 miles until you come to Highway 35/22. Turn left (east) and proceed to Gas City. Here, you should avail yourself of a brief stop at the *Gas City Museum,* 210 W. North A Street, one block north of Highway 35/27, (765) 674-1428. It offers a look at the area's past forays into gas and oil exploration—thus, the name of the town. For such a small town, there's sure a host of stuff crammed in, from displays on former politicians to glass factories, the old city hall, and information on world skating champion Jackie Champion, a former resident. Open 1-4 p.m. weekends. Gas City also has a mini-zoo along South Broadway Street; kids will love feeding such animals as deer, llamas, emus, pygmy goats, mute swans, and peacocks.

Return to Highway 9 and drive south 4 miles to Highway 26. Turn left (east) and go a little more than a mile to Fairmount. At the four-way stop, go south on Main Street 4 blocks. This is James Dean territory and the reason most people wind up in these parts. He may have been born in Marion to the north, but Fairmount has by far the lion's share of his heritage and cool stuff to see. What's included here is just a short list of James Dean-related items to be seen or experienced. You don't even have to be a fan to appreciate it—like him or not, he represented something to the American psyche, though we don't always seem to know exactly what it is.

First stop is the *James Dean Memorial Gallery,* 425 N. Main Street, (765) 948-3326. Here you'll find the world's largest collection of memorabilia and archives pertaining to the intense young man who died young and dramatically, perhaps the way he would have wanted it. Everything you could imagine pertaining to James Dean is here: clothing, novelty items, original movie posters, high school items, dolls, even a life mask. The gift shop upstairs is absolutely amazing with all the Dean-themed treasures to take home—souvenir numero uno on this tour, to be sure. Open 9 a.m.-6 p.m. daily. Admission.

A couple other places in Fairmount bill themselves as Dean-themed museums—you can't miss the signs. The *Fairmount Historical Museum,* 203 E. Washington Street, (765) 948-4555, is a good place to start. In addition to artifacts from JD's life, it has the usual collections of regional history but also, interestingly enough, an exhibit on Garfield the Cat creator Jim Davis (never did get it clear if he's from here or not, but gotta love any exhibit with the paunchy, soporific feline).

Fairmount High School, which Dean attended 1945-49, located on Vine Street between Adams and Jefferson Streets, closed in 1986 but still stands. The park along North Main Street is now James Dean Memorial Park and has an oversized bust of Dean by Hollywood artist Kenneth Kendall. At 124 W. First Street is the Friends Church, where Dean's funeral was held on October 8, 1955.

If you've seen enough James Dean memorabilia and flotsam, you can concoct a mini-tour of sites. Along County Road 150E is the Winslow Farm, Dean's boyhood home; it isn't open to the

Angry Young Man

Only child James Dean was born on February 8, 1931, in Marion, Indiana, but shortly thereafter his father—a dental technician—moved the family south to Fairmount. After five years the family moved to California but ultimately James was sent back to live with his paternal aunt and uncle in Fairmount, where he attended middle school before entering Fairmount High School in 1945. He was much more focused and successful in extracurriculars: art, drama, band, and sports, for which he was cited at 1949 graduation exercises.

He moved to California and entered Santa Monica City College to study pre-law. We all know how that turned out. He switched to UCLA, where the acting bug bit, and to a major in theater arts. With his burning good looks, he eventually landed his first acting gig—for a Pepsi commercial, which paid $30—and then bit parts. In New York he had much more success, appearing in dozens of TV dramas and in two Broadway plays, including his first, *See the Jaguar.* While in *The Immoralist,* his second play, famed director Elia Kazan spotted him and the world of celluloid was never to be the same again. He took Dean back to Hollywood to star in *East of Eden* and a star was born in every sense of the term. We all know his other roles—*Rebel without a Cause* (who hasn't dreamed of replying "Whattaya got?" to Karl Malden's "What are you rebelling against?") and *Giant.* What most people don't know is that all three movies were made over a period of 18 months.

On September 30, 1955, Dean was driving his new 550 Porsche Spyder near Salinas, California, where he planned to race. He died when a Ford pulled onto the highway in front of him. *Rebel without a Cause* opened the next week. His body was returned to Fairmount and now lies in Park Cemetery, a half-mile south of town.

public but you can take pictures from the driveway by the barn.

Farther along this highway is the Back Creek Friends Church, which holds a memorial service for James Dean every year on September 30.

No James Dean pilgrimage is complete, of course, without a visit to his grave at Park Cemetery. It's located one-half mile south of Highway 26 on County Road 150E. People still come in droves to lay flowers.

Drive east on Highway 26 out of Fairmount for about 7.5 miles and follow the signs to Matthews. If you miss them, when Highway 26 turns to the north, take County Road 950E south. After our brief Hollywood foray, we're back on rural Indiana back roads in search of a cool old covered bridge. And this is a good one. Signs will direct you through the tiny town of Matthews to the corner of Third and Front Streets and the leviathan 181-foot-long *Cumberland Covered Bridge.* Built in 1877, it was completely refurbished in 1999 and sits resplendently over the Mississinewa River. It is Grant County's last remaining covered bridge. Among its interesting historical tidbits is the fact that it was very nearly lost in 1913 in a devastating flood. Swept from its abutment, it floated a quarter mile downstream, but hardy locals hitched horse teams to it and dragged it back. The bridge is feted with an annual festival the weekend after Labor Day.

From County Road 950E, return to Highway 26 and continue north. In about 2.5 miles, 26 turns east. Follow that for about 18 miles to Highway 167. Turn right (south) and drive for 5 miles to Dunkirk. Along the way, you'll pass through Hartford City and begin to get a handle on the story of all this Indiana glassmaking. Following the discovery of abundant natural gas in the area (they thought it permanent; it wasn't) in the late nineteenth century, glass houses (factories to you and me) sprang up all over the region due to the availability of cheap fuel. The industry—the U.S.'s oldest industry, they say—became an economic base. The *Glass Museum* of Dunkirk, 309 S. Franklin Street, (765) 768-6872, can tell you all about it. In addition to learning about Indiana glassmaking, you can view antique leaded glass windows, dozens of hanging lamps, and more than 5,000 pieces of glass in all shapes and forms, all from the more than 100 factories once located throughout this county and surrounding counties. Hours are 10 a.m.–4 p.m. Tuesday–Saturday, May 1–October 31. Admission.

From the north edge of Dunkirk, take County Road 400S and go east. Continue past Highway 1 to Highway 67. Go left (north) and drive into Portland. Portland generally engenders little more than a lash-the-wheel-and-doze attitude as travelers fly through; it's worth a peek, however. The entire downtown is basically a historic district. Note the town's arched bridge. Locals are rightfully proud of it; it's the only concrete bowstring-truss bridge in the state. Check out the *Jay County Courthouse* downtown. The first one was made of logs, while this, the fourth, is a stately Indiana limestone edifice listed on the National Register of Historic Places (check out the stained-glass dome). East of here along Main Street is the *Center for the Arts,* 138 E. Main Street, (219) 726-4809, where exhibits by U.S. and international artists are on display. Eight blocks east the *Jay County Historical Society Museum,* 903 E. Main Street, (219) 726-7982, is a cheery place and has an assortment of county historic artifacts—not to mention friendly volunteers working the desks. Hours are 10 a.m.–4 p.m. Monday–Thursday. On an equally historic if more somber note, the *Museum of the Soldier,* 521 E. Arch Street, (219) 726-2575, has military displays with some items dating back to the Revolutionary War. It's open the first and third weekends of the month.

If nothing else, check out the *Ritz Theatre,* 200 N. Meridian Street, (219) 726-7849. This Art Deco vintage marvel still shows flicks and has comfy rocking chair seats.

From Portland, go north on Highway 27 for 7.5 miles to Bryant. If you've got a brood along, it may be time to quiet the complaining or tussling in the back seats. A perfect way to tire out energetic little 'uns (not to mention mom and dad) is found at *Bearcreek Farms,* 8339 N. 400E, (219) 997-6822 or (800) 288-7630. This city-state-sized place is a mega-entertainment complex consisting of an amusement park (get ready to shell out when the kids see *that!*); an entertainment theater with a slate chock-full of foot-stomping musicals, regular big band performances, and even some national touring artists; an antique car museum; a turn-of-the-twentieth-century village mock-up; an antique carousel; one-third size replica train rides; and a museum-worthy collection of musical instruments. Whew! In the likely event that you're plumb tired out from all the action, you can crawl into one of their cozy cottages or log cabins while the kids run screaming toward the swimming pool.

Continue north on Highway 27 to Geneva. At the *Limberlost State Historic Site,* 200 E. Sixth Street, (turn right off Highway 27 downtown), (219) 368-7428, you can tour the Limberlost Cabin, home for two decades to Gene Stratton Porter, one of the Hoosier state's most famous authors. In this two-story dwelling she penned the novels *The Girl of Limberlost, The Song of the Cardinal,* and *Freckles.* In addition to novels, she wrote poetry, did photography, and was a seminal figure in ecology, even designing her house to use native materials and blend into the surroundings. Porter lived here 1893–1913, moving only when the surrounding swamp—which she loved and used as the setting of many of her books—was drained. Interesting historical tidbit: the name Limberlost came from an incident when a hunter named Limber Jim was lost in the bogs and spinneys of the

A buggy ride through Amish country.

swamp for three days; he couldn't be rescued because he mistook the search parties for hostile Indians. Hours are 9 a.m.–5 p.m. Tuesday–Saturday, from noon Sunday, mid-March to mid-December.

Continue north on Highway 27. Just north of Geneva, go right (east) on County Road 950S to County Road 900S and turn right. Go a half-mile east and look for signs on the south side of the road for *Amishville.* This area is home to one of Indiana's densest concentrations of Amish culture, and the Amishville complex, 844 E. 900S, (219) 589-3536, is a 125-acre working family farm open to the public for tours, hay rides and buggy rides, fishing, and camping. There's also a restaurant—Der Essen Plaz, or "the Eating Place"— where you'll get to know first-hand how stick-to-your-ribs delicious Amish homestyle food is. Tours start in a restored farmhouse and generally take in a mini-petting zoo of farm animals before a bouncy buggy rolls through the acreage, taking in everything from an 1850s gristmill grinding wheat to fence repairing. Of course, most important, it's a first-hand way to experience the life of the "Gentle People" who choose to live in a way so different from mainstream U.S. culture.

Before or after a visit to Amishville, consider a leisurely let's-get-lost-and-see self-guided tour through the surrounding farm roads. The roads are narrow, winding, and rise and fall like a roller coaster at times, but the gorgeous, lush topography more than makes up for it. At Amishville, ask for directions to Ceylon Covered Bridge to the north. Obviously, be very careful to watch for buggies along the side of the road. Always assume there will be a buggy around the next bend or over the next rise. And please, *slow down.*

Return to Highway 27 and continue north for 5 miles to Berne. In the early 1850s the area around Berne became home to numerous Swiss Mennonite families who came, recognized its resemblance to the fecund land they had known back home, and put down roots. So heavy was the Swiss concentration here that guidebooks of the early and mid-twentieth century remarked on the noticeable Swiss accent of the populace. A lesser-known tidbit: Berne's Mennonite publishing house was until recently the only one for Mennonite communities in North America. It's now a gem of a stop on any road-trip itinerary, so quaint that a First Lady of Indiana once called it "one of the seven hidden treasures of Indiana."

The best way to gain an appreciation is to stop by the *Berne Chamber of Commerce,* 175 W. Main Street, (219) 589-8080, and see if any special celebrations or events are scheduled—you'd be amazed how many celebratory hootenannies they have around here, and chances are very good that *something* will be going on. Swiss Days takes place in late July and is a can't-miss for fun and culture; you have to like an ethnic festival that has its own bowling tournament.

While at the chamber, get directions to the wonderful *Swiss Heritage Village,* 1200 Swiss Way, a reconstructed village of 15 (and more all the time) buildings on 26 acres, all dating to the latter half of the nineteenth century. Period-garbed docents lead tours throughout the grounds, where you can witness living history demonstrations of cheesemaking, sheep shearing, spinning, broom making, and more. But it's much more than this. There's a six-acre nature center with ponds, wet-lands, and woods repopulated with native species of the period; kids like the bird feeding station.

There's almost always a special event going on. Hours are 9 a.m.-4 p.m. Monday-Saturday, May-October. Admission.

From Berne, go west on Highway 218 for 5 miles to Highway 116. Turn right and go about 4 miles to Vera Cruz. Follow the signs to *Ouabache State Park*. This overlooked little park, 4930 E. Highway 201, (219) 824-0926, is bordered by the Wabash River on the southwest. It may be small but there is a three-mile bike trail, camping, skiing, hiking trails, canoe/boat rentals, a swimming beach, pool, and waterslide. The fishing here is said to be excellent. In the early twentieth century, the park was the site of wildlife conservation experiments and there is an excellent wildlife preserve—even bison are here! By the way, a note on the pronunciation: "WAH-bahsh" is perfectly acceptable—the Indiana Department of Natural Resources even says so officially—but around here you're likely as not to hear "oh-BAH-che."

Go north on Highway 201 for a mile or so to Highway 124; turn left (west) into Bluffton. At Highway 1, turn right and proceed about 1 mile to Highway 116. Turn left (west) and drive about 5 miles to Highway 224 at Markle. Continue on 224 toward Huntington. At Highway 5, turn left (south) and drive a short distance. Along the route, you're passing some special topography. Just after turning onto Highway 116 you pass through what once were epic oak stands (a couple of towering giants still stand in the area).

West of Markle, Highway 224 parallels the J. Edward Roush Lake Project, the result of an impoundment plan that created a long, narrow chunk of green space across two counties. Here you'll find the *Little Turtle State Recreation Area* and wildlife viewing areas along the *Kekionga Trail.*

Here you have a chance to visit the fine *Wings of Freedom Museum,* 1365 Warren Road (near the Highway 224 and Highway 5 interchange), (219) 356-1945, at the Huntington Municipal Airport. In addition to lots of aviation artifacts, photographs, and displays on engines, there are displays on the Tuskegee Airmen and on the Women Airforce Service Pilots. The anchor to the museum's displays is the P-51D Mustang Scat VI flown by WW II ace General Robin Olds, who scored 24 kills in it. Hours are 10 a.m.-4 p.m. Saturday, 1-4 p.m. Sunday, May 1-October 1. Admission.

Return to Highway 224 and follow 5/224 into downtown Huntington. Huntington was originally called Wepecheange, which roughly translates as "Place of Flints," Realizing that the name did not exactly flow like honey, city fathers changed it to Huntington in 1831. It honors Samuel Huntington, a member of the Second Continental Congress. An early guidebook was obviously impressed by the place, remarking that "this relatively small community has the hustle and atmosphere of a much larger city, and the imposing courthouse is more suggestive of a state capitol than a Hoosier county seat." Huntington is now well known as the birthplace of former U.S. Vice President Dan Quayle and, as would be expected, the city plays up that fact to draw tourists.

In downtown Huntington, follow Highway 5 to the city center and head for the *Huntington County Visitor and Convention Bureau,* 407 N. Jefferson Street, (800) 848-4282. You can pick up a brochure with a good city and county map. Also inquire about the historic district and highlights when strolling around. The following two spots are in walking distance.

Most visitors want to see what Dan Quayle was really all about. From the visitor center go north three blocks, then east two blocks. The *Dan Quayle Center and Museum,* 815 Warren Street, (219) 356-6356, claims to be the only vice presidential museum in the country. The exhibits don't focus solely on Mr. Quayle, but give an excellent overview of the history of the vice presidency. How much do you really know about vice presidents or the office? Me neither. Of course, they love to tout the fact that Indiana has produced five veeps—yes, including the butt of so many jokes. (Careful—they are understandably sensitive about that around here.) Hours are 10 a.m.-4 p.m. Tuesday-Saturday, from 1 p.m. Sunday.

About six blocks east of the visitor center is the *Huntington County Historical Museum,* 315 Court Street, (219) 356-7264, which has an exhibit about local resident John Kissinger who, while serving with Teddy Roosevelt in Cuba, underwent yellow fever experiments. He eventually suffered such a horrible case of the disease that he was discharged and pensioned; Dr. Walter Reed touted him as a national hero for his heroic battle and bravery in volunteering for the grim duty. There are other exhibits on local history. Hours are the same as the Dan Quayle Center.

From Jefferson Street in Huntington, go north to West Park Drive. Turn left and drive southwest for 2.5 miles to the junction with Highway 9. A big attraction for the area, the *Forks of the Wabash Historic Park,* (219) 356-1903, recreates the relationship between the Miami Indians and the settlers (not to mention the U.S. government). Downtown the local chief, Francis LaFontaine, is buried in a local cemetery and his house can be viewed on one of those walking tours. On the site are a log house and home of a Miami chief, hiking trails, and picnic area.

Go south on Highway 9 for about 9 miles to County Road 500S. You'll be passing through yet another hydro-inspired recreation area—the *Salamonie River State Forest,* which offers a host of excellent features. Highway 9 crosses Majenica Marsh at the southeast tip of Lake Salamonie.

Turn right onto County Road 500S. After about 2 miles, turn right at Highway 105. Here, along the southern edge of the lake, you immediately come to a hunting area and an official wildlife viewing area near the gate entrance along Highway 105. At the lake are bridle trails, jillions of campsites, cross-country skiing, fishing, hiking trails, a nature center, a beach, and more.

While at the visitor center, get directions to Hanging Rock southeast of Lagro. It's among a number of klintar in the area (klintar are mound-shaped hills that are remnants of coral reefs formed during the Silurian Age). Hanging Rock is used by climbers, though budding geologists love the entire region for its amazing rocks.

From the visitor center return to County Road 500S and turn west. Drive to S. America Road and turn right (north); continue into Lagro. Lagro was one of the primary towns on the Wabash/Erie Canal, a crucial transportation conduit that allowed settlers and commerce to circumvent the dense old-growth forests. Planners had been discussing the feasibility of the canal as early as the 1780s but it took till the 1840s till traffic started, er, flowing. Built mostly by immigrant Irish, Lagro still retains a fairly heavy Hibernian influence. Saint Patrick's Catholic Church in Lagro was one of the Midwest's earliest churches. Kerr Lock in town is one of the very few surviving from the original canal.

Turn west onto Highway 24 and drive about 6 miles to Highway 13. Turn south on 13 and proceed into downtown Wabash. Wabash is historic as the first electrically lighted village in the world. You can see one of the original lights in the lobby of the Wabash County courthouse. Downtown Wabash is picture postcard pretty. Visit the spot downtown where treaties were signed—such as Treaty of Paradise Springs—and take a leisurely stroll on the *Paradise Springs Riverwalk.* It's lovely. If nothing else, catch a flick at the historic Eagles theater downtown; it's housed in an original vaudeville facility.

Optional Quick Trip: On a decidedly different bent, on your way out of town to the south you could opt for a side trip along Bowman Road/County Road 850S to the *Frances Slocum Cemetery.* Frances Slocum is a name well known in the county. She was kidnapped by Indians in Pennsylvania and was found here in Wabash 50 years later. She and her family are buried in this cemetery.

At the intersection of Highways 13 and 15 in downtown Wabash, go south on Highway 15 for about 12 miles to County Road 600N. Turn right (west) and drive a short distance to the *Mississinewa Lake Project.* A number of historical sites are here. At this spot on December 18, 1812, the Miami nation made a brave but futile stand to preserve their land as well as their way of life. The U.S. Army, fearing that the Miami would become both hostile to settlers and involved in the War of 1812, sent a 600-man contingent led by Lieutenant Colonel John B. Campbell to attack and destroy villages up and down the Mississinewa River. In the end only one battle was fought, with some 30 Miami dying (out of an estimated 300), along with 8 U.S. soldiers. Though the casualty rate wasn't decimating for the Miami, it prevented them from acting against the U.S. and it struck enough fear into Miami leaders that they would eventually give in to U.S. treaty demands. *Mississinewa 1812* is a festival with a battle reenactment held in early October; it's the largest War of 1812 event in North America, with over 30,000 people attending. Call (800) 822-1812 for information.

Nearby is the *Miami Indian Cemetery,* 3750 W. County Road 600 N, the largest Native American cemetery in Indiana and the resting place of Miami Chief Meshingomesia, among others. On site is a restored one-room Indian schoolhouse, (800) 253-3578, built in 1860 when the land was part of an Indian reservation. It's the last wood-frame Indian schoolhouse in Indiana and can be viewed May–September (admission). Hiking trails, hunting, and fishing are also available on site.

Return to Highway 15, turn right, and cruise about 6 miles back into Marion, the start of this tour.

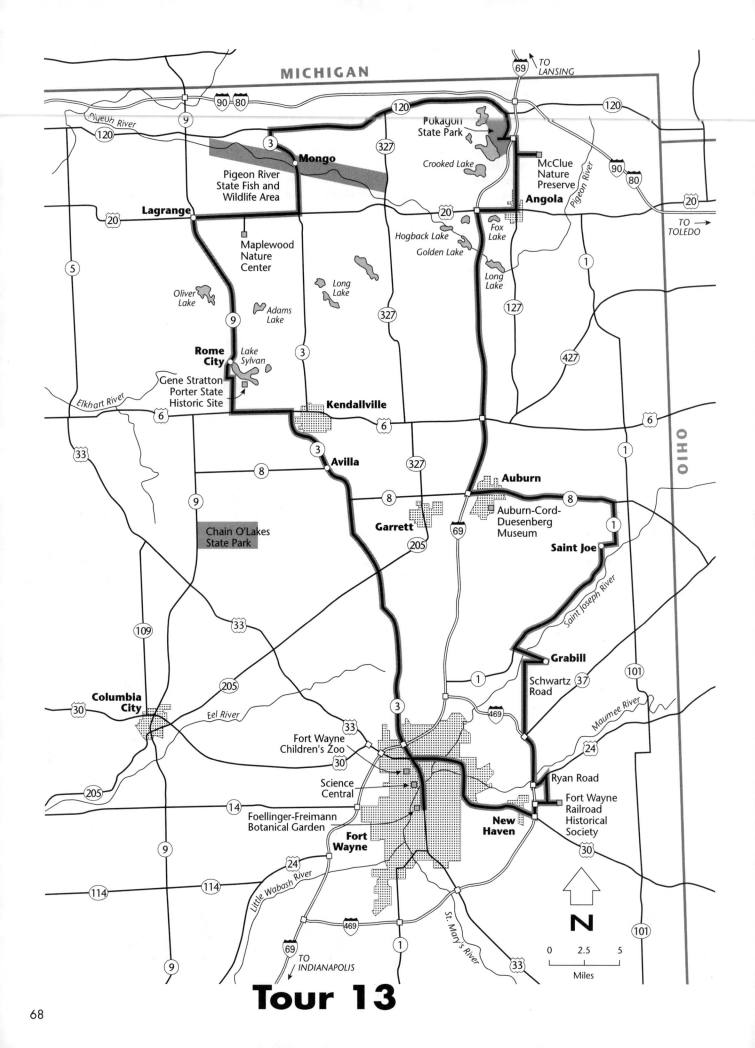

MICHIGAN

TO
LANSING
69

90 80

9

Pigeon River

120

120

3

Mongo

Pigeon River
State Fish and
Wildlife Area

Lagrange

20

Maplewood
Nature
Center

5

Oliver
Lake

9

Adams
Lake

Rome
City

Lake
Sylvan

Gene Stratton
Porter State
Historic Site

Elkhart River

6

33

6

Kendallville

3

Avilla

8

9

Chain O'Lakes
State Park

109

205

Columbia
City

30

Eel River

205

30

205

14

Foellinger-Freimann
Botanical Garden

Fort
Wayne

9

24

114

114

Little Wabash River

9

69

TO
INDIANAPOLIS

120

327

Pokagon
State Park

Crooked Lake

McClue
Nature
Preserve

20

Angola

Pigeon River

90 80

20

TO
TOLEDO

Hogback Lake

Golden Lake

Fox
Lake

Long Lake

1

127

Long
Lake

427

3

327

6

1

327

8

Auburn

8

8

Garrett

205

69

Auburn-Cord-
Duesenberg
Museum

1

Saint Joe

1

Saint Joseph River

Grabill

Schwartz
Road

37

1

469

Fort Wayne
Children's Zoo

Science
Central

New
Haven

Ryan Road

Fort Wayne
Railroad
Historical
Society

Maumee River

24

101

101

469

1

St. Mary's River

30

33

OHIO

6

N

0   2.5   5

Miles

Tour 13

Tour 13
From the Heartland to Lake Country

Fort Wayne–Grabill–Saint Joe–Auburn–Pokagon State Park–Lagrange–Rome City–Fort Wayne

Distance: 154 miles

Our tour begins in Fort Wayne, which truly could be called the Crossroads of America (in fact, it often is) for its strategic location for water, rail, and highway transportation. With these elements in place, it was among the first automobile manufacturing centers in the country. Fort Wayne is also known as the City of Attractions; for a city its size it has an extraordinary number of worthy spots to check out. We traipse eastward to a great museum where visitors may actually drive a diesel locomotive. Then downshifting, so to speak, we visit a quiet, charming Amish community filled with quaint shops and restaurants. Next we stop in Auburn, home to one of the nation's first car manufacturers, and then head into the heart of Lakes Country, Steuben County, home of more than 100 lakes, endless recreation, and more state parks, nature reserves, and wildlife viewing areas than one would think a county could hold. We top it all off with a glimpse at the home of one of the Hoosier State's favorite daughters, novelist/naturalist/photographer Gene Stratton Porter, now a State Historic Site.

Begin this tour at the Fort Wayne Visitors Center in the downtown area. Because the site lay at the confluence of three rivers, the Saint Joseph, Saint Mary's, and Maumee, the original settlers of the region—the Miami Indians—recognized it as a crossroads, one chief saying it was "that glorious gate . . . through which all the good words of our chiefs had to pass." This strategic location was at the western end of the Great Black Swamp, on a major route between the Great Lakes and the Mississippi Valley, and at a portage site through which virtually all human traffic had to pass. Originally, the site was called Kekionga, literally "blackberry patch," but the word carries sacred meaning. The city's key location for transportation was further cemented with the building of the Wabash and Erie Canal; being at the highest point of the canal, it was dubbed Summit City. Stretching from Toledo, Ohio, to Lafayette, Indiana, the canal used Fort Wayne as a crucial supply and repair junction. Rather than doom the city, the arrival of the railroads helped it thrive—by 1871 a half-dozen lines made Fort Wayne one of the nation's true rail crossroads (some called it the Altoona of the West).

Fort Wayne's wonderful Foellinger-Freimann Botanical Conservatory—an Eden any time of the year.

Lincoln Highway

Indiana can take at least partial credit for another legendary American ribbon of transportation, the Lincoln Highway, a 3,385-mile transcontinental highway between New York City and San Francisco. Carl G. Fisher, founder of the Indianapolis Motor Speedway, was the brains behind it. Originally conceived in 1913, Fisher was heartily supported by major automobile manufacturers (naturally), who raised money and lobbied Congress to get involved.

Other transcontinental highways had been proposed before, but Fisher's was the first one with an organized plan for support—and finance; the organization Fisher founded shrewdly used the media as a PR instrument to drum up support. Overcoming resistance to privately financed highways was no small feat. Many wealthy industrialists who one would presume could have benefited from these new highways quite rationally questioned giving the job of public works to private firms.

The concept of roadways was still somewhat alien at this time anyway. By 1910, 180,000 cars were registered in the United States, the majority of which were Model-Ts (Henry Ford was one of the industrialists dead set against highways built by private firms with public funds). But of the 2.5 million miles of existing roads, less than 7 percent were "improved" (meaning graveled rather than dirt). And there was no rhyme or reason to where roads went. Certainly there were no gas stations, repair shops, or even maps. You think you get lost without your gazetteer now? Think of back then, when the road you were on was actually a choice of which pasture-to-pasture trace to rattle down. Twenty states didn't even have road departments. Yet, somehow, they pulled it off.

Often called the Main Street of America, the Lincoln Highway was originally called the Coast to Coast Rock Highway and designed to create a network of existing roads into one improved artery at a time when having roads at all was something. The cost for just materials (excluding labor and machinery) was a mind-numbing $12 million and Fisher wanted it done in under three years, in time to allow 25,000 cars to cross the country for an international exposition. A myriad of state and county roads and highways were eventually cobbled together and, after a bit of disagreement and the implementation of a national numbering system in 1926 the highway that roughly corresponds to today's U.S. Highway 30 was born.

The original Indiana section of the highway zigzagged from Fort Wayne to Ligonier, Elkhart, South Bend, and Valparaiso. Looking like the bight in a rope, it roughly followed Native American and trapper trails. It was by no means the straightest line—by train the distance from Fort Wayne to Chicago was 145 miles, by the road it was 195—but it was the most efficient for road travel. In the 1920s a new road was hacked out parallel to the route of the Pennsylvania Railroad, and a controversial new numbering system was adopted for good—here it became U.S. Highway 30. A good spot to view it is in Lake County, west of Dyer on the Illinois-Indiana boundary; it was constructed to be an "ideal" segment of a highway and was billed as almost futuristic when unveiled in December 1922 and billed as the Greatest Section of Road in the World. Only 12 miles long, it was built of concrete laid 10 inches thick and 40 feet wide (four lanes, incredible for the time), and came replete with landscaping, illumination, and an adjacent footpath—eerily prescient of today's highways, though they obviously overestimated the public's desire to walk/jog/bike alongside four lanes of belching traffic.

Most folks don't know that Johnny Appleseed, the proselytizing purveyor of fruit, is buried right here in Fort Wayne. Two other interesting historical tidbits: it has always been one of the state's most heavily unionized cities, and it claims to be the place where night baseball was born. Yes, on June 2, 1883, a team of pros from Illinois squared off against a team of students from Fort Wayne Methodist Episcopal College under some of the first electric lights ever placed over a public park. It was witnessed by more than 2,000 spectators. The WPA guidebook dryly noted that "in brilliancy the spectacle was a great success, but as a specimen of ball playing it was poor indeed." Indeed. By the way, the pros won—11-10.

The best way to begin the tour is to park in one of the many inexpensive parking ramps or downtown lots. Two are in the same block as the *Fort Wayne Visitor Center*, (219) 424-3700 or (800) 767-7752, www.visitfortwayne.com, which is located at the corner of Washington Boulevard—one of the main drags downtown—and Calhoun Street. (Pay particular attention to one-way streets in Fort Wayne.) The visitor center, as one has come to expect in Indiana, is fully equipped with brochures and solicitous advice. They've got superb maps, so claim one.

Ask at the center if it's possible to view the historic Grand Page organ at the 1928 *Embassy Theater*, 121 W. Jefferson Street, (219) 424-6287. The theater is a cultural center with ballet, theater, an orchestra, and more. The original architecture and detailings have been lovingly restored and the result is smashing. You could also ask for directions to the one sight not covered in our tour: *Lakeside Rose Garden*, (219) 427-6000, 1401 Lake Avenue. These rose gardens—actually groupings of gardens—are one of the nation's largest with more than 2,500 plants of 225 varieties.

Then put on your walking shoes. The city of Fort Wayne has a jaw-dropping number of attractions to check out; this is often said about cities, but it's decidedly true here. Many of the sights are within a few blocks of each other, so you should plan to do some walking to catch all the sights.

If you're interested, the visitor center has a wonderful brochure outlining three ambitious downtown neighborhood walks detailing not just historic structures but also points of beginnings for the community. They're really quite fascinating. The one thing most people want to see is the *Allen County Courthouse* a few blocks north of the visitor center at 715 South Calhoun Street. The fourth courthouse to serve, this one is absolutely smashing. The cool blue marble exteriors are lovely enough, but try to get a peek inside at the stained glass windows and artwork. It's generally open 8 a.m.–4:30 p.m. weekdays.

Walk one block south from the visitor center to the *Foellinger-Freimann Botanical Conservatory*. This wonderful exhibit, 1100 S. Calhoun Street, (219) 427-6440, is a glass-enclosed retreat in the heart of the city. The large enclosure houses three separate botanical areas: Desert House, Tropical House, and Floral Showcase. Flowers are always nice in winter, the tropical house is particularly nice on a cool autumn/spring day, and the waterfalls are absolutely cacophonic. Kids love the interactive exhibits like Wood the Talking Tree; actually, I liked it, too. Hours are 10 a.m.–5 p.m. Monday–Saturday; noon–4 Sunday. Admission.

Go across the street to Cathedral Square. Here the *Cathedral of the Immaculate Conception* is the cornerstone. The Gothic architecture features Bavarian-made stained glass—said to be the finest in the Western Hemisphere—and wood carved sanctuary and Stations of the Cross. A small museum houses religious artifacts dating back to the mid-thirteenth century. Hours for the museum are 10 a.m.–2 p.m. Wednesday–Friday and 1-3 p.m. second and fourth Sundays; the church is open 7 a.m.–4 p.m. daily.

From the south side of Cathedral Square, go four blocks east on Lewis Street, then two blocks south on Clay to E. Douglas Avenue. This next attraction is a bit far for some people to walk, so you could backtrack in a car or catch it if you're approaching downtown from the south. The *Fort Wayne African/African-American Museum,* 436 E. Douglas Avenue, (219) 420-0765, honors the contributions of local African Americans and Africans in general. The Underground Railroad is prominently featured, and there's a host of locals-done-good in a variety of areas. Open 9 a.m.–1 p.m. Tuesday–Friday, noon–4 p.m. Saturday.

Walk one block north and two blocks west on Washington Boulevard. The *Firefighters Museum,* 226 W. Washington Boulevard, (219) 426-0051, tells the lengthy history of firefighters. After the benchmark events of September 11, 2001, paying a visit here takes on a special poignancy. And it should still bring out the kid in all of us. The facility is housed in an old engine house. The food's pretty good at the upstairs Old Number 3 Cafe, too.

One block to the west is the *Allen County Public Library,* an excellent place for some research into family because it has the country's second-largest genealogy collection.

From the Firefighters Museum, walk 4 blocks east on Washington Boulevard to Barr Street, then go north two blocks to Berry Street. Here you'll find the attraction that brings most visitors to the city—the *Lincoln Museum,* (219) 455-3864. The 11 permanent exhibits here are fantastic and regularly win awards for museum design or education. Kids and adults love to help fight a Civil War battle, or just take on more quotidian tasks, such as handling the presidential mail or decorating the White House. Four theaters supplement the enormous amounts of information presented in exhibits with excellent audiovisuals. And for souvenirs this is the place—the museum store is purportedly the largest of its kind in the state. Open 10 a.m.–5 p.m. Tuesday–Saturday, 1-5 p.m. Sunday. Admission.

Just across the street sits the underappreciated (how could it not be, with one of the best Lincoln museums for a neighbor?) *Allen County Historical Museum,* 302 E. Berry Street, (219) 426-2882. It's housed in the 1893 city hall and has a host of rooms set up to review the city and regional history—especially through its characters. Most of us travelers wind up spending a little time in the hoosegow; you too can "do time" in the original jail. Open 9 a.m.–5 p.m. Tuesday–Friday, noon–5 p.m. weekends.

At this point it may be prudent to retrieve your vehicle. The remainder of the sites we'll visit in Fort Wayne are quite a hike from the downtown.

Go one block north to Main Street and turn right (east); continue for one block. The huge Performing Arts Center is the home of the worthy *Fort Wayne Museum of Art,* 311 E. Main Street, (219) 422-6467. The permanent collection totals nearly 1,500 pieces and emphasizes nineteenth-century art. The overview of one year's traveling exhibitions is impressive in scope and includes more photography than many museums. A slew of extra activities is ongoing. Hours are 10 a.m.–5 p.m. Tuesday–Saturday, noon–5 p.m. Sunday. Admission.

Walk (or drive) north on Lafayette Street for two long blocks alongside Headwaters Park, then cross the bridge over Saint Marys River to Lawton Park. As you approach the Lawton Park, you'll see a historic reconstructed fort on the riverbank. At the western edge of the park sits *Science Central,* 1950 N. Clinton Street, (219) 424-2400, a hands-on center full of challenging activities that make science, math, and technology just a bit less frightening for kids and us techno-phobes. A personal fave is the Walk-like-an-

The spires of Fort Wayne's Cathedral of the Immaculate Conception.

Astronaut area—totally fun, though only the kids may go on it. Open 9 a.m.–5 p.m. Tuesday–Saturday, noon–5 p.m. Sunday. Admission.

Walk (or drive) back to the visitor center at the corner of Washington Boulevard and Calhoun Street. Drive west on Washington to Van Buren Boulevard. Turn right and head north. After crossing the Saint Marys River, Van Buren becomes Sherman Boulevard. Continue on Sherman to the *Fort Wayne Children's Zoo.* The zoo, located to the west, 3411 Sherman Boulevard, (219) 427-6800, is a 42-acre spread and award-winning menagerie for tots and tykes, with over 1,300 animals representing species around the planet. Jungle and rainforest exhibits focus on orangutans and tigers. You can hop aboard a "jeep" and ride into Africa (you'll come out unscathed). Kids seem possessed with getting to the Australian adventure area—yep, you can touch a kangaroo. The zoo possesses the world's only Endangered Species Carousel. Open 9 a.m.–5 p.m. daily, late April to mid-October. Admission.

Just to the east is the *Jack Diehm Museum of Natural History,* 600 Franke Park Drive, (219) 427-6208, where the fish and mammals may be stuffed and mounted but are no less educational. A host of geological and anthropological exhibits are also found here. Open the same seasons as the zoo, noon–5 p.m. Wednesday–Sunday. Admission.

Continue north on Sherman Boulevard to Coliseum Boulevard (Highway 930) and turn right. Just before the road crosses over the Saint Joseph River, you'll notice the *Allen County War Memorial Coliseum/Expo Center/Stadium,* 4000 Parnell Avenue, (219) 482-9502, which has numerous attractions throughout the year, from big-time college athletics to minor league hockey, basketball, and baseball.

Continue east on Coliseum Boulevard. After crossing the Saint Joseph River you come to Johnny Appleseed Memorial Park. Johnny Appleseed (born John Chapman in Massachusetts in 1774) was an eccentric personality who, motivated by Fort Wayne's religious fervor, ambled throughout the Midwest to preach the gospel and plant apple orchards in 1801. Early on he was drawn to religious philosophy, some say after being kicked in the head by a horse (and, they continue, seeing a vision of endless fields of apple trees in blossom). He wandered throughout the countryside (mostly west of the Alleghenies), dispersing fruit seeds over nearly 100,000 square miles and looking for all the world like a hirsute Huck Finn, sans footwear (though Huck didn't preach his own version of the Gospel, to be sure). He died in 1845 and is buried elsewhere.

Continue east on Coliseum Boulevard (Highway 930) as it bends to the south, then east. After its junction with I-469, continue east a little more than a mile to Ryan Road. Turn left (north) and go to Edgerton Road. Turn right and go past Berthaud Road to the *Fort Wayne Railroad Historical Society.* This overlooked museum features the wildly popular NKP 765 steam locomotive. You can get caboose rides or even climb into the engineer's cabin and grab the controls of the 400-horsepower diesel switcher (if you're 18 or older)—you can ride the beast for up to an hour after receiving instruction. Even for nonfans of the Iron Rooster it's kind of cool, given how up close and personal you can view it. Otherwise, the two-track locomotive shop and rolling stock museum maintains equipment that once helped make Fort Wayne a center in the nation's railroad network. How about a 44-ton diesel switcher or a leviathan 200-ton crane? There's a whole lot more too, something that whole families enjoy. The facility is open most Saturdays, March–October.

Return to Ryan Road by way of Edgerton Road, turn right (north), and drive to the next intersection, with Harper Road. Turn left on Harper and proceed a little more than a mile to Highway 24. Then turn quickly onto to I-469 and drive north for about 4 miles to Highway 37. Turn east, then immediately go north on Schwartz Road. Continue north for 5 miles to Witmer Road, then turn right (east) to Grabill. Grabill is legendary as one of Indiana's quaintest spots: it's a veritable Currier and Ives print come to life. Surrounded by Old Order Amish farms, the picture-postcardaesthetics draw throngs of road trippers for its many shops laden with antiques and Amish and artisan crafts. Be careful—there's a lot of Amish buggies rolling about these parts. Grabill is also home to one of the state's—nay, the Midwest's—best arts and crafts festivals, the *Grabill Country Fair,* in September.

Take Grabill Road west 2.5 miles to Highway 1. Turn right and proceed 10 miles to the town of Saint Joe. One of the most unique stops on any tour is *Ralph Sechler and Son, Inc.,* 5686 Highway 1, (219) 337-5461, purveyors of gourmet pickles for eight decades. You can visit the huge plant and showroom and learn how they pump out more than 40 varieties of pickles. Sechler's original homestead still stands, and it's astonishing to realize that Ralph used to pack all the pickles himself in the basement. The business has certainly come a long way.

Take Highway 1 east and then north out of town for about 4 miles to Highway 8. Turn left (west) on 8 and continue for about 8 miles to Auburn. Auburn, the oldest town in De Kalb County, was one of the nation's earliest auto manufacturers. The Auburn Automobile Company, which operated from 1900 to 1937, made extraordinary luxury automobiles. The original 1930 Art Deco showroom and factory headquarters is now the *Auburn-Cord-Duesenberg Museum,* 1600 S. Wayne Street, (219) 925-1444. Autophiles will be in heaven—Duesenberg, Packard, Cord, Cadillac, Auburn, Rolls-Royce, all the sybaritic rides are here, more than 140 vehicles ranging from the carriages of the 1890s to sports cars. The Auburns and Cords are highlighted, as they drew most attention to Indiana's nationally recognized auto industry. At one point, Hollywood celebs absolutely had to have these luxury cars; a personal favorite is John Lennon's 1956 Bentley (doesn't really fit, does it—John Lennon in a Bentley?). The annual *Auburn-Cord-Duesenberg Festival* takes place over Labor Day weekend and is one of the state's most popular. One highlight of the festival is the World's Largest Collector Car Auction, with more than 5,000 cars for sale. Hours are 9 a.m.–5 p.m. daily. Admission.

Northeast of the museum is another collection that's sure to delight gearheads and their families, the *National Automotive and Truck Museum,* 1000 Gordon M. Buerig Place, (219) 925-9100, housed in the former Auburn automobile factory. You'll find two acres of autos from the 1940s to the 1960s and trucks of all eras. Hours are 9 a.m.–5 p.m. daily. Admission.

If you're in Auburn the last week of September, stop by for the *De Kalb County Free Fall Fair,* which began in 1932 and is one of two remaining street fairs in the state. You can find a midway, free concerts, 4-H competitions and livestock judging, farm equipment shows and displays, and a grand parade Saturday night; the fair actually begins the fourth Monday of September, so it's a week-long blowout.

Continue west on Highway 8 to I-69. Turn north and drive about 20 miles to exit 148 (Highway 20); turn right and go east 2.5 miles to Angola. Angola is the seat of Steuben County, otherwise known as Indiana's Lakes Country. More than 100 lakes pepper the landscape here, offering endless boating, fishing, canoeing, and more. Before you head out to scope out the endless acres of blue, give Angola a look-see. All roads lead to Columbia, the enormous figure atop the *Soldier's Monument* in downtown Angola; this enormous set of sculptures honors the county's war dead.

One block south is the *Steuben County Tourism Bureau,* 207 S. Wayne Street, (800) 581-0908. It has an excellent magazinelike brochure with maps of many local lakes and other detailed information (it also has free postcards of the Soldier's Monument). If nothing else, stop by because it's housed in the old county jail, an 1877 structure listed on the National Register of Historic Places. (Historical tidbit: at one time the sheriff lived here with his father, a four-star U.S. Army general.) The bureau can give directions to the five other county buildings listed on the National Register. The highlight for most travelers is the *Steuben County Courthouse,* an 1868 edifice that is a replica of Boston's Faneuil Hall. The *Cline Memorial House Museum,* 313 E. Maumee Street, honors Cyrus Cline, U.S. Representative from 1905 to 1917. It's loaded with early twentieth-century memorabilia.

From Angola, drive north on Highway 127 for 5 miles to County Road 400N; turn right and go for 1 mile. Here you'll find *McClue Nature Preserve,* an 80-acre swath of wetlands and an excellent spot to experience birds and wildlife. Marked trails and brochures are on site. At Pokagon

State Park (see below) you can arrange a personal tour. Along this road you'll also find *Wing Haven,* a nonprofit preserve organization whose acreage is also open to the public. The holdings include most of Seven Sisters Lakes, lots of trails, a log home, and assorted buildings. An open house takes place the first Sunday of every month.

Return to Highway 127, turn right, and continue a short distance to Pokagon State Park on the left. Within the boundaries of popular *Pokagon State Park,* 450 County Lane 100 Lake James, (219) 833-2012, are Lake James and Snow Lake. In addition to the camping, cross-country skiing, hiking trails, beach, horseback riding, and nature center, you'll find something unique for the Hoosier State—tobogganing at 40 miles per hour on a 1,700-foot, double-track toboggan track. (It opens Thanksgiving Day and doesn't even require snow, since they can slick it down with snow machines.) There's also a popular state park inn if camping isn't for you. *Potawatomi Nature Preserve* offers prime viewing of wildlife and wildflowers.

Return to Highway 127, turn left, and go 1.5 miles to Highway 120. Turn left (west). Some of northern Indiana's best natural areas are in Steuben County, and a couple are found along our drive here, which traces the northern edge of the glacial erratics that helped form the many lakes in the region. Two miles north of Highway 120 on County Road 750W is the *Ropchan Memorial Nature Reserve,* with high ridges of woodland around a primeval-type icy lake. You'll find a tamarack forest with thick moss.

Continue west for 17 miles to Highway 3; turn left (south). A short jog off the highway brings you to the otherworldly *Pigeon River Federal Wildlife Area and Tamarack Bog Nature Preserve,* two superb areas for getting off the beaten path and exploring the natural world; there is a designated wildlife viewing area.

Continue south on Highway 3 through Mongo to Highway 20. Turn right (west) and proceed 7.5 miles to Highway 9 in Lagrange. Turn left (south) on Highway 9 and drive 10 miles to Rome City. Along the way you'll pass the *Maplewood Nature Center* south off Highway 20 (follow the signs); it's also a good spot to explore the natural world. Another possibility for a backwoods traipse is the *Olin Lake Nature Preserve* west off Highway 9, south of Lagrange.

Southeast of Rome City, the *Gene Stratton Porter State Historic Site,* on Pheasant Point Road, Highway 9, (219) 854-3790, marks another home of the Hoosier State's beloved author, naturalist, and photographer. (The other is in Geneva, east of Marion.) In her lifetime, Porter wrote novels, nature works, poetry, and essays as well as newspaper and magazine articles. Eight of her works were adapted for film and she has a reported readership of some 50 million. She was also a seminal figure in nature photography and conservation ecology.

As with the other cabin, Porter designed and built this cabin, *The Cabin in Wildflower Woods,* here on Sylvan Lake with a splendid bucolic location—you can see wildlife and wildflowers just walking the grounds. The exterior of the two-story cabin is Wisconsin cedar logs; paneling throughout is of local wild cherry. The interiors are original and have been painstakingly restored; you'll gape at the three amazing fireplaces: one of polished English brick, one of stone and Native American artifacts, and one of puddin' stone (whatever that is, but it sounds cool). On display are numerous items from Porter's life—books, photos, and more. A visitor center in the old carriage house has more information on the renaissance woman's life. Hours are 9 a.m.–4:30 p.m. Tuesday–Saturday, 1–4:30 p.m. Sunday, mid-March to mid-December.

Continue south on Highway 9 to Highway 6. Turn left (east) and drive about 5 miles to Highway 3 just west of Kendallville. Turn right on 3 and continue for 30 miles back to downtown Fort Wayne.

Tour 14
Touchdown Jesus
and the Gentle People

South Bend–Mishawaka–Elkhart–Bristol–Goshen–Middlebury–Shipshewana–Topeka–Ligonier–Nappanee–Wakarusa–South Bend

Distance: 144 miles

This tour of "Michiana," that border region of Michigan and Indiana where state lines matter little and regional cultures blend, could quite rightly be called the most representative of all that Indiana has to offer. Its highlights include no less than Jesus signaling a touchdown, a close encounter with the Old Order Amish, classic midwestern rural landscapes, and assorted historical and/or industrial museums for good measure. We start out in South Bend, the home of the University of Notre Dame, one of the state's most visited sites. Whether or not you're a football fan (remember, everyone's a football fan with a visit to the Golden Dome) South Bend and Notre Dame rate a visit. Athletics count, of course, but Notre Dame has always represented something honorable and loyal in the American ethos. With all the hubbub surrounding South Bend, it's easy to overlook Elkhart, its sibling city to the east. That would be a mistake. Not only is it another representative in the Indiana gallery of small-city-with-way-more-attractions-than-it-rightfully-should-have, but it also is the gateway to one of the nation's densest concentrations of Amish culture. It's essentially unthinkable to miss a visit, short or otherwise, to the Gentle People. We top it all off with a spin through quiet small towns with the friendliest of folks, some intriguing museums, and a dose of natural beauty to boot. All in all, this could be the most challenging, but equally rewarding, circle tour of Indiana.

Start the tour in downtown South Bend. An essential first stop will be the *South Bend/ Mishawaka Convention and Visitors Bureau,* 401 E. Colfax Avenue, Suite 310, Commerce Center, (219) 234-0051 or (800) 828-7881, www.livethelegends.org.

But first some background. I cannot tell you how many times I've run into tourists who hadn't planned on stopping in Indiana on their coast-to-coast U.S. blitzkrieg. But, while blazing down the Indiana Turnpike, they suddenly see signs pointing toward this shrine of American college football. And like the voice from the cornfield in *Field of Dreams* that impels otherwise rational people to do things they hadn't dreamed of (of course, sports are a force to be reckoned with), *something* draws them off the mad swells of interstate traffic and into this picturesque community. Even interna-

tional tourists are somehow captivated. A soccer-faithful Belgian who knows absolutely nothing about American football can be heard to say, "Well, South Bend, I mean, it's Notre Dame; it's football; it's *America,* isn't it?" Indeed.

South Bend may be home to the Fighting Irish (for those who just arrived from another planet, that's the nickname of the athletic teams of the University of Notre Dame), but it was French *voyageurs*—explorers who paved the way for trappers, Jesuits, settlers, and assorted scoundrels—who first established a presence in what would eventually be a shrine of American college football here. Lying at the southernmost bight of the Saint Joseph River, it offered explorers a natural waterway conduit. No less than Père Marquette and Louis Jolliet, the famed explorers of the Mississippi and its environs, passed through in 1673. Not long after, in December 1679, explorer/adventurer/author René-Robert Cavelier de Sieur La Salle made a portage between the Saint Joseph and Kankakee Rivers on his way to the Mississippi and the great unknown. La Salle forged a treaty between the Miami natives and the Illinois Confederation, creating a multinational force to oppose the eastern tribes, which were supported by the English.

As in other Great Lakes regions, the first permanent settler did not have politics on his mind but furry gold—beaver pelts. The fuzzy little critters' soft fur had created a fashion frenzy in the East (and as far away as Paris) and in 1820, Pierre Freischutz Navarre, an agent for the American Fur Company, arrived to establish a trading post. Over the next decade, various machinations in the fur trade resulted in settlers relocating here, using Fort Wayne as a stopover. The city had innumerable names before the U.S. Post Office finally stepped in and renamed it South Bend; settlers had been calling it the Bend since its inception.

The city's true founding father, Alexis Coquillard, along with a partner, bought John Jacob Astor's fur trading agency, no small venture, which lasered attention onto the burgeoning city. Prescient city planners, Coquillard and partners built dams, ferries, and an industrial base upon which to found their community. (One early result of their efforts: the Studebaker Company was founded here in 1852 as a modest blacksmith and wagon shop; today AM General manufactures Hummers, those

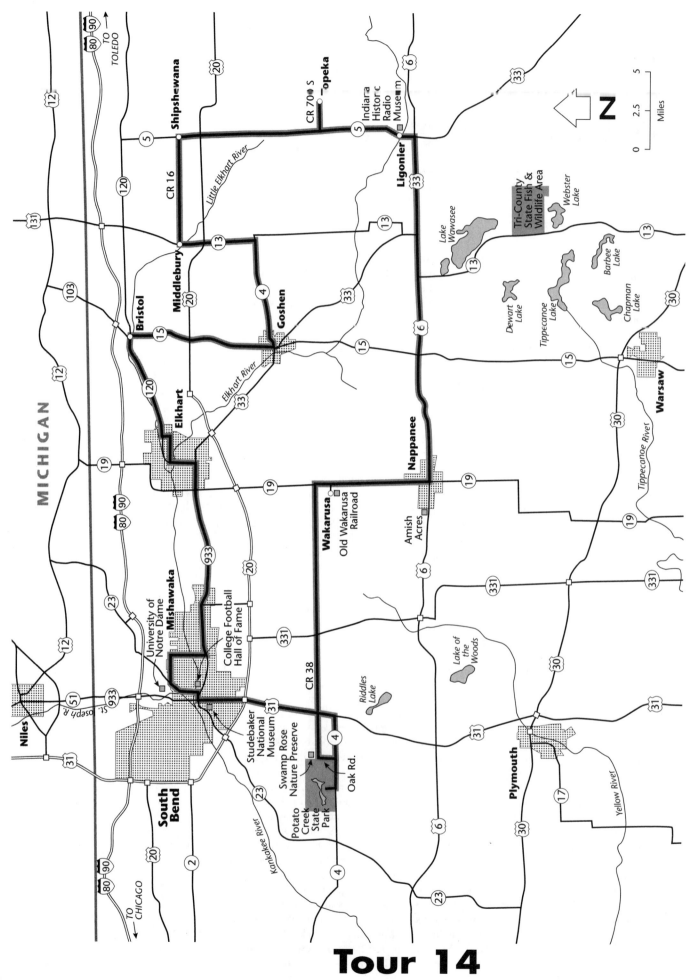

MICHIGAN

TO
TOLEDO

TO
CHICAGO

Shipshewana

Topeka

CR 700 S

Indiana
Historic
Radio
Museum

Ligonier

CR 16

Little Elkhart River

Tri-County
State Fish &
Wildlife Area

Lake Wawasee

Webster
Lake

Dewart
Lake

Tippecanoe
Lake

Barbee
Lake

Chapman
Lake

Middlebury

Bristol

Goshen

Elkhart

Elkhart River

Warsaw

Tippecanoe River

Nappanee

Mishawaka

University of
Notre Dame

College Football
Hall of Fame

Wakarusa

Old Wakarusa
Railroad

Amish
Acres

Niles

St. Joseph R.

Studebaker National
Museum

Swamp Rose
Nature Preserve

Potato
Creek State
Park

Oak Rd.

CR 38

Riddles
Lake

Lake of
the
Woods

Plymouth

Yellow River

South Bend

Kankakee River

Tour 14

beasts of military burden, here.) In the early 1840s Edwin Sorin, a priest of the Congregation of the Holy Cross, arrived to establish a school, for both Potawatomi Indians and local settlers. (The first student was city father Alexis Coquillard.) And we all know what the result of that mission was.

At the convention and visitors bureau, you'll need the staff's help in planning what is usually a pretty lengthy day of exploring. First, ask if the local farmer's market is open that day. The largest farmer-owned market of its kind in this country, it's an excellent place to load up on picnic goodies for lunch. Generally it's open Tuesday, Thursday, and Saturday year-round, also Friday in summer. A handful of South Bend's attractions are located downtown, so the following tour presumes a parking of the car and a pair of good shoes.

From the visitors bureau on 401 E. Colfax walk west over the Saint Joseph River a short distance, then turn left on S. Saint Joseph Street; walk one block. Here you'll find what are likely the city's two primary attractions after Notre Dame. If you're a football fan—and again, when in South Bend, who *isn't?*—your first stop is definitely the *College Football Hall of Fame,* 111 S. Saint Joseph Street, (219) 235-9999 or (800) 440-3263. Canton, Ohio, is the logical choice for pro football's Hall of Fame, where NFL junkies jump in apoplectic glee as they walk toward their shrine; ditto for South Bend, the hallowed ground of college football. Even Notre Dame football bashers have to admit that they always pay attention when Fighting Irish highlights are replayed on television. As the saying goes, "Every day is Saturday here."

The Hall of Fame has the usual relief-sculpture busts and detailed historical exhibits, but it's the other stuff that really delights. Slobbering fans often find themselves unable to leave the Stadium Theater, a 360-degree experience-in-the-round that leave them breathless. I've seen adults actually push kids out of the way at the Practice Field (note the capital letters), where you can get into the game and test your football skills. Show up during August for *Enshrinement Weekend,* a several-day blowout feting stars, new and old. It's great fun and a great way to experience a key undercurrent of South Bend culture. Hours are 10 a.m.–7 p.m. daily, June 1–December 1, till 5 p.m. the rest of the year, with extended hours on weekends of Notre Dame home games. Admission.

On the opposite side of the street is the *South Bend Regional Museum of Art,* 120 S. Saint Joseph Street, (219) 235-9102. Within the sleek and chic-looking multiuse Century Center are a performing arts center and park area. The permanent exhibits focus on local, regional, and national artists, with emphasis on nineteenth- and twentieth-century American art, but visiting exhibitions can run the gamut from photography to internationally renowned artists. Hours are 11 a.m.–5 p.m. Tuesday–Friday, from noon weekends.

The *East Race Waterway,* on the east side of the river, is the only manmade whitewater raceway in North America. Not only are international and national competitions held here, but recreational kayaking is possible.

From the corner of W. Jefferson Boulevard (just south of the Hall of Fame) and S. Saint Joseph Street, walk three blocks west to S. Main Street, then five blocks south. Many forget that northern Indiana was once an automotive capital, and South Bend was among its leaders. The *Studebaker National Museum,* 525 S. Main Street, (219) 235-9108, pays homage to a classic American beauty. Starting out as a modest carriage company, the company ultimately moved into wagons before the auto industry took it into enormous but sleek cars and trucks, all of which are on display in this amusing museum. Even the Studebaker family's Conestoga wagon is here. Rarities like President Lincoln's carriage (the one in which he rode to Ford's Theater), a 1934 Bendix experimental car, and the prototype Packard Predictor are definite must-sees. A nice addition is a hands-on science center for kids. Hours are 9 a.m.–5 p.m. Monday–Saturday, from noon Sunday. Admission.

Walk five blocks north on S. Main Street to W. Washington Street. Turn left (west) and walk five blocks. Spread out over 10 acres is the amazing *Northern Indiana Center for History,* 808 W. Washington Street, (219) 235-9664, a complex anchored by the restored posh 38-room *Copshaholm Mansion,* now a museum filled with original antiques, artwork, and more. The formal gardens on the grounds are lavish and lovely. Also on site is a restored worker's home—an interesting place and a refreshing change from museums that focus on the rich but somehow forget the poor, who were likely living in the same place. A children's museum offers hands-on activities. An archaeological and anthropological wing examines the region's natural history. *Whew!* This is an ambitious and eclectic place; seriously consider checking it out if you have a chance. Hours are the same as those for the Studebaker Museum. Admission.

Walk one block north to W. Colfax Street, turn right, and return to the area of the visitor bureau. Drive to Michigan Street just west of the Saint Joseph River and turn right. Go a short distance to Angela Boulevard and turn right, then left on Notre Dame Avenue to a visitor parking lot on the right-hand side. You are here, that fabled shrine of college football—the *University of Notre Dame.* Oh yeah, and the academics aren't bad either! For over 120 years Notre Dame and South Bend have co-existed in a synergistic "town and gown" relationship. Visitors could spend an entire day taking in all that the subdued, leafy 1,250-acre campus offers. Drop by the nearby *Eck Visitor Center,* (219) 631-5726, for parking details and maps or directions to the various sights.

A highlight of northern Indiana—a glimpse of Notre Dame's Golden Dome.

First stop for most visitors is the hallowed *Golden Dome,* otherwise known as the Main Building. There is no more gorgeous color than the halcyon rays streaming off the graceful rondure on a crisp, sunny autumn morning. Note the 12 incredible allegorical corridor murals, painted by Vatican artist Luigi Gregori (he spent more than 15 years at Notre Dame). Near the turn of the twenty-first century, some $58 million was spent to restore the grand dame to its previous Victorian stateliness. Just west is the *Grotto of the Lady of Lourdes,* a reproduction of the one in France. Nearby is the *Log Chapel,* at the edge of Saint Mary's Lake; it's a reproduction of the chapel built in 1830 by Father Stephen Badin, the first Roman Catholic priest ordained in the United States. His remains rest under a stone slab in the middle of the chapel floor. It's open only for Notre Dame events. If you continue walking south along the lake, you'll come to a Knute Rockne Memorial.

The other architectural and historical gem to the campus is likely the *Basilica of the Sacred Heart.* It's more than a century old and contains more detailed murals from the artist Gregori. Shaped like a cross, the layout follows the plan of the French ambulatory and chevet chapels. The

stained glass was brought from France. The oldest carillon in North America rests in the spire. Sacred relics and artworks are contained within.

Newer additions to Notre Dame include the *Snite Museum of Art,* (219) 631-7960, which contains nearly 20,000 pieces, with particularly nice religious artwork. You'll also find works by masters such as Picasso and Chagall. Hours are 10 a.m.–4 p.m. Tuesday–Wednesday, to 5 p.m. Thursday–Saturday. Visit the *Hesburgh Library,* (219) 631-6258, which houses 2 million volumes and is nationally regarded for its holdings; its 11-story granite mural depicts the "Word of Life."

But back to football. Yes, you can inquire at the Eck Visitor Center about a chance to nose around Notre Dame Stadium, the House that Rockne Built. You can absolutely feel the history and tradition as you stand on the turf or sit in the stands. If you have even a modicum of football fan in you, you'll get chills. And don't leave without getting a glimpse of "Touchdown Jesus" from the stands. Gazing north you can spot a mural that you would swear shows Jesus signaling a touchdown for the Fighting Irish. If the stadium isn't open, head for the *Joyce Center,* which holds Notre Dame athletic memorabilia.

Note that Notre Dame isn't the only college in town. Across town is *Saint Mary's College,* founded in 1844 by the Congregation of the Sisters of the Holy Cross. It remains one of the few colleges for women only in the nation and is perennially ranked by national media as one of the country's best liberal arts colleges. Its campus is every bit as lovely as Notre Dame's.

From Notre Dame, an optional side trip would be to *Highland Cemetery,* west of the Saint Joseph River along Portage Street (get directions from the visitor center). Serious football fans will want to avail themselves of the trip, for it is the final resting place of the most legendary college football coach of all time—Knute Rockne. In no way is it possible to overstate the importance of Rockne's reign as Notre Dame's coach. In many ways he redefined the game of football and the way Americans regarded the college version of it. Say the name Rockne and folks will think of the Four Horsemen or the Seven Mules or, sadly, of his all-too-early demise in a plane crash. Also here is Council Oak, a tree under which La Salle forged his treaty between the Miami and Illinois Confederation (and, thus, the French). A lovely return trip would be via Riverside Drive to the east, via Pinhook and Keller Parks. Paralleling the Saint Joseph River, it's a serpentining road with gorgeous views; canoe rentals can be found along the route.

Drive south on Notre Dame Avenue to Angela Boulevard. Turn left and drive east for 2 miles past Highway 23 to Ironwood Drive. Turn right (south) and go about 1.5 miles to E. Mishawaka Avenue. Here you'll find *Potawatomi Park and Zoo,* (219) 235-9800, which houses conservatories, tropical gardens, a nature/learning center (geared for kids), and animals from virtually every continent. Hours are 10 a.m.-5 p.m. daily, April-December. Admission.

Continue south on Ironwood Drive to Highway 33/933; turn left and follow 33/933 east for about 1.5 miles to Merrifield Avenue; turn left to Merrifield Park. Within Merrifield Park is the *Shiojiri Niwa Friendship Garden,* a 1.5-acre Japanese garden; you can also swim, fish, boat, and ice skate. Otherwise, South Bend's neighbor to the east is often overlooked but you'll find a spot or two of interest. One thing of interest locally is Mishawaka's population: a healthy Flemish enclave populates neighborhoods downtown. At 1402 S. Main Street is *Hannah Lindahl Children's Museum,* (219) 254-4540, with lots of educational displays and hands-on exhibits for kids, many themed on regional Native American culture and natural history. More Japanese culture is to be examined in its Japan House. Open Tuesday-Thursday in June, Tuesday-Friday in September-May, and the first and third Saturday of the month; closed July-August. Admission.

Return to Highway 33 and drive east for 10 miles into Elkhart. In town, go east on W. Franklin Street (Highway 33) to S. Main Street in the downtown area. Elkhart is the gateway to the large communities of Amish to the south, but it has a lot to offer in its own right. Located at the confluence of the Saint Joseph and Elkhart Rivers and on Christiana Creek, it has long been famous for its proximity to water and is often called the City of Bridges. This ready-made water power lured manufacturers and the city still today has a diversified base of factories. Interestingly, some 15 firms in the city produce more than 50 percent of the nation's band instruments—cornets, trumpets, and more.

There is a tourism office but it's a bit out of the way for our purposes. If you need it, head north on Highway 19 to the Indiana Turnpike (exit 92). The *Amish Country/Elkhart County Visitors Center,* (219) 262-8161 or (800) 860-5949, www.amishcountry.org, behind the Cracker Barrel restaurant, has a full-sized vacation planner for you; you can also book B&B rooms here and pick up audio tour guides of the region.

Park your vehicle near Main Street, a good spot from which to visit the local attractions. For a good education on Elkhart, consider the unique *Time Was,* 125-A N. Main Street, (219) 293-6005, the city's repository of city history. It's housed in two anachronistic apartments downtown above an 1899 building. History buffs will have a field day with the mountains of photos, newspapers, yearbooks, and more. Open by appointment only. The *Midwest Museum of American Art,* 429 S. Main Street, (219) 293-6660, with more than 1400 works in its holdings, mostly focuses on nineteenth and twentieth century American and European art. The permanent collection subdivides the history of American art into eight periods throughout its galleries. Its Norman Rockwell and Grandma Moses paintings are particularly popular. Hours are 11 a.m.-5 p.m. Tuesday-Friday, 1-4 p.m. weekends. Admission.

Three blocks to the south is the *National New York Central Railroad Museum,* 721 S. Main Street, (219) 294-3001. You can wander through exhibits that detail the creation of New York Central, Penn Central, Amtrak, and Conrail railroads. Three locomotives are on site, including the only known 3001 L-3a Mohawk steam locomotive. Other holdings include early twentieth century rail coaches, a loading deck replica, and a reconstruction of a train station office. A melange of railroad memorabilia is also found here. Hours are 10 a.m.-2 p.m. Tuesday-Friday, 10 a.m.-4 p.m. Saturday, from noon Sunday. Admission.

Nearby, a block south and about two blocks west, is another attraction that celebrates a mode of transportation but of an entirely different sort. It is the cultural linchpin to the Great American Road—the RV, the recreational vehicle, the perfect answer for the American who wants it all and wants to take it with him, too. The *RV/MH Hall of Fame Museum and Library,* 801 Benham Avenue, (219) 293-2344, is a fascinating way to get an overview of the vehicles we're all familiar with but know very little about. Who knew that RVs date from the 1910s? For many people this is the highlight of this tour. Hours are 9 a.m.-5 p.m. Monday-Friday.

Now on to two spots north of the Saint Joseph River. One is just across the river and a short distance east off N. Main Street. *Ruthmere,* 302 E. Beardsley Avenue, (219) 264-0330, is a lovingly renovated 1908 Beaux Arts mansion. It was built by one of the organizers of Miles Laboratories and is truly spectacular: Cuban mahogany paneling, silk upholstered walls, gilt, gesso, and painted ceilings to mention but a few of the extraordinarily lush details. The house was even designed with a player piano/organ that conducts sound throughout the house via floor vents. The art collection—much of it from presidential collections—rivals any museum's holdings. Tours at 10 and 11 a.m. and 1-3 p.m. Tuesday-Saturday, at 2 and 3 p.m. Sunday, July-August. Admission.

Are you ready for some serenity—and more walking? If so, great. If not, you can use your vehicle because this place is about a mile north of the river. The *WoodlawnNature Center, 604* Woodlawn Avenue, (219) 264-0525, is located just west off Johnson Street/Highway 19. It's a 10-acre nature sanctuary with hiking trails, wildlife viewing and natural history/anthropological exhibits detailing mastodons, Native Americans, geology, and more. Hours are 11:30 a.m.-4:30 p.m. Tuesday-Saturday, March-October; 1:30- 4:30 p.m. Tuesday-Saturday, rest of year.

Amish Etiquette

The Amish are very friendly and curious about you too. This doesn't mean, however, that you have carte blanche to invite yourself into their lives. The Amish view a photograph as a potential for graven images (a biblical taboo) and, worse, self-pride.

More important: *slow down.* Most roads are hilly, winding, and/or narrow (likely all three). Always assume there's a buggy with a family and young child in it just over the next hill or around the next bend.

Return to your vehicle and, from S. Main Street, drive to Middlebury Street, turn east, and drive about 1.5 miles. Northern Indiana was a major automobile manufacturing base, and two places in Elkhart pay homage to this heritage. The *S. Ray Miller Auto Museum,* 2130 Middlebury Street, (219) 522-0539, is a collector's delight, with more than 40 vintage autos, including 18 national vintage auto show winners and 13 "100 point classic car of America" winners. The collection includes such luminous automobile engineering marvels as Duesenberg, Auburn, Cord, Pratt, Elcar, Marmon, Stutz, and more. Among the memorabilia is one of the largest collections of original car emblems in the world.

From Middlebury Avenue, drive east for about 1.5 miles to Highway 13 (Middleton Run Road). Turn left (north) and go to Highway 120. Turn right and drive for 7.5 miles to Bristol. In Bristol, the *Elkhart County Historical Museum,* 304 W. Vistula Street, (219) 848-4322, has a largish collection of historical items in a refurbished Victorian home; there's also a cottage outside as well as re-creations of a schoolroom, general store, and typical 1930s home. It has a lot of military uniforms, too. Open Tuesday–Friday and Sunday.

From the intersection of Highway 120 and Highway 15 in Bristol, drive south on 15 for 10 miles to Goshen. This little city is famed for its maple trees and hefty Mennonite presence (Goshen College was founded and run by Mennonites). It has great walkways and bike paths if you're athletically inclined. It's also one of northern Indiana's hotspots for shopping. The *Old Bag Factory,* 1100 Chicago Avenue, (219) 534-2502, is a collection of shops housed in an anachronistic 1896 warehouse; its popularity stems from the fact that at many of the shops you can actually watch artisans at work. Even for shopping-phobes, it's a great treat. Other high-end craft and quilt shops are found downtown.

At the intersection of Highway 15 and Highway 4 in Goshen, turn east on Highway 4 and go 12 miles to Highway 13. Turn left (north) and proceed 5 miles to Middlebury. Legendary

in these parts is *Das Dutchman Essenhaus,* (219) 825-9471, west of Highway 13 on Highway 20. This huge complex started as a restaurant serving up copious quantities of dense and luscious Amish fare; now it includes a bakery, shops, carriage/buggy rides, a miniature golf course, a hay maze, and petting zoo for the kids (there are more than 225 animals of 79 species, including Power-Man, the 20-inch-tall horse that they believe to be the world's smallest). The complex is so big it even has its own covered bridge. A former Amish farmhouse has been converted to a comfy inn for the road-weary.

In Middlebury, turn right on County Road 16 (it becomes County Road 250N in Lagrange County) and drive east for about 6 miles to Shipshewana. Turn right (south) on Highway 5. Here is the heart of Amish country in northern Indiana and a tiny community that seems to draw countless zillions of tourists, where rattling Amish carriages are at times outnumbered by belching tour buses. *With so much Amish traffic around, this is a good place to really, really watch your driving and use some extra caution.* Most tourists are barreling through on their way to the very worthy *Menno-Hof* near the intersection of Highways 20 and 5, (219) 768-4117. If you know nothing of the Mennonite/Amish culture, this stop is a must. It's an extraordinary museum and cultural center—without the staid, antiseptic atmosphere that some museums have, this one really comes alive and may just leave a lump in your throat.

Inside the enormous buildings are two dozen exhibits detailing the arduous struggle of the people who were forced to flee Europe and make their way to the New Land. You can enter a mock-up of a dungeon where Swiss authorities imprisoned thousands of believers from the sixteenth century on. Another life-size display lets you enter the cramped quarters of a ship sailing for freedom. Still other exhibits portray typical cobblestone streets of the villages the believers left behind. Even the little ones aren't forgotten—there's a loft chock-full of toys for kids to play with while the elders get their education. Highly recommended. Hours are 10 a.m.–5 p.m. Monday–Saturday.

Otherwise, Shipshewana is the place to experience the other favorite tourist thing: an Amish auction. Once weekly the streets are jam-packed with buggies and wagons as the Amish descend to horse-trade and 11—yep, count 'em—auctioneers work the crowd simultaneously; around this sprouts what seems to be the planet's largest flea market (more than 1,000 vendors haggle in a great, spirited cacophony). It's all great, great fun. This is probably why the village has the apt moniker Trading Place of America. Every Wednesday morning year-round there are auctions (horse, pony, hay, and tack); there are flea markets Tuesday and Wednesday, May 1–late October.

A sign—of the old times—in Amish country.

At the hitching post in an Amish parking lot.

If you tire of walking, a number of buggy, carriage, and wagon tour operators in the village will take you from place to place.

Continue south on Highway 5 for 10 miles to County Road 700S and turn left (east). Drive about 2 miles to Topeka. Topeka has the same Amish culture, a couple of excellent places to check out, *and* . . . no tourists. One of the most fascinating ways to get a glimpse of Amish/ Mennonite culture is to visit an Amish-oriented hardware store. Think about it. No electricity, no phones, no modern conveniences. Where in the world would you be able to find an authentic, nineteenth-century-style cast-iron wood-burning stove? Or how about a real, honest-to-goodness scythe? Well, Topeka has the *Honeyville General Store.* You can buy bulk foods, actual penny candy, even old-fashioned ice cream. If you want to see those funky old "antique-new" stoves, head over to *Topeka Seed & Stove,* 514 E. Lake Street. Even more intriguing might be *Hoosier Buggy Shop,* 5345 W. 600S, where the owner and his four sons repair, restore, and build carriages and buggies. Since you're probably wondering, a buggy costs around $3,000 brand new, though a bells-and-whistles model can run upwards of $6,500. This shop's buggies are so well known that you can see them in Disney World.

Return to Highway 5 and continue driving south to Ligonier. Ligonier is a blip on the map—sneeze and you may miss it. How, then, do they manage to have four museums? That's an awful lot of history for a town of its size. The biggest draw is right along Highway 5. Housed in the same building as the Ligonier Visitor and Convention Bureau is the *Indiana Historic Radio Museum,* filled with a collection of more than 400 radios of the 1920s to the 1940s. *Stone's Trace Tavern* dates from the 1840s and has a cool collection of memorabilia dating to the Pony Express—nothing like it in these parts, that's for sure. Next to the Fashion Farm Restaurant is *This Old House Museum,* filled with items of two prominent families. There's also a city historical museum, but you'll probably be too tuckered out to give it a try. If you've seen one museum too many—not unlikely given the numbers—the town has a grand, kitschy festival. Ligonier was once home to a marshmallow factory and each Labor Day weekend they still have a celebratory blowout feting that fact; it's wonderful.

Continue south on Highway 5 a short distance to Highway 6. Turn right (west) and proceed for 24 miles to Nappanee. This little burg with the cool name lies amidst lush fields of onion and, interestingly, mint. It grew around the railroad and has a manufacturing base to buttress its agricultural foundation. Trim, compact, and relaxed, it's been noted by no less than *Time* magazine as one of the top 10 small towns in America. The concentration of Amish culture is, if anything, intensified around here.

Thus, it's a perfect setting for *Amish Acres,* (219) 773-4188 or (800) 800-4942, one mile west of downtown on Highway 6. Another get-to-know-the-locals experience, this one allows a glimpse up close on a renovated Amish homestead. Tours start with video documentaries on Amish/Mennonite culture. You can then pile into a horse-drawn cart to bounce around the 80 acres, examining rebuilt original farm buildings and watching farmers and crafters at their work. Literally dozens of living history demonstrations are offered, from lye making to candle dipping; a personal favorite has always been those remarkable quilts the Amish women make—if you're ever going to drop some heavy coin on a worthy souvenir, that's what I'd recommend. Expansion of the offerings now lets you eat copious meals at the on-site restaurant (the *Chicago Tribune* rated their shoo-fly pie tops after reviewing 139 towns and covering 8,000 miles) and even enjoy a musical comedy April–November. The general store has been called "tops" by Yahoo and was profiled in *U.S. News and World Report.* Hours are 10 a.m.–5 p.m. daily, March–December; restaurant and performance times vary. Admission.

From Nappanee, drive north on Highway 19 for about 7 miles. As you approach Wakarusa, you come to Maplewood Drive and the *Old Wakarusa Railroad,* (219) 862-2136, which invites visitors to experience a 1.5-mile steam train ride. The cars are open for viewing; the engine is an 1862 model. The route is short but lovely, including a lengthy tunnel. Hours are 11 a.m.–sunset Monday–Saturday, April–December. Admission.

Continue on Highway 19 for a short distance to County Road 38/Osborne Road. Turn left (west) and drive 13 miles to Oak Road. Turn left and head south to Highway 4 and the entrance to *Potato Creek State Park.* This park, (219) 656-8186, is located approximately 10 miles south of South Bend. Along the way from Wakarusa you pass by the Swamp Rose Nature Preserve along New Road and established wildlife viewing areas along Highway 4. This state park has outstanding natural areas and is exquisite for birding and wildlife viewing; kids will like the nature center at the northern end of the lake, which has informative displays along with a songbird and small mammal viewing area. Trails run throughout the old fields, mature hardwood woodlands, restored prairies, and diverse wetlands; those in the hillier sections are great and one leads to the Swamp Rose Nature Preserve. A paved bicycle trail is also popular. Keep your eyes peeled for kingfishers and great blue herons around the 327-acre lake. In addition to regular camping, the park has family housekeeping cabins.

Go east for 5 miles on Highway 4 to Highway 31; turn left and drive for about 10 miles back to South Bend.

The Gentle People

Many Americans' impression of Amish culture—yes, it isn't just religion, it's a culture—comes from a Hollywood film (*Witness* with Harrison Ford), and gross misunderstandings are the result. Even the many people who come to this area to experience Amish life go away still puzzled about these fascinating people.

No one knows for sure just how many Amish are spread out across the Midwest. (I use the word *Amish* to refer to both Amish and Mennonites, with whom Amish are often confused. It is beyond the scope of this aside to distinguish the two anthropologically, and I apologize for that.) Conservative efforts peg the number at close to 100,000, mostly in Ohio, Indiana, and Wisconsin.

Both Mennonites and Amish come originally from in and around Switzerland. A 1600s schism resulted in their splitting off religiously from the Swiss Anabaptists in a dispute over baptism. Like many religious "radicals" they were persecuted, to the point of being executed for heresy. Finding no safe haven in other surrounding countries, there was yet a second sub-split, with one group fleeing to the Alsace region of France. It was there in 1693 that a conservative faction of that group took the name of its leader, Jacob Amman, adopted his severe social and familial code, and looked for a better life across the sea.

The base of Amish culture is the community, with two overriding tenets: separation and obedience. The outside world isn't "evil" but it does have a negative influence and distracts one from true actions. Obedience is even more important. The Amish follow an oft-misunderstood idea

called *gelassenheit,* loosely translated as "yielding" or "submission." This forms a core to the Ordnung ("order"), the unwritten set of social mores that one must strictly adhere to or risk being shunned.

Many kinds of Amish exist. Old Order Amish are more conservative, but more and more progressive communities are taking hold. For example, some will ride in cars, though they won't drive them. Some will use electricity, if it isn't theirs. Some own property. All Amish still cultivate the ethic of hard work, thrift, and community support. The Amish and their schools have been in the courts for decades; one case reached the Supreme Court. Amish children can go to public schools or to one of the 100 or so one-room schoolhouses taught by an Amish woman, aged 16 or older. They learn in English and German (to read the Bible); Pennsylvania Dutch is spoken at home. They pay no social security tax, nor do they receive payments; they pay all other taxes.

It is these enigmatic and seemingly contradictory beliefs which have engendered a sometimes strained relationship between Amish and their neighbors (called English, high people, or Yankees). Locals may bristle when requests for rides or phone use become too frequent. Though some Amish accept rides, most use hired drivers (usually $.45 to $.60 per mile).

"English" could learn a lot from their Amish neighbors in general. During the Great Depression in the 1930s, the Amish fared better than most. Their refusal to use credit left them debt-free; those who needed help got it from that famous Amish banding-together to assist one of their own.

Tour 15
Cars, Circuses, and Barns

Kokomo–Greentown–Peru–Rochester–Mentone–Culver–North Judson–Winamac–Logansport–Kokomo

Distance: 208 miles

We start our tour in the city with the name that everyone has to love—Kokomo, a name so syncopated it's been used in nearly a dozen hit songs, even if the song has nothing to do with the theme. Some of the greatest glasswork and automobile finery in the United States came out of this city of inventors. From here the road leads us to the City of Circuses, Peru, winter home to some of America's greatest shows on earth. From here we switch gears to get an up-close view of an Indiana specialty—the round barn—at a museum dedicated to this fast-disappearing architectural gem. From here we roll through verdant agricultural fields to experience a quirky regional economic linchpin—the egg. The fecundity turns to natural beauty at a handful of wildlife preserves and a pair of state parks, and in between the nation's only crack cavalry troop makes for a fascinating and unique stop-off. We clamber aboard trains for more railroad history and then trip to Logansport to see some intricately carved carousel animals (and perhaps scuba dive in a glacially cold lake) before returning to Kokomo, tired to be sure, but thrilled with another day of diverse Indiana adventure.

Start your tour on the northeast side of Kokomo on Highway 31 at the *Kokomo/Howard County Convention and Visitors Bureau.* Located at 1504 N. Reed Road (Highway 31), (765) 457-6802 or (800) 837-0971, www.kokomo-in.org, the bureau has a vacation planner packet with the usual brochures but also with a wonderfully detailed map.

Kokomo bills itself as the City of Firsts. Consider the short list of first inventions/discoveries/developments that the city officials proudly trumpet: first car, invented by Elwood Haynes, road tested on July 4, 1894, on Pumpkinvine Pike; first pneumatic rubber tire, invented by D. C. Spraker, president of Kokomo Rubber Tire Company in 1894, who wrapped three-ply rubber, canvas, and other vulcanized rubber strips around a pole; first aluminum casting, invented by William "Billy" Johnson at the Ford & Donnelly Foundry in 1895; first carburetor, invented by George Kingston in 1902; first stainless steel, invented by Elwood Haynes in 1912 because his wife demanded dinnerware that didn't tarnish; first stellite cobalt-based alloy, another Elwood Haynes discovery; first aerial

bomb with fins, developed here in 1918; first mechanical corn picker, developed by John Powell in the early 1920s; first canned tomato juice, developed by Kemp Brothers Canning Company in 1928 at the request of a physician searching for baby food for his clinic; first push-button car radio, developed in 1938 by Delco Radio Division, GM; first all-metal lifeboats and rafts, developed in 1943 and dubbed the Kokomo Kid; first signal-seeking car radio and first all-transistor car radio, both developed by the Delco Radio Division; and finally, the first American howitzer shell, at least one used in actual combat, developed here by Superior Machine Tool Company in 1918.

Whew! All this technology and manufacturing was brought forth by plentiful cheap natural gas, discovered regionally in 1886. Manufacturing continues to buzz even today; *Industry Week* magazine placed Kokomo first in the nation in manufacturing productivity and put the city on a "gold medal" industry list among, ahem, Detroit, Toronto, and Tokyo. Wow!

From the visitors bureau, go just down the street to the *City of Firsts Automotive Heritage Museum.* One of two local museums highlighting the auto industry, this one, 1550 N. Reed Road, (765) 454-9999, also celebrates Kokomo's automotive heritage, with more than 80 classic and antique cars, many of which were produced locally. Included in the holdings are a 1932 Chrysler Custom Imperial 8 (only two others survive), a Haynes car that climbed Pikes Peak, some classic motorcycles, and an original 1902 Haynes-Apperson. You'll also find the façade of Elwood Haynes cottage, a replica 1930s gas station, and a re-created 1950s diner. Hours are 10 a.m.–5 p.m. daily. Admission.

Drive south on Highway 31 to Sycamore Road; turn right and go west through downtown to 1200 W. Sycamore Street. The Howard County Historical Society's holdings are on display at the *Seiberling Mansion,* 1200 W. Sycamore Street, (765) 452-4314, an 1891 neo-Jacobean Romanesque Revival mansion. Built by a wealthy industrialist, this served as a family home and later as a university; it fell into disrepair and was nearly demolished until local groups saved it and lovingly

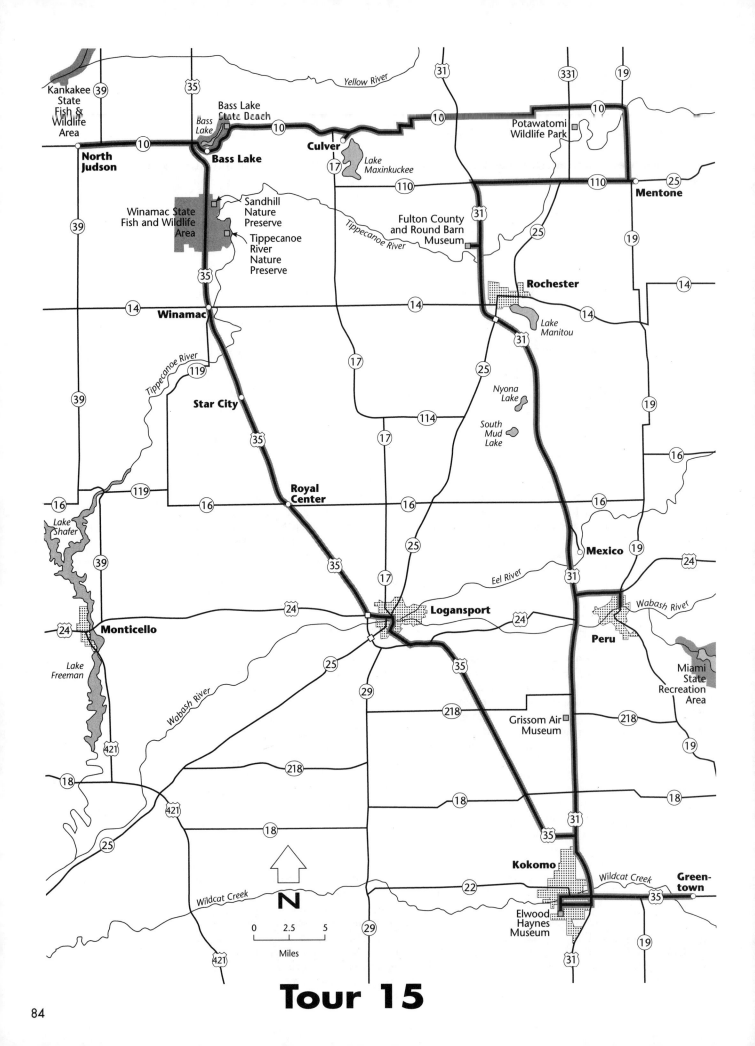

Kankakee State Fish & Wildlife Area

North Judson

Bass Lake
Bass Lake State Beach
Bass Lake

Culver

Lake Maxinkuckee

Potawatomi Wildlife Park

Mentone

Yellow River

Sandhill Nature Preserve

Tippecanoe River Nature Preserve

Winamac State Fish and Wildlife Area

Tippecanoe River

Fulton County and Round Barn Museum

Winamac

Rochester

Lake Manitou

Star City

Tippecanoe River

Nyona Lake

South Mud Lake

Lake Shafer

Royal Center

Mexico

Monticello

Lake Freeman

Wabash River

Logansport

Eel River

Peru

Wabash River

Miami State Recreation Area

Grissom Air Museum

Kokomo

Wildcat Creek

Green-town

Elwood Haynes Museum

Wildcat Creek

N

0   2.5   5
Miles

Tour 15

84

restored it. The hand-carved woodwork and Moorish brass hardware are telling examples of period design; the stained glass work is extraordinary. In addition to the interiors, local and regional historical exhibits and antique cars are on display.

Return east to the downtown via Walnut Street, one block north of Sycamore. You'll pass by the anchor, the county courthouse, and check out the historic architecture in the 39 blocks comprising the city center. The courthouse itself is an Art Deco jewel of limestone, marble, and stainless steel; its bronze doors show meticulous craftsmanship, and the skylights display a century of Indiana glasswork. Head over to the *Lerner Building* at 107 E. Sycamore Street to see the area's oldest bicycle shop, which also has a collection of antique bicycles.

From the corner of Walnut Street and Washington Street/Highway 22 (one block west of the county courthouse), drive south on Washington for 2 miles to W. Hoffer Street. Turn right and go two blocks, then turn left (south) on S. Webster Street. You'll come first to Kokomo's premier attraction—the *Elwood Haynes Museum,* 1915 S. Webster Street (in Highland Park), (765) 456-7500, and the nearby Kokomo Center for the Arts, 525 W. Ricketts Street, (317) 457-9480. The Haynes museum contains original automobiles, including a 1923 Haynes Roadster and the 1905 Haynes Model L. Displays on his industrial research offer glimpses of his creative genius. For a historical side trip, get directions to the spot east of town where Haynes tested his first car; a memorial marks the spot. Hours are 1–4 p.m. Tuesday-Saturday, till 5 p.m. Sunday. The *Center for the Arts* is just north and has revolving exhibits in its art galleries. Hours are 1–5 p.m. Tuesday–Friday, till 4 p.m. Saturday.

Also in Highland Park is Old Ben, aka the World's Largest Steer. In 1902 a purebred registered Hereford bull and ordinary shorthorn cow produced no ordinary offspring. Weighing 125 pounds at birth, Ben had to sit on his knees to nurse after only a week. Within four years he weighed 4,000 pounds. He became nationally famous and a local railroad built a spur line to his barn to pick him up and deliver him to fairs and agricultural exhibits. Tragically, he slipped on ice and fractured a leg in 1910 and had to be put down. He was too large to be weighed, but it's estimated that he topped out at nearly 4,700 pounds. He was an incredible 16 feet long. Old Ben was turned into hot dogs, but his hide was stuffed and he became a gift of the city. He now sits in his own special pavilion.

In the same park is another Brobdingnagian object—the *Sycamore Stump,* the remains of a sycamore tree found just off Highway 22 west of Kokomo, near Wildcat Creek. Figuring its age is impossible—a conservative estimate is 434 years, while some have posited an age of 1,500 years. No matter what the age, at 51 feet in circumference,

you've got to see it to believe it. In 1916 it was moved to the park (no mean feat, since it weighs several tons). For a while it was used as a telephone booth, but repeated vandalism forced the city to put it in protective custody of sorts and it now sits fenced off.

One block south from the Haynes Museum, proceed east about 0.5 mile on East Boulevard to Union Street. Turn left, go one block to Poplar Street, turn right (east), then turn left onto S. Market Street. At 1310 S. Market Street you'll be at the *Kokomo Opalescent Glass Co.,* (765) 457-1829. At one time the glass industry, encouraged by cheap natural gas in northern Indiana, rivaled all other industries. This factory dates to 1888 and is the only remaining "gas boom" factory in the county today. The company outlasted all others by betting on sheet glass (think stained glass) and were proved right. When the industry went belly up, they thrived. It is a one-of-a-kind tour to be sure. (No open-toe shoes are allowed.) Tours at 10 a.m. Wednesday and Friday.

Return to East Boulevard and turn left. Proceed east to Highway 31, turn north, and go to Highway 35. Turn right (east) and drive 7.5 miles to Greentown. This is another town that benefited mightily from epic pockets of natural gas under the earth. One local company's wares are now museum-quality pieces on display at the *Greentown Glass Museum,* (765) 628-6206, 112 N. Meridian Street. The Indiana Tumbler and Goblet Company produced its wares for about nine years around the turn of the century. Collectors highly prize the exquisite pieces for their distinctive hues. The factory primarily made crystal clear and translucent colored glass, and its "chocolate" and "golden agate" (called Holly Amber) are especially prized. These last two were developed and perfected by Jacob Rosenthal, a glass chemist who worked here only three years, Chocolate (opaque brown) glass was produced during his three years, Holly Amber for only six months, which explains why it's so prized and difficult to find. Open 10 a.m.-noon and 1-4 p.m. Tuesday-Friday, 1-4 p.m. weekends, May 15-October 31; 1-4 p.m. weekends only, November-December and March-April.

Double back on Highway 35 to Highway 31, turn north, and go for 14 miles to the *Grissom Air Museum.* This huge complex, (765) 688-2654, next to Grissom Air Reserve Base, is a fascinating way to get a glimpse at 50 years of aviation history—military aviation mostly. Nearly 20 historic aircraft are on display; the highlight is likely an original B-17 Flying Fortress standing guard outside (nope, it doesn't fly). Everybody loves to clamber into the cockpit of a Vietnam War-era Phantom jet. The laundry list of memorabilia and exhibits can easily take up a whole afternoon. Best of all—it's free. Open 10 a.m.-4 p.m. Tuesday-Saturday; closed in January.

Continue north on Highway 31 for 6 miles to Business Highway 24. Turn right and proceed into Peru. Peru is a lovely little community near the confluence of the Mississinewa and Wabash Rivers. Near this site in 1812 Chief Tecumseh stoked a fire for the last great council of the Mississinewa, his ultimate attempt to organize the Midwest tribes into a confederation and side with the British against the United States. The other nations, remembering the Battle of Tippecanoe, refused to continue the warring; Tecumseh left for Canada and joined the British.

Peru later became famous for circuses. Along with Baraboo, Wisconsin, another crucial wintering ground for circuses, Peru was home of the Hagenbeck-Wallace Circus and once had acres of large red warehouses to house animals and equipment over the winter, giving rise to its fun moniker, Circus City. The Wallace circus dates from 1882 when a traveling circus couldn't pay its bill at Ben Wallace's stable; an instant business opportunity dropped into his lap when he took it over. Within a decade, four of the top circuses in the country wintered here. Locals still tell stories about

Mr. Inventor

One can't help but notice that of all the inventions and discoveries that Kokomo has churned out in the last century, a noticeable number are the result of one tireless tinkerer and garage genius: Elwood Haynes. He is credited with designing and building the first car (this is, of course, hotly disputed by other claimants) but as a specialist in metallurgy he would later develop numerous metal alloys; on a humorous note, one of his early discoveries, stainless steel, came at the behest—or, rather, demand—of his wife, who was tired of tarnished tableware.

But it is for his car that Haynes became legendary. While others do pish-posh his title, strictly speaking he did invent the first clutch-driven automobile with electric ignition right here in Kokomo. He originally dreamed up the somewhat radical (for the time) idea in 1892. Experimenting with everything from steam to electricity, he finally settled on his single-stroke engine and set to building the horseless wonder. On July 4, 1894—how fitting is that, the Yankee inventor rolling it out on the U.S.A.'s birthday—he hauled his leviathan creation (the engine alone weighed 240 pounds) into the countryside, along the wonderfully countryesque named Pumpkinvine Pike, and roared off on a 1.5-mile rip-snorting ride, topping off at a whopping 8 miles per hour. He tinkered some more and began manufacturing in 1895 with Elmer and Edgar Apperson, two brothers who owned the Riverside Machine Shop. In 1897 they had built and sold the princely number of three cars. But by 1900 his business had taken off and they had plans to produce 50 cars annually. The first automobile manufacturing plant in Indiana had been founded. Ultimately, it's not hyperbole to give him lion's share of credit for making northern Indiana and Indianapolis a leader in the automotive industry. That legendary first car now sits in the Smithsonian.

The Haynes-Apperson Company split up later and Haynes's plants closed in 1925; Delco Radio later purchased the buildings and Chrysler bought even more of the assembly lines.

greeting legendary cowboy star Tom Mix—who had joined the Sells-Floto Circus with a Wild West show—at the railroad depot. Stop by the third week in July for the wildly popular *Circus City Festival;* it has a fun three-ring amateur circus, midway, crafts, and a wonderful circus parade the final day.

If that weren't enough, Peru was the birthplace of Cole Porter, the internationally known writer of such song classics as "Anything Goes," "Night and Day," and 1,500 more. His expansive home here was converted into apartments following his death; he's buried locally in Mount Hope Cemetery.

Exhibits on all of these famous happenings and people can be found at the *Miami County Museum,* 51 N. Broadway Street, (765) 473-9183. The circus attraction memorabilia are particularly engaging and good for kids as well as adults. It has more than 75,000 items—a stunning amount for a local historical museum. It doesn't overlook anything, to be sure, with exhibits covering natural history of 15,000 years ago right through the circus days. Twenty-five reconstructions of storefronts are found on the second floor; it's a good glimpse at bygone days of small-town Indiana. You'll also find a nice art room with displays of paintings by George Winter and Indiana author James Whitcomb Riley. Quaint items include an old penny-scale to weigh yourself and an orchestrian piano you can play for a quarter.

Among the Cole Porter memorabilia are his 1989 Grammy award, other awards, photographs, and his 1955 Cadillac, which he shipped to Europe for three vacations. Hours are 9 a.m.–5 p.m. Tuesday–Saturday. Even better for circus buffs (or those who never really have grown up) is the *International Circus Hall of Fame,* three miles east on Highway 24, (765) 472-7553. Lines of circus wagons are about the grounds and there are oodles of colorful memorabilia—certainly enough razzmatazz to keep the kids interested. Everybody loves the circus performances in summer; we're all kids when clowns show up, aren't we? Hours are 10 a.m.–4:30 p.m. Monday–Saturday.

From downtown Peru, return to Highway 31. Proceed north on Highway 31 for about 20 miles to County Road 375N, four miles north of Rochester. Rochester is certainly worth a look-see, and although it's a friendly and comfortable place, it isn't Loyal. But before the Rochester folks get irate, let me explain. Four miles north of Rochester, along Highway 31 at the Tippecanoe River, is the *Fulton County Round Barn Museum,* 37 E. 375N, (219) 223-4436, which includes a wonderful round barn museum and a reconstructed living history village called Loyal. Most travelers come to snoop around round barns, and it's hard not to; not only are they architectural marvels, but at the rate they're disappearing, this once-proud part of Midwest heritage will be lost forever. Fulton County, incidentally, with 17 round barns, once had more of this eye-catching type than any other county in Indiana (and Indiana had more than any other state—225); sadly, only 8 remain in the county (and only 100 in Indiana). Thus, the county historical board has taken upon itself quite a mighty but admirable task in preserving what's left.

The Round Barn Museum was built in 1924 by the C. V. Kindig Company and donated to the commission when a tornado ripped off its roof. Inside you can get a look at horse-drawn implements, a 1912 truck, farm tools, a 1915 buggy, and even an original covered wagon. Loyal has an assortment of villages dating between 1900 and 1925. There's the old Rochester depot with 160 feet of extant track and a caboose and boxcar. Other highlights are the Kewanna jail, a stagecoach inn, a dentist's office (gruesome to think about), a cider mill, windmill, and even a round chicken house. Show up the second Saturday of each month to get a blacksmithing demonstration. A reference room has newspapers dating back to 1877, and a permanent display room has great local tidbits of history. For example, Rochester and the circuses have ties to Elmo Lincoln, who was the first Tarzan. And you can learn the story of Lake Manitou, a sacred lake and epicenter of Native American legend.

In mid-September the museum complex hosts Trail of Courage, an important and popular living history festival of pre-1840 settlement life. A variety of encampments spring up and let you experience life during the French and Indian and Revolutionary Wars, a voyageur camp, and a handful of typical Native American villages. Pioneer days crafts and skills are on display, and the muzzle-loading and tomahawk-throwing competitions will leave the little ones pop-eyed. Each year one Potawatomi family is memorialized for the forced relocation of the Native Americans to the West on what became known as the Trail of Death.

For aficionados of round barns, come mid-June is the Round Barn Festival in downtown Rochester and at the museum. There are more encampments, old time crafts, and interesting sideshows, such as blanket trading. General hours for the museum are 9 a.m.–5 p.m. Monday–Saturday. Remarkably, it's free.

Get back on Highway 31 and continue north for another 4 miles. At Highway 110, turn right (east) and drive for 10 miles to Mentone. Mentone certainly offers one of the most intriguing spots to visit on this tour. Tourists blowing through town generally screech to a halt in front of a 12-foot-high, 1.5-ton concrete egg right along the main road. They stand in front of it, scratch their heads, gaze around, and wonder why a giant egg graces the village's roadway. It's actually quite simple: In the early part of the twentieth century, eggs (and chickens in general) were a mainstay of the local economy. It has subsided somewhat, but a lion's share of the county's residents still garner income from chickens and eggs

The quirky legacy of the egg in Mentone.

in all their forms. A festival in June to fete the honorable egg is great fun. You can stop by the *Mentone Chamber of Commerce* office for brochures of educational and stimulating agricultural driving tours of the county.

Just west and south one block along Oak Street you'll see the *Lawrence D. Bell Aircraft Museum,* (219) 353-7551, not hard to see if you look for the Huey chopper parked out front. Bell, a local boy who made good, was an aviation pioneer with a nearly endless list of aviation firsts; later he founded the Bell Aircraft Corporation, which is legendary for taking commercial helicopters into its future. The models of Bell Aircraft planes and choppers are exquisitely detailed and informative.

Drive back west on Highway 110, then immediately right (north) on Highway 19. Just after crossing the Tippecanoe River, turn west onto Highway 10. There is a boat launch along the river where you can put in a canoe as well. About two miles after you turn west on Highway 10 you pass by a turnoff to *Potawatomi Wildlife Park,* an established wildlife viewing area rife with shorebirds, ducks, and herons. Beaver lodges are fairly prevalent. The ponds, wetlands, and bottomland forest are absolutely filled with songbirds.

Continue west on Highway 10 for about 19 miles to Culver. This town is home to *Culver Military Academy,* located along the shore of 1,800-acre Lake Maxinkuckee, (219) 842-3311. The spacious grounds are laid out in English collegiate design and are surrounded by dense spinneys; it's fun just to stroll the 300-acre grounds looking at the historic architecture. The academy is of note today for its horsemanship program—the only one like it in the country. Now that there is no U.S. cavalry, these troops are the escorts of presidents and nobility. You may get an appreciation of the pageantry at demonstrations of the Black Troop guard, held Sunday afternoons, May–October.

If military precision isn't your cup of tea, Lake Maxinkuckee makes for a great day of leisure. Just across from the military academy, the lake beckons with its public beach, sandy beach, and wooded park. You can rent canoes and boats.

Drive west on Highway 10 for another 10 miles to Bass Lake. You'll find Indiana's fourth-largest natural lake, so not surprisingly the swimming and wading are just fine (bathhouse provided) at *Bass Lake State Beach,* (219) 772-3382; there's also camping. Save your entrance ticket for free admission to Tippecanoe River State Park (more on that below).

Keep going west on Highway 10 for 11 miles to North Judson. More railroad heritage is to be found at the *North Judson Hoosier Valley Railroad Museum,* (219) 223-3834, 507 Mulberry Street, a railroad restoration organization with 30 pieces of rolling stock, much of which is awaiting restoration. Freight cars, cabooses, operable diesel switch engines, and an Orton locomotive crane are the most prized possessions, along with a 1947 C&O K-4 class locomotive. The volunteer staff is constantly laying track and switches on the abandoned right-of-way of the Erie Railroad. Open 8 a.m.–5 p.m. daily.

Return east on Highway 10 to Highway 35 at Bass Lake. Turn right (south) and head to Tippecanoe River State Park. Along the way you'll pass by both the *Sandhill Nature Preserve* and the *Tippecanoe River Nature Preserve,* both established wildlife preserves. The prairie, some of which has undergone restoration, is a prime habitat for the Franklin's ground squirrel, which is on the endangered species list. Besides the pervasive deer, you can also see beaver and red fox. The hiking trails of the state park, (219) 946-3213, are excellent, as they wend through oak forests, marshes, and dry sand prairie (there's even a modest sand dune); Trail 8—the Bluestem Trail—leads to the Sandhill Nature Preserve, while Trail 4 leads to the Tippecanoe River Nature Preserve. Tippecanoe State Park is also outstanding for canoeing though, sadly, no rentals are available in the park itself (lots of liveries are found nearby). As you float down the river imagine yourself a seventeenth-century French voyageur, as this route was crucial for fur trading.

Continue south on Highway 35, through Winamac, Star City, and Royal Center to just west of Logansport. Turn left (east) on Business Highway 35 and proceed into downtown Logansport. The first thing you notice is that you can't seem to enter the city without crossing a bridge, given its location on the Wabash and Eel Rivers. So it is, naturally, the City of Bridges. The city was named for Captain James John Logan, a U.S. Army officer who also happened to be a nephew of the great chief Tecumseh. He was killed in the War of 1812; a friend named the town after winning naming rights in a shooting competition. The *Logansport/Cass County Chamber of Commerce,* 300 E. Broadway, (800) 425-2071, has lots of tourist information.

But most folks come to see the genuine Gustav Dentzel hand-carved animal carousel in *Riverside Park,* Eleventh and High Streets. Fully restored, this operational masterpiece has 43 exquisite animals and dates from 1896. There are also a brass ring, band organ, and kiddie train. Hours are 6–9 p.m. Monday–Friday, 1–9 p.m. weekends, Memorial Day–Labor Day; 1–5 p.m. weekends the rest of the year. Admission.

In addition, check out the *Museum of the Cass County Historical Society,* 1004 E. Market Street, (219) 753-3866, which includes an 1853 home, a cabin, a schoolroom, antique china, Native American artifacts, and an automobile built by the ReVere Motor Company, which operated in Logansport for a decade in the early 1900s. Hours are 1–5 p.m. Tuesday–Saturday, as well as first Sunday of the month.

From downtown Logansport, take Business Highway 35 south to Highway 435 soon after crossing the Wabash River. Turn left on 435 and proceed to Highway 35. Turn left on 35 and drive southeast for about 25 miles back to Kokomo.

Tour 16
Covered Bridges and
Wide-Open Roads

Rockville–Mansfield–Bainbridge–Greencastle–Cunot–Terre Haute–Dana–Turkey Run State Park–Rockville

Distance: 175.5 miles

The covered bridge at Bridgeton, in Parke County.

We begin this tour with the covered bridges that have made Indiana famous. Concentrated in Parke County, they draw tens of thousands of bridge peepers and photographers every year. Pick a direction, any direction, and there you'll find historic covered bridges, old gristmills, friendly shops dispensing crafts and antiques, and oodles of grand festivals showing the rustic and charming side of the state. We'll then see some very old natural beauty, a German buzz bomb, and one of the oldest and most precious churches east of the Mississippi (which is also in a darn lovely little town).

Hankering for more scenery, we wend down the road past some state recreation areas to the isolated Cataract area, where we can enjoy the state's tallest waterfall ... and, of course, a covered bridge. We head west into the "high land" of Terre Haute, once the dividing line between French colonial provinces of Canada and Louisiana. Terre Haute

holds special significance for members of labor unions and their supporters—this was the birthplace and home of Eugene V. Debs, founder of the country's first labor union and a one-time presidential candidate. And many hoops-crazy folks should be alerted to the fact that Larry Bird, of Boston Celtics fame, played his college basketball here, at Indiana State University. Then it's on to one of Indiana's true natural treasures, Turkey Run State Park.

Begin this tour in Rockville, about 50 miles due west of Indianapolis. This is serious covered bridge country, and Rockville is its epicenter. Parke County is absolutely littered with covered bridges (with three more at Turkey Run State Park; see Tour 17), officially tallying 32, locals say. Some tourists spend a lifetime "collecting" them; it takes me nearly a lifetime to find some of them! Vehicles

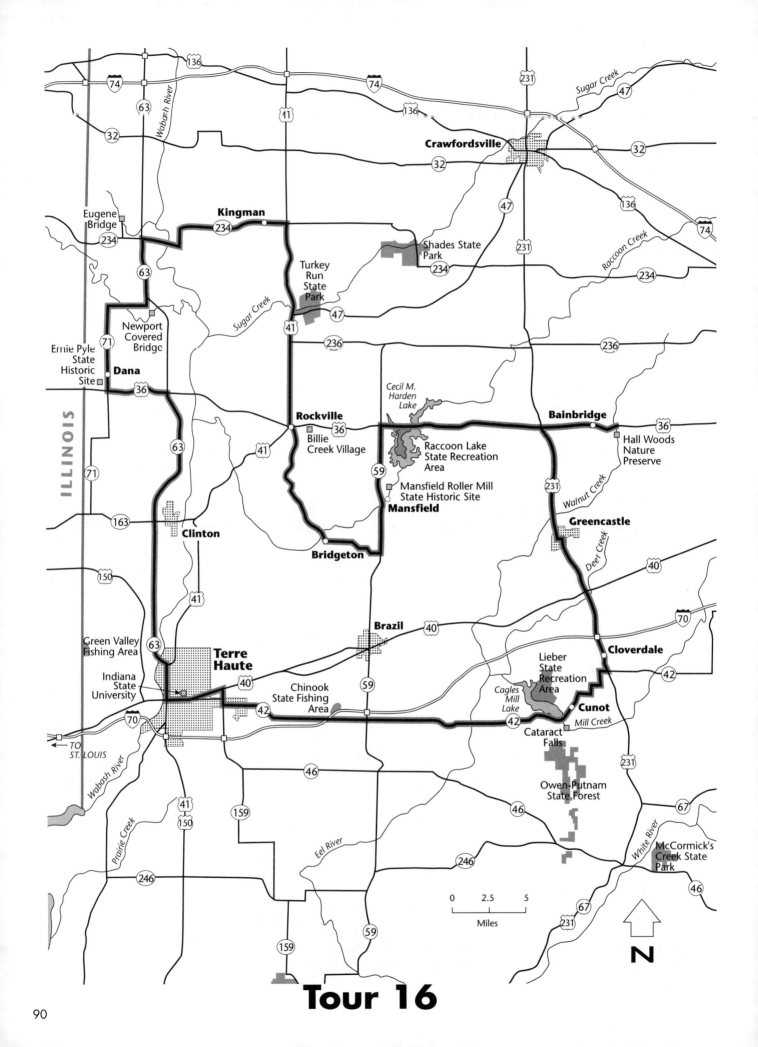

Tour 16

descend on Rockville, on weekend mornings especially in summer and fall, but this picturesque little place doesn't seem touched by the hoopla at all. An absolute must is the *Covered Bridge Capital Tourist Centre/Parke County,* (765) 569-5226, www.coveredbridges.com, in the old railroad depot along the main road in the village center. They've got oodles of great maps and chatty advice. Most certainly pick up a map of their five recommended and mapped bridge tours. The five tours go in every direction throughout the county and each is 25–30 miles long. You get to see four to six bridges per, so it balances out nicely. Each tour destination also features other regional highlights.

NOTE: No map can prepare you for the spiderweb of winding, gravel, single-lane roads (some of them don't even qualify as roads) awaiting you out there. Just remember that getting lost is sometimes half the fun. Also note that the map on page 90 of this book does not contain the five Parke County routes. The last one listed here—the Black Route— is perfect for getting to the next leg of our tour, so save that one for last.

The Brown Route is a classic favorite of many people. It leads westward out of town to take in a pair of bridges and an old schoolhouse and—a personal favorite—briefly follows the bed of the old Wabash Erie Canal. Communities along this route are legendary for their pig roasts during festivals.

The Red Route leaves to the southwest and passes through or by six bridges (one of which stands next to a waterfall), the Bridgeton Mill, the diminutive village of Mecca with its precious one-room schoolhouse, an old country store, and an 1878 house.

The Blue Route takes you back up to Turkey Run State Park and is often called the most scenic of the tours. You also can pass through the area of a historic Quaker community.

The Yellow Route takes you to five bridges, including the longest double span and longest single span anywhere. You also pass through the historic Quaker community. Ask at the visitor center about the beef served at festivals. In Tangier locals bury beef underground and cook it 14 hours; it sounds a bit off-putting, but it's delicious.

The Black Route heads southeast, taking in a couple more bridges and a historic mill in Bridgeton (the last family-owned and operating gristmill in the county, dating to 1823—you can see the burr stones grind corn, wheat, rye, and buckwheat), a scenic wildlife area, before leading to Mansfield, home of the *Mansfield Roller Mill,* an imposing 1820 mill that still grinds wheat and corn the old-fashioned way. It sits next to a lovely waterfall. Late April sees a huge festival blowout— the simultaneous *Mountain Man Rendezvous,* when costumed Grizzly Addams wannabes wander about town mingling with delighted tourists, and the ever-popular *Mushroom Festival*—great fun to hunt for the delectable fungus. *Use this route to lead to the next segment of our tour.*

If auto touring is cramping your legs, haul out the bike and grab another map produced just for you and your own county bike tour. It roughly follows many of the same auto tours but obviously lets you enjoy them at a much more leisurely pace. An organized bike tour takes place the first Saturday in May. The course is flat to rolling with several substantial climbs; SAG vehicles assist.

But wait—Rockville isn't just about bridges. Before leaving Rockville, plan to visit *Billie Creek Village,* one mile east of town on Highway 36, (765) 569-3430, a re-created settlement of nearly 40 Parke County buildings: farmhouses, a general store, a fudge shop, churches, schoolhouse, house of Governor Wright, and many more. Costumed docents give demonstrations of period life, and artisans regularly appear. In short, something is always

Another of Parke County's covered bridges.

going on. They've even relocated three of the county's most legendary bridges here. Kids love the wagon rides. If you're exhausted, a cushy inn is on site. Hours are 9 a.m.–4 p.m. daily. Admission.

If you like festivals, you've certainly come to the right place. Pick a weekend—any weekend—and chances are something will be going down. *Billie Creek War Day* takes place the second weekend in June and is Indiana's largest Civil War Reenactment. The village also hosts the *Steam Harvest Days and Tractor Show* on Labor Day weekend. The *Parke County Maple Syrup Festival* takes place in late February and early March; nothing finer than licking your sweet lips as you tour a maple syrup farm while headed toward one of those grand covered bridges. The granddaddy of all local festivals is the *Parke County Covered Bridge Festival,* a 10-day blowout sponsored by nine towns beginning the second Friday in October.

Head southeast out of Rockville on County Road 40E, eventually following the Black Route signs along several different county roads. After about 16 rollicking miles heading south, then east, you'll come to Highway 59. Turn left (north) and proceed for about 8 miles to Highway 36, passing through Mansfield on the way. Turn right (east) on 36 and cruise for 15 miles to Bainbridge. Approximately two miles east of Bainbridge is the *Hall Woods Nature Preserve.* You'll not likely find a more magnificent spot for wildlife viewing than here. The jewel in the crown is its great blue heron rookery but more than 120 species of birds are here. Botanists will go gaga at the tree species, some of which contain enormous representatives, among the tallest and largest in Indiana. Oh, yeah, and there are two more covered bridges.

Return on Highway 36 back through Bainbridge and go about 4 miles west to Highway 231. Turn left (south) and drive 9 miles to Greencastle. This town is another Indiana gem, loaded with historic architecture; its most prominent community feature is the sedate campus of DePauw University. Many people use it as a base to explore the natural wonders of the *Lieber State Recreation Area* to the south. Historical tidbit: John Dillinger once robbed a bank here.

Stop by the *Putnam County Convention and Visitors Bureau,* 2 S. Jackson Street, (765) 653-8743. Nearby is your first stop, a genuine World War II German buzz bomb outside the courthouse—no idea why. The bureau can hook you up with maps and directions to other town sites and to the nine covered bridges surrounding the town.

You can tour the dozen or so historic structures on the *DePauw University campus,* several of which date to the turn of the nineteenth century. The Methodist church on campus is the oldest of that denomination in Indiana. The state's Journalism Hall of Fame is also here. Tours daily (half day Saturday) except Sunday; call (765) 658-4006 for information.

From Greencastle, continue south on Highway 231 for 11 miles to Highway 42 just south of Cloverdale. Turn right (west) on 42 and proceed about 5 miles to Cunot. You're in the land of the *Lieber State Park Recreational Area,* (765) 795-4576, a thousand acres of lush forest surrounding the 1,500-acre *Cagles Mill Lake.* Just follow Highway 243 a short distance north of town. Surrounding this are about 7,500 acres of state forest and federal flood control reservoir management at the Cagles Mill Lake Area. You can go swimming, fishing, boating (rentals are available), and hiking; a unique feature here is the Water Safari Boat Tour of the lake. You can reserve campsites.

Quick Trip Option: For a real treat, head to *Cataract Falls,* south of Cunot. They are difficult to reach, so your best bet is to go back to Cloverdale and go south on Highway 231 for about 5 miles to County Road 1050N. Follow the signs for 3.2 miles to the falls. Two sets are found here: Upper Falls, the state's highest, drops 86 pounding feet; Lower Falls are less ambitious but no less lovely. A Civil War-era general store and a covered bridge are special treats for this day.

From Cunot, take Highway 42 west for about 27 uneventful miles to Highway 46 just east of Terre Haute. Turn right on 46 and go 1.5 miles to Highway 40; turn left (west) and proceed into downtown Terre Haute. Terre

Terre Haute's Social Conscience

Coal was discovered in the Terre Haute region in the early 1800s, but serious efforts at extraction wouldn't start till the post–Civil War years. Railroads allowed for full-scale coal shipping, at which time industry in Terre Haute kept pace with the rest of the country. At one time 30 million tons of coal were extracted and shipped for World War I. But with labor comes strife, and Terre Haute had plenty of it, though at first its strikes were relatively peaceful.

It wouldn't last. Boom/bust cycles of labor always cause tensions and the strike of 1935 was no different. In the city that was home to Eugene V. Debs, it was a given that labor would eventually square off with companies.

The general strike of 1935 was the first of its kind east of the Rockies. More than 600 workers walked out of a stamping shop for a 10 percent raise and unionization. The company brought in strikebreakers. In response, labor unions called off 26,000 workers in a general strike the *New York Times* called "nearly 100% effective." Then the governor of the state brought in national guard troops and declared martial law; tear gas was used and arrests were made. Even when striking eased, the governor continued with martial law. Later, mediators from the National Labor Relations Board sided with the striking unions; the Supreme Court agreed in spirit but not in law.

Haute—or "high land," as the plateau upon which the city sits was dubbed by French fur traders forging into the wilderness along the Wabash River—is a southern key to the Wabash River valley and its heritage. Terre Haute gained notice mostly as a union town. The first Indiana Grange was started in a nearby township in 1869, and famous labor leader and resident Eugene Debs started one of the nation's first worker unions; highly effective industrial strikes in the early twentieth century gained national recognition. Terre Haute is also the hometown of Paul Dresser, composer of "On the Banks of the Wabash," Indiana's state song, and brother of Theodore Dreiser, author of several important twentieth-century novels, including *Sister Carrie* and *An American Tragedy.*

Almost an afterthought by many travelers, the city of high land has an astonishing number of worthy sights, given its relatively small population (approximately 55,000). Stop by the *Convention and Visitors Bureau,* 643 Wabash Avenue (Highway 40), (812) 234-5555 or (800) 366-3043, www.terrehaute.com. Historic architecture is everywhere you look in the *Farrington Grove Historic District,* a 70-square-block area of more than 800 original structures, many of them lovely antebellum homes. The visitors bureau has brochures detailing all structures.

You can get an overview of the entire region's history at the *Historical Museum of the Wabash Valley,* 1411 S. Sixth Street, (812) 235-9717. Travelers are treated to re-creations of a general store, post office, and numerous other downtown businesses; antiques and assorted historical memorabilia line cases throughout the well-planned museum. It's *huge,* occupying more than a dozen rooms. Hours are 1–4 p.m. Tuesday–Sunday, February–December.

Just north of Highway 40, the first national road and the dividing line between the north and south sections of Terre Haute, sits the *Eugene V. Debs Home,* 451 N. Eighth Street, (812) 232-2163. This well-maintained house was home to the legendary socialist and labor leader. In addition to Debs memorabilia, other pieces pay homage to labor leaders in the workers rights movement. Hours are 1–4:30 p.m. Wednesday–Sunday.

Indiana State University, north of downtown just off Highway 40, is the alma mater of Indiana's most famous son of basketball—Larry Bird. He *almost* led the school to the 1979 NCAA national basketball championship, but Magic Johnson and Michigan State prevailed, starting a rivalry that would last over a decade in the NBA. You'll see lots of Larry Bird-themed items around downtown, including one entire restaurant and hotel. The campus has a *Center for Performing and Fine Arts,* which has art exhibits, a rare dictionary collection, an anthropology museum, and an observatory.

More art is on display at the *Sheldon Swope Art Gallery,* 25 S. Seventh Street, (812) 238-1676,

which emphasizes American art beginning in the nineteenth century. Special events, films, lectures, and various other happenings make it worth a peek. Even the building it's housed in, a gorgeous 1901 Italian Renaissance building, is a piece of art. Hours are 10 a.m.–5 p.m. Tuesday–Friday (till 8 p.m. Thursday), noon–5 p.m. weekends.

The *Rose-Hulman Institute of Technology Gallery,* 5500 Wabash Avenue, (812) 877-1511, has even more artwork—much of it Hoosier-centric. If you want see Indiana artwork, this is a good place. Hours are Monday–Friday, 8 a.m.–5 p.m.

Taking Poplar Street (Highway 42) east you'll come to *Dobbs Park,* a wonderful 100-acre nature center, one quarter of which is a state preserve and wetlands area. Nature trails snake through woodlands. Kids love the interpretive nature center and butterfly/hummingbird garden. There's also a small Native American museum detailing Eastern Woodland Native American cultures. Just west of here, *Deming Park* is even larger and has a whole host of recreational activities, plus miniature train rides.

Fairbanks Park, at First and Farrington Streets, has a memorial to Paul Dresser; on the site is a restored nineteenth-century workman's home. Note that the bedrooms upstairs are reached from outside.

From downtown Terre Haute, take Highway 63 north about 24 miles to Highway 36. Turn left (west) on 36 and proceed for 4.5 miles to Highway 71. Turn right (north). Along Highway 36, you'll see roads to no fewer than four other covered bridges; keep your eyes peeled for them. On Highway 71, in the town of Dana, you'll soon come to the boyhood home of Ernie Pyle and a memorial to this beloved Hoosier. Famed as a World War II correspondent—the correspondent GIs trusted as one of their own—Pyle was born and raised here and he's now memorialized at the *Ernie Pyle State Historic Site,* (765) 665-3633. The original farmhouse is a visitor center; two Quonset huts have also been relocated here and house lots of World War II-era artifacts and exhibits on his actions during the war—before Japanese machine gun fire cut him down on Okinawa. A plaque reads: "At this spot, the 77th Infantry Division lost a Buddy, Ernie Pyle, 18 April, 1945." One thing that most people don't know is that Pyle was actually a famous vagabond. For seven years he and his wife drove around the United States as he wrote a column entitled "Hoosier Vagabond" (which ties in nicely with this book). This quote remains a personal mantra: "I have no home. My home is where my extra luggage is, and where the car is stored, and where I happen to be getting mail at the time. My home is America." Hours are 9 a.m.–5 p.m. Tuesday–Saturday, mid-March to mid-September.

Continue north from Dana for 7.5 miles on Highway 71. Just after the highway bends to the east and crosses the Little Vermillion River, you can take an access road to the south and see the *Newport Covered Bridge.*

Highway 71 soon merges into Highway 63. Continue north on 63 for 4.5 miles to Highway 234. If you crave yet another covered bridge, jog west off Highway 234 into Cayuga, then north into Eugene to see the *Eugene Bridge.*

At the junction of Highways 63 and 234, turn right (east) on 234 and drive for 11.5 miles, passing through Kingman, to Highway 41. Turn south and proceed for about 6 miles to *Turkey Run State Park.* This is arguably the busiest and hardest-working park in Indiana. If it isn't, it sure seems as if it is. All of Indiana—and at times perhaps the Midwest—troops through spring, summer, and fall to gaze at the Narrows Bridge, surely one of the most popular tourist attractions the state has to offer. You can spin around and get a look at two others.

The park's natural beauty is sublime—sandstone formations are some of the earth's loveliest creations, and the sheer-walled ravines take your breath away. The *Rocky Hollow-Falls Canyon Nature Preserve* is equal to the untouched beauty of nearby Shades State Park (Tour 17). Old growth walnuts and sycamores tower over rain forest-quality mosses and ferns; you become somnolent in the quietude of hemlock groves.

Of note is the exposed sandstone. It's called Mansfield sandstone after a nearby community of the same name. Eons ago silt and sand at the mouth of the ancient Michigan River were gradually compacted into rock. With it was vegetative and animal matter that slowly turned into coal, helping the region economically multimillennia later—you can still see striations of coal veins as you hike the park's interiors. Later, rivers came through and etched their marks on the park. Punchbowl is a huge pothole formed by glacial erratics and is a great geological primer.

The park has 11 trails, ranging from easy to very rugged. Trail No. 3 is a nasty little one with a high degree of rewards. Trail No. 1 goes past one big tree, some lovely sycamores, and leads to a covered bridge. Trail No. 2 traces a cliff line, so be cautious. Trail No. 8 is a personal favorite; quiet and untrampled, it follows a small creek. For hardcore hikers only is Trail No. 9, a one-miler that's incredibly rugged but lets you see old growth stands.

One of Indiana State Parks' popular inns is also here; a great time for a splurge, no? You can also spend an afternoon at the nature center, which has wildlife exhibits, or in the cool star-projection room.

Return to Highway 41 and turn left (south); continue for about 10 miles back to Rockville.

Tour 17
Battles and Bridges

Lafayette–West Lafayette–Battle Ground–New Richmond–Linden–Crawfordsville–Shades State Park–Covington–Attica–Lafayette

Distance: 156.5 miles

A denizen of Wolf Park, near Lafayette.

Our tour starts in one of the most important and historically significant regions of the Wabash River valley: the banks of the Wabash River at Lafayette, once a principal node on the river's transportation network. In the eighteenth century, the French established a fort, the first military establishment in Indiana, and one of the Midwest's most decisive battles between the U.S. military and Native Americans took place nearby. Later, rivermen gave it a rough and tumble reputation. The Lafayette area provides an excellent means of experiencing the history of Indiana's (and the Midwest's) rich inland waterways.

Hoosier Hysteria crops up as we visit the tiny town chosen by Hollywood to represent the typical Indiana village in the movie *Hoosiers*. We also meet Ben-Hur (in a way) and look at one of the nation's most interesting jails. Many people (locals, as well as travelers) say the area's Shades State Park is one of the most extraordinary in Indiana, primarily for its eerily primeval nature preserve and world-famous ridge topography. Before finally loop-

ing home, we get to view a bit of wilderness as original natives and settlers saw it—through a freakish sandstone arch.

Start your tour at the junction of I-65 and Highway 26 just east of Lafayette. Northeast of the junction is the *Greater Lafayette Convention and Visitors Bureau,* 301 Frontage Road (behind the Cracker Barrel restaurant), (765) 447-9999 or (800) 872-6648, www.lafayette-in.com. Its tour planner has an excellent fold-out map of the city and county.

The site of what today is Lafayette played a crucial role in the settlement and development of present-day Indiana. The Wabash River valley was a crucial conduit to the Mississippi River from the Great Lakes, and the French established Fort Ouiatenon here, the first military post in Indiana. The Lafayette area was the scene of the 1811 Battle of Tippecanoe, a major defeat for Native Americans of the Northwest Territory. The Wabash River later impelled settlement and development of a major

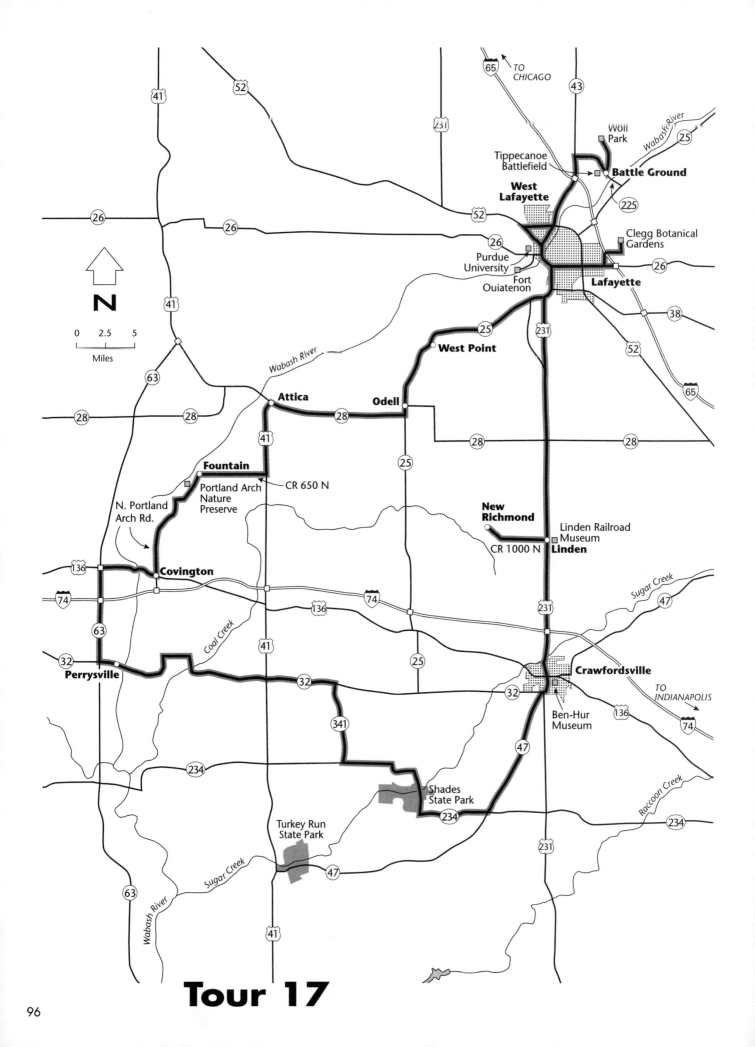

Tour 17

steamboat transportation network for agricultural products. The town was formally founded in 1824 by William Digby and named for the Marquis de Lafayette, the French general who had assisted the U.S. colonies in the Revolutionary War. The surrounding countryside is some of the state's richest farmland. On the west side of the Wabash River sits Purdue University, another of Indiana's Big Ten universities.

Take Highway 26 a short distance west to Creasy Lane. Turn right and go north to Eisenhower Road, which then jogs left and becomes County Road 400E. Follow the signs to Clegg Botanical Gardens; total distance is about 2 miles. If you have time, you can drive north from here on city roads to the *Clegg Botanical Gardens,* 1782 N. County Road 400E, (765) 423-1325, 15 acres of glacial residual topography covered with tracts of redbud and dogwood—it's an explosion of nature in spring and fall. Trails snake through the terrain and lead to a lovely lookout point. Best of all, it's free.

Return to Highway 26, turn right, and proceed west to *Columbian Park.* Opposite Home Hospital, this park has a zoo, playgrounds, an aquatic center, an amusement park, a nice cove, and great picnicking.

Continue west on Highway 26 to downtown Lafayette. The downtown is a historic district maven's dream. Six historic neighborhood districts are outlined on the CVB's map (you can also get an audio tour guide at the CVB), and you can spend the better part of a day just wandering the streets and looking at the historic architecture. A personal favorite is the *Tippecanoe County Courthouse,* more than a century old and another piece of architectural eye-candy. What is most charming is the fact that, at the time it was designed, public input was asked for, and locals filled 45 pages of a book with their wishes—much of it was followed, and that's the way government should work. With the vibrancy and charm that a Big Ten university town offers, there's no hurry anyway, and you've got loads of chic shops and eateries to keep you going as well.

Otherwise, your first stop downtown should be the *Art Museum of Greater Lafayette,* 101 S. Ninth Street, (765) 742-1128, in the Ninth Street Hill Historic Neighborhood. American and Indiana art is featured in permanent collections; another area of focus is American art pottery. A year-round schedule of temporary exhibits highlights major art, historical themes, regional cultures, and local artists. A children's area allows for self-exploration in art. Hours are 11 a.m.–4 p.m. Tuesday–Sunday.

Just north of here is the Gothic Revival mansion—the Fowler House, as it's known locally—housing the *Tippecanoe County Historical Museum,* 909 S. Street, (765) 476-8416. It was built in 1851 by Moses Fowler and has a variety of historical items of regional interest. Hours are 1–5 p.m. Wednesday–Sunday. Admission.

Four blocks west is the engaging *Red Crown Mini-Museum,* a "walk-by" antique car museum, housed in one of only seven remaining Standard

The Battle of Tippecanoe

On November 11, 1811, soldiers under the command of William Henry Harrison fought the Shawnees under the command of the Prophet, brother of legendary Indian chief Tecumseh. When the smoke cleared, the Indians had been pushed into the swamps and the U.S. Army had suffered heavy casualties. As more than one historical account has noted, however, nothing had really been settled except that the natives had had their spirit essentially broken, resistance thereafter abated, and they were ultimately relocated.

The Prophet and Tecumseh were born in Ohio. Originally named Laulewasikaw, the Prophet was what could be termed a back-to-the-lander, preaching a return to the halcyon days of native self-sufficiency and harmonious living. He didn't want conflict with whites but like so many natives he eventually felt forced into a corner. This was in no small part due to the influence of Tecumseh, who very nearly succeeded in forging a confederation of tribes between the Great Lakes and the Gulf of Mexico to oppose westward expansion; most tribes sympathized but were tired of fighting. The Prophet soon found his ideas being politicized into war phraseology.

In 1808 the two brothers established a village at the mouth of the Tippecanoe River. The trouble was, word reached the governor that the natives were cooperating with the British in Canada and so demanded meetings in Vincennes, during which nothing was settled. Tecumseh returned to the village and subsequently the United States forcibly removed Indians from their main hunting grounds, perhaps the major reason impelling legions of natives to come to Tecumseh.

Tecumseh proposed more meetings with the governor and, after traveling to the South to discuss the issue with natives there, wanted to go all the way to Washington to meet with President James Madison. Before that could happen, Governor Harrison sent in the troops. A contingent of 900 men was dispatched to the village. Before sunrise on November 7, the encampment of soldiers was attacked by Indians from the Prophet's village; the Army lost 61 men, with 127 wounded. The next morning the soldiers burned the deserted village. Tecumseh still had not returned from the South.

Following the battle, forced relocations proceeded. Perhaps the only permanent lingering effect of the battle was the phrase "Tippecanoe and Tyler too." President Harrison rode that slogan into the White House three decades after his most famous battle.

Oil Products buildings (dating from 1927).

If you're here on a Tuesday, Thursday, or Saturday in May to October, stop by the *Farmer's Market* just northwest of here. Or, you can continue west to the Wabash River to a pedestrian bridge to *Tapawingo Park.* This whole area is undergoing dramatic development that will add to the riverfront area attractive new shops, restaurants, open spaces, a park, riverwalk and overlook, and more.

From Tapawingo Park, the paved *Heritage Trail* leads south along the river to the Tippecanoe Battlefield. Plans are to extend this all the way along the river to Fort Ouiatenon. It's great!

Drive across the river on Highway 26 to West Lafayette. After a short distance, go to River Road, turn left (south), and proceed 4 miles. Here you'll find *Fort Ouiatenon,* River Road S, (765) 743-3921, site of the state's first (1717) military installation. Archaeologists estimate the area was once home to 2,000 to 3,000 people. At a crucial transport network, a half-dozen Native American tribes called the spot home. Now a 30-acre park, it has a replica blockhouse with interpretive exhibits. In fall the *Feast of the Hunter's Moon* festival is an encampment detailing life of the French and natives. By the way, it's pronounced "wee-ah-the-non." (It was named for the Wea village across the river.)

Return via River Road to Highway 26 in West Lafayette; turn left and go a few blocks. Turn right (north) onto Northwestern Avenue and drive to the *Purdue University Visitor Information Center.* Located at 404 Northwestern Avenue, (765) 494-4636, the center can arrange tours and dispense information. The campus is an enormous place indeed; at over 1,580 acres, it even has its own airport. Wandering the grounds you can check out the art galleries in Stewart Center, the Krannert Building, and Creative Arts Building II. The *Purdue Memorial Union* has sweeping Gothic walls and an old-world feeling.

Continue on Northwestern Avenue to Highway 231 and go about 1 mile to Lindberg Road; turn left and proceed to the *Celery Bog Nature Area.* This is one of Indiana's most significant natural areas. Trails lead through the ecologically pristine zones and provide for excellent birdwatching. A nature center has exhibits on the natural history of the area (who really knows what a bog is?) and is a good place to find out where the wild things are for critter viewing.

Return to Highway 231, turn left, and drive a short distance to Highway 52. Turn right (east) and go about 2 miles to Highway 43. Go north on 43 about 5.5 miles to its junction with Highway 225. Turn right (east) and go about 2 miles into Battle Ground. Turn left on Jefferson Street and go for 1.5 miles to County Road 800N. Turn right and go to *Wolf*

Park. This education and research park, (765) 567-2265, focuses on the majestic and oft-misunderstood wolf but you'll also find a bison herd, coyotes and foxes. The visitor center gives an overview of the wolf and its incredible social structure as well as its integral position in the ecosystem. If you arrive on a weekend you can get a second treat—you may be able to watch wolves eat and play. Howl Nights at 7:30 p.m. Saturday year-round are great fun; it's incredible to hear the lonesome howls and then the responding howls (even coyotes get in on the act). At 1 p.m. Sunday from May 1 to November 30 special wolf-bison presentations are given. No, they don't allow the wolves to attack the herd, but you can watch in fascinating, up-close detail how they "test" the herd and how the herd responds. Open 1-5 p.m. daily, May 1–November 30.

Go back to Jefferson Street and proceed through Battle Ground; on the western edge of town, you'll come to the *Tippecanoe Battlefield National Historic Landmark.* Here's the site of the epic battle between the forces of William Henry Harrison and the bands of Tecumseh's confederation. The museum, (765) 567-2147 or (800) 872-6569, on site has uniforms, weapons, and other memorabilia of the conflict, and you can walk the battlefield, which is marked off to explain how forces moved about. Exhibits detail period life and offer background about the battle. Exhibits tracing Harrison's 1840 presidential campaign include a display on a famous Whig rally he held here—it is credited in part with placing political hyperbole and sloganeering into campaigning. Hours are 10 a.m.–5 p.m. daily, May–October; reduced hours rest of the year, so call ahead.

Return to Battle Ground and go to Highway 225. Retrace your route back to Highway 43. Turn left and drive back to Highway 26 in West Lafayette. Turn left (east) on 26 back across the Wabash to Highway 231 in Lafayette. Go south on 231 out of town for 19 miles to County Road 1000N. Turn right and head west to New Richmond. This tiny community is yet another tie to the film *Hoosiers.* Interiors and exteriors were filmed in and around the village though the gym used for the movie is in Knightstown (see Tour 10). You may recognize a few landmarks driving around town and the countryside. The local chamber of commerce can point you in the right direction to take in the movie locations. Stop by in late September for its fun *Hickory Festival* (the town was called Hickory in the movie—see the town's welcoming sign now).

Return to Highway 231 and drive a short distance south to Linden. The chugging iron horse is again on display here at the *Linden Railroad Museum,* (765) 339-7245, housed in the original town depot. Built in 1907, the depot is the oldest intact junction depot in Indiana. It now houses var-

Touring one of Indiana's many great parks.

ious kinds of railroad equipment and memorabilia from the two railroads that once served the community, the Monon and the Nickel Plate. The agent's room now contains a $^3/_4$-inch-scale steam model of the Monon 440 locomotive with passenger coach. Nickel Plate artifacts are housed in their own room. Lines created by model railroad clubs have been known to snake throughout the whole place. Hours are 1-5 p.m. Friday–Sunday, May–September. Admission.

Continue south on Highway 231 for 10.5 miles to Crawfordsville. This attractive community is rightfully dubbed the Athens of the Hoosier State for its culture—noted literary figures have resided here—as well as its beauty. General Lew Wallace wrote *Ben-Hur* here; Maurice Thompson and Meredith Nicholson are other noted Hoosier authors who put the place on the map. It can also proudly claim to be part of the first air mail delivery in the United States. In August 1859 Professor John Wise took off in his balloon, the *Jupiter,* from Lafayette with a mail pouch filled with nearly 150 letters and packages, intending to show the U.S. Postal Service it could be done. Around six hours later he landed near Crawfordsville. Hardly a success—he hadn't intended to come anywhere near Crawfordsville. Still, Wise insisted on taking credit for delivering mail by air and the postal service formally recognized the attempt, if not the success.

Wabash College was one of the state's first colleges, founded in 1882, and is a rarity—a school for men only.

The Crawfordsville-Montgomery County Visitors Center, 412 E. Main Street, (765) 362-5200 or (800) 866-3973, www.crawfordsville.org, can point you in the direction of any of the town's many attractions. Most folks come to see the *Ben-Hur*

Museum/General Lew Wallace Study, E. Pike Street at Wallace Avenue, (765) 362-5679. This is the study of General Lew Wallace (he wrote the novel that turned into the epic Hollywood tale here, thus the name), who was also a scholar, statesman, and soldier. He served in the Indiana senate and later became U.S. minister in Turkey, among many other renaissance-man type undertakings. In addition to *Ben-Hur,* he wrote three other novels and an unfinished autobiography. The museum has memorabilia from his colorful life as well as lots of exhibits on his most famous work. Hours are 1-4:30 p.m. Tuesday–Sunday, April–May and September–October; 1-4:30 p.m. Tuesday and Sunday, 10 a.m.–4:30 p.m. Wednesday–Saturday, June–August. Admission.

The *Old Jail Museum,* 225 N. Washington Street, (765) 362-5222, is a restored 1882 jail probably unlike any other you've ever seen. It was the first of seven "rotary" jails built in the United States. The two-tiered cellblock consisted of a turntable divided into 16 wedge-shaped units. The turntable is housed within a stationary steel cage with one opening per story. To get a certain cell, you just rotate the whole shebang to bring it to the front. This was used until 1939. Lots of other county artifacts are in the museum, but watching that baby turn, that's what everybody wants to see. Hours are the same as for the Ben-Hur Museum.

The final historical stop in Crawfordsville is *Lane Place,* 212 Water Street, five acres of grounds and buildings of Henry S. Lane, a state and U.S. congressman, governor, and senator (as chairman of the first national Republican conventions in 1856 and 1860, he was instrumental in getting Abraham Lincoln nominated). A million dollar (literally) renovation project over the past quarter century is just about finished; it looks smashing. The main mansion has original furnishings and family artifacts; on the grounds is Speed Cabin, once used on the Underground Railroad. Hours are 9 a.m.–4 p.m. Monday–Friday in summer; hours are reduced other times. Admission.

Continue south on Highway 231 until Highway 47 splits off from it. Go south on 47 for 7.5 miles to Highway 234. Turn right (west) and drive for about 6 miles to *Shades State Park*. Along this route lots of lovely bucolic postcard-quality vistas await you; every hairpin turn seems to offer another brilliantly red barn, or a yard filled with antique farm machinery, or artistically lovely scarecrows. If you're looking for natural *isolated* splendor, you need go no further than this wonderfully rugged, pristine park, (765) 435-2810. The area is so challenging topographically, with valleys enshrouded constantly in darkness due to soaring walls of gorges and ravines, that early explorers named the area Shades of Death and learned mysterious legends from local natives.

This 3,000-acre state park is less developed than Turkey Run State Park, its well-known counterpart to the south (see Tour 16), and thus you'll find fewer visitors. Highway 234 bisects the park and to the east is one of the state's most rewarding hiking opportunities—the Pine Hills State Nature Preserve, nearly 500 acres of backcountry hemlock and pine and a series of four untouched craggy ridges (backbones) that slice into the sky upwards of 100 feet. You can see hawks soaring on thermals above the ridges—quite a sight indeed.

The hiking trails—there are 10 of them—are superb. They may not be long, but they're certainly challenging. Many lead to almost a dozen resplendent cascades within the park's confines. And we haven't even mentioned the canoeing yet. Sugar Creek meanders through the park and is thought by canoeists to be the best in the state. A favorite

run is to float from here south to Turkey Run; it's absolutely lovely. Numerous liveries rent canoes and equipment; make certain you get up-to-the-minute advice on water conditions. Semi-rough camping is available in the park.

As you leave Shades State Park, you cross the Deers Mill Bridge, a lovely 1878 span that is 275 feet long and quite likely one of the most photographed in the state.

Continue west on Highway 234 for about 5 miles to Highway 341. Turn right (north) and cruise for 5 miles to Highway 32. Turn left (west) and drive for 15 miles to Highway 63. Turn right (north) and go 5 miles to Highway 136. Turn right (east) and go 2.5 miles to Covington. Turn left on N. Portland Arch Road and drive about 8 miles northeast to *Portland Arch Nature Preserve* near Fountain. This bit of geological oddity is the result of millennia of waterworks, a natural carving seen so often in the western states. Streams have created a 30-by-12-foot opening in the sandstone, creating a natural bridge. Even better are the wild lands surrounding the spot—tough sandstone cliff facings and imposing stands of trees; even better, you can espy several rare plant species such as Canada blueberry here. You can even find an old settlers' cemetery somewhere off in the preserve. Hiking trails lead off from parking lots.

Drive east on County 650N for 4.5 miles to Highway 41. Turn left (north) and proceed to Highway 28 in Attica. Turn right and drive east for 9 miles to Highway 25. Turn left on 25 and go north for about 14 miles through Odell and West Point to Highway 231. Turn left and follow 231 for a couple of miles back to Lafayette.

Tour 18
The Dunes and Beyond

Gary–Indiana Dunes National Lakeshore–Chesterton–Michigan City–La Porte–Valparaiso–Merrillville–Crown Point–Griffith–Munster–Hammond–Gary

Distance: 132.5 miles

Traveling from Illinois to Michigan along I-90 or the Indiana Tollway, it's hard to imagine anything other than an unrelieved industrial landscape. Equally difficult is remembering that you're still technically traveling along a littoral Great Lakes road—what with the acres of hillocks of iron ore tailings, villages of ore-loading elevators or warehouse complex, half-mile-long ore dock fingers poking into the lake, not to mention other aging residuals of the glory days of iron rusting gracefully in the weeds.

Ah, but options are there, for those aficionados of things back road, or at least for those wishing to flee the insanity of U.S. interstate culture. Highway 20 and Highway 12 in tandem trace the cusp of Lake Michigan—the Hoosier State's only Great Lakes coastline—for just over 45 miles from Gary to eye-catching Michigan City. A short drive, but what a stupendous necklace of miles. Highway 12 (aka the Dunes Highway) takes travelers through most of the scenic grandeur.

More workmanlike Highway 20 has fewer sights at the western end, but this highway roughly follows the original path of the Oregon Trail; as you tool along the road, gaze at the prairies and impressive lake vistas and imagine yourself in the well-worn boots of the European pioneers as they struggled through, overjoyed to finally gaze at the big lake, an important landmark early in the trip westward. Along the way we also drift through a private community, an enclave of early twentieth-century architecture. Indiana Dunes National Lakeshore is a mandatory stop, if for no other reason than to stand atop Mount Baldy and feel the chilled Lake Michigan air ruffle your hair and breathe life back into your road-weary body.

We head south and west, into classic moraine and other glacial topography, a lovely melange of bucolic meadow and active agriculture—popcorn country. On the roll westward back to Gary we'll come across museums, historic architecture, covered bridges, sacred shrines, and one or two surprises.

Start the tour just east of Gary, at the interchange of I-90/65 and Highway 12/20. Gary (population 117,000), along with East Chicago, at one time comprised the heart of the Midwest's steel industry, equidistant from the ore fields of the

Upper Midwest and the coal of the east. In 1901 U.S. Steel Corporation chose this area as the site of its main steel processing plant. Construction began in 1906, took three years, and cost over $110 million. Around the company's infrastructure grew a new community, comprised mostly of immigrants. Many other cities in the upper Great Lakes followed the same pattern, but the speed at which Gary grew was beyond explosive. The workers' enclaves were separated from the plants by the Calumet River. To its credit, the steel company platted the community using the most modern (for 1906) theories of civic engineering. Gary became nationally recognized in the early twentieth century for its pioneering, progressive schools. It's still Indiana's third-largest city, though population has dipped to its present number from a one-time high of around 150,000.

Much-maligned Gary takes it on the chin, image-wise. The stereotypes persist. Gary is poor, Gary is segregated, Gary is dangerous. Then there is the fact that it's hard to see the lake without an ominous, gargantuan industrial structure to spoil the vista. Heck, most Indiana guidebooks avoid mention of the phlegmatic town altogether (including official state tourist publications); the ones that do mention it simply list the latest attempt to rejuvenate the economy: casinos. But don't let it depress you; gritty Gary was and still is a major Great Lakes industrial town, important and necessary. Industry has waned but can still be observed from the roadway. Casinos do also exist for those inclined. And despite the herculean efforts of U.S. Steel, not all the sandy shoreline was buried under topsoil—one tiny stretch of dunes still exists along the lakefront. Furthermore, it is the birthplace of Michael Jackson.

Begin to head east on Highway 12/20 toward the *Indiana Dunes National Lakeshore.* Starting just east of Gary, and ending up near Michigan City, the Indiana Dunes National Lakeshore is absolutely Indiana's crown jewel. This national treasure pops up in several different areas along the way. But from the window you'd hardly know it. Its main segment is a jaw-droppingly gorgeous 15,000 acres stretching approximately 10 miles along the lake. Indiana may have been shorted in quantity of Great Lakes shoreline, but it more than made up

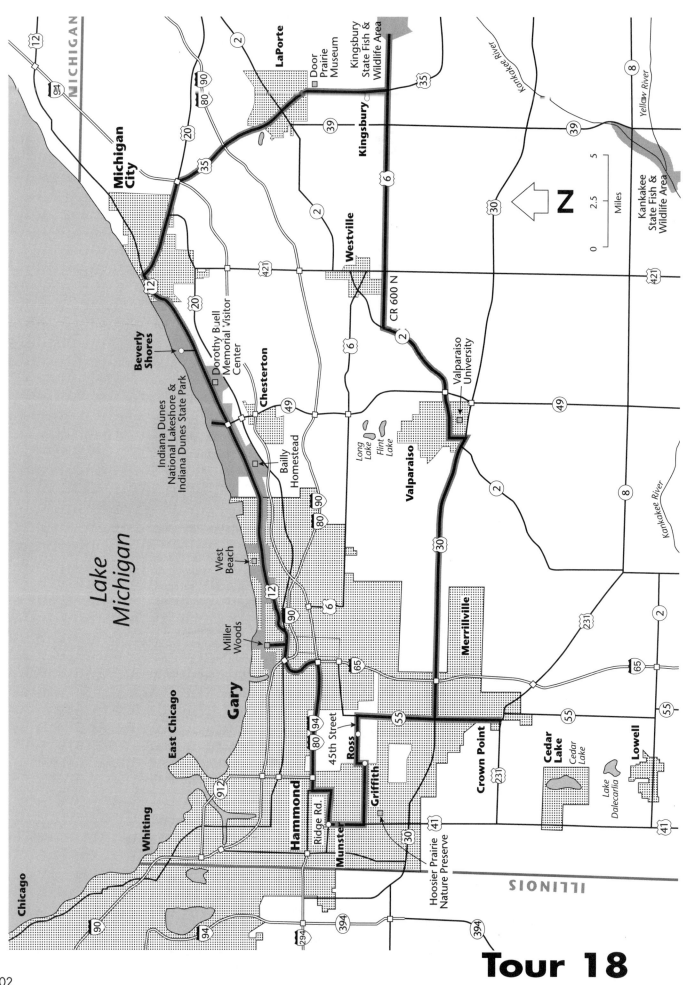

Lake Michigan

MICHIGAN

Chicago

Whiting

East Chicago

Gary

Hammond

Munster

Ridge Rd.

Griffith

Ross

45th Street

Miller Woods

West Beach

Indiana Dunes National Lakeshore & Indiana Dunes State Park

Beverly Shores

Dorothy Buell Memorial Visitor Center

Chesterton

Bailly Homestead

Westville

Valparaiso

Valparaiso University

Long Lake

Flint Lake

Merrillville

Crown Point

Cedar Lake

Cedar Lake

Lake Dalecarlia

Lowell

Hoosier Prairie Nature Preserve

ILLINOIS

Michigan City

LaPorte

Door Prairie Museum

Kingsbury State Fish & Wildlife Area

Kingsbury

Kankakee River

Yellow River

Kankakee State Fish & Wildlife Area

CR 600 N

N

0 2.5 5

Miles

Tour 18

A gorgeous landscape along West Beach Trail, Indiana Dunes National Lakeshore.

for it in quality. (The dunal topography here arguably rivals any on the Great Lakes, including Michigan's Gold Coast along Lake Michigan, famed for its gorgeous sands and sunsets; equally remarkable, the lovely scenery survived in one of the most heavily industrialized regions in America.) No less than Carl Sandburg rhapsodized about the place: "Those dunes," Sandburg wrote, "are to the Midwest what the Grand Canyon is to Arizona and the Yosemite is to California. They constitute a signature of time and eternity."

The lakeshore is an oddball display of variegated botany and topography, and has a flavorful cultural history to boot. The so-called Wisconsin glacier, the last dominant glacial epoch in the Upper Great Lakes, began 75,000 years ago, and what it did and did not do resulted in the resplendence of the shoreline today. Wind and wave, courtesy of the prevailing northwesterly winds of Lake Michigan, whip away at the shorelines of Wisconsin and northern Illinois. Back dunes form when seedlings are blown in and, nourished by Great Lakes water, take root at right angles to the wind, eventually establishing diverse biotic communities that hold the sands together. The dunes fronting Lake Michigan are constantly changing, part of the charm of the area.

Native Americans traversed the area as far back as two millennia; by 1800 the Potawatomi, who held sway throughout much of the southern and southwestern parts of Lake Michigan, had established upwards of 50 villages in the area. Eventually Europeans, initially the French, established a stronghold in the area, mostly as a fur trading outpost. The French are memorialized by a historical marker in Indiana Dunes State Park, separate from but completely surrounded by the national park. They were eventually defeated by the British, who left the malarial, swampy region completely to the Native Americans, until the upstart Americans gained their independence and started snooping around the region.

After a short distance on Highway 12/20, follow Highway 12 as it branches off. Proceed about 0.5 mile to Lake Street; turn left and head into *Miller Woods.* After setting out, you should know that the lakeshore's main visitor center is another 10 miles farther east on Highway 12. (There are also two other information centers in the area; more about them later.) The Dunes complex is so spread out amid private property that you may want to visit the facility for information first, then return to the Miller area—or plunge into the Dunes experience at any point along the way.

If you're doing a linear tour, first up is *Miller Woods,* the westernmost portion of the lakeshore just outside of Gary. It's located near the community of Miller (actually still part of Gary). The little enclave of Miller is attractive and warrants a stop for lunch at one of its many chic eateries; after you've loaded up on carbs you can walk the nature trails in the woods. The *Paul H. Douglas Center for Environmental Education,* on Lake Street near Miller Woods, (219) 938-8221, has educational information and runs many excellent programs to promote an understanding and appreciation of the place. Hours here are 10 a.m.–4:15 p.m. weekdays.

Back on Highway 12, continue east for about 1 mile to County Line Road; turn left and head into *West Beach.* (This is one of the only fee areas in the national lakeshore; after 6 p.m. it's free.) Stop at the visitor center and pick up some trail maps because West Beach has three trail loops. The Long Lake Trail Loop is less than two miles long and goes through an ancient marsh and mature oak forest. The topography and length are similar along the West Beach Trail Loop, which traces at least in part the northern edge of Long Lake before linking up with the most popular trail, the Dune Succession Trail, a one-miler linking beach, dunes, and lake which in its brevity still provides for a bit of a sweat and a primer in millions of years of geological progress. Succession is the means by which a group of plants and animals in one place is gradually replaced over time by another system; pick up one of the informative maps and explanatory brochures detailing the vegetation and geology—you'll be fascinated.

Other beaches at the park include those at the Indiana Dunes State Park (see below), Kemil Beach, Lake View Beach, and Central Beach, the most popular as it's contiguous to Mount Baldy, the lakeshore's most salient feature.

Return to Highway 12 and go east for 7.5 miles to Mineral Springs Road; turn right. Here you can visit an early pioneer cemetery and two early nineteenth-century homesteads. Acadian fur trader Joseph Bailly built the *Bailly Homestead* here in 1822 because it was at the confluence of two Native American footpaths and a canoe route. The Bailly family lived here until 1918. Several extant buildings have been renovated and can be toured. *Chellberg Farm* was established by Swede Anders Chellberg in 1885 and is best known today for its spring demonstrations on making maple syrup.

A good place to begin your exploration here is the *Bailly/Chellberg Visitor Center,* adjacent to Bailley Homestead, (219) 926-7561. It's also a good spot to get advice and printed matter. Hours are 11 a.m.–4:30 p.m. daily, Memorial Day to Labor Day; weekends only, Labor Day–October and March–May.

Quick Trip Option: Just a bit south of all the sandy fun is Chesterton, considered the gateway to the national lakeshore but equally well known for its festivals. Its *Hometown Christmas Festival* is great fun but throngs descend on the town for its amazing *Wizard of Oz Festival* the third weekend of September. There is a modest *Wizard of Oz museum* in the downtown, 109 E. 950N, with memorabilia from the legendary film. Otherwise, just stroll about the historic districts downtown; the gentrified community smacks of a bygone era. One highlight is the *all-steel home,* 411 Bowser Avenue, a house truly all steel right down to the furniture; this housing unit is representative of the style of home made available to GIs returning from World War II. For more information contact the Porter County Convention, Recreation, and Visitor Commission, 800 Indian Boundary Road, (800) 283-8687.

From Mineral Springs Road, return to Highway 12 and turn right. Go about 3 miles to Highway 49 and turn left into the *Indiana*

Dunes State Park. This resplendent park, smack dab in the middle of the national lakeshore, has a diverse ecosystem characterized by desert flora, giant wood ferns, and white pine trees. Compared with the national lakeshore, it's diminutive at 2,000-plus acres, but its Mount Tom tops even legendary Mount Baldy (see below) at 192 feet! Other trails lead to the Big Blowout, a bowl-shaped cavern formed by erosion, and numerous stands of pines. There's plenty of camping in the state park, along with a nature center, a three-mile-long swimming beach, and hiking/biking trails. Bordering the park along Highway 12 a half-mile west is Cowles Bog, another nature preserve, this one the very site that inspired local naturalists to call for the establishment of a national park. Here there is a moderate to rugged hiking trail; three loops top out at five miles. You'll find interdunal ponds, marshes, a stand of northern white cedars, forested dunes, fore dunes, and an open beach along the trails.

Other trails within the state park or national lakeshore boundaries include nearly a dozen precious ribbons leading through spectacular natural beauty. A personal highlight is the *Heron Rookery Trail,* an easy two-mile linear trail running parallel to a river on the south side. It is made up of a forested watershed and reclaimed farmland; birding and wildflower gazing are outstanding here. Note that the north side of the river is a bird sanctuary and entry is prohibited. Another highlight of the natural world is Pinhook Bog, south of Michigan City via Highway 421 and access roads. It is Indiana's only true bog and has a fascinating mile-long trail.

But the highlight of the federal park is 125-foot-high *Mount Baldy,* an epic dune that, due to prevailing wind currents, retreats away from the lake a few feet per annum. Located along north-south migratory flyways, these dunes attract huge numbers of birds. Numerous trails are used by both cross-country ski aficionados and hikers. Three beaches offer swimming. A few human highlights also stand out, all east of the visitor center. Just about any day around here you can watch local teens racing down the dunes on plastic snow sleds; it may be ecologically debatable but it's also addictive.

The park has a nature center, (219) 926-1952, with library, exhibits, children's activity room, and a bird observation area. Hours are flexible month-to-month but roughly 9 or 10 a.m.–noon in summer, tapering off as the seasons progress. March is a riot of maple syrup making; it's great family fun.

A fee does apply to the state park. Camping is available year-round but restricted to April 1–October 31 at the national lakeshore.

Return to Highway 12 and turn left. Drive a short distance to Kemil Road; turn right and you'll be at the *Dorothy Buell Memorial Visitor Center.* Whether you stop by early or late in your dunes exploration, the center, (219) 926-7561, provides great information about the national lakeshore. The facility is open daily year-round, 8 a.m.–6 p.m., Memorial Day through Labor Day, until 5 p.m. thereafter. Travelers will find audiovisual exhibits and plenty of informational brochures; there's also an 11-minute introductory video on the lakeshore and its ecosystem. Keep an eye out for a copy of *Singing Sands Almanac*; this newspaper-size informational brochure has not only good details but also calendar listings of the unbelievably large number of activities and events taking place in the area.

Continue east on Highway 12 for about 8 miles to downtown Michigan City. Along the way, you pass Beverly Shores (population 900), a quaint community sunk in the middle of the national lakeshore, though only two-thirds of it is technically part of the shore. The remainder is a posh private community dating from land speculation days of the early 1920s when real estate magnates from Chicago descended on the region. Of particular note is the architecture, with lots of Spanish-style stucco houses. But most people come to ogle the *Houses of Tomorrow*, a half-dozen dwellings featured in the 1933 World's Fair that were boated across Lake Michigan from Chicago after the fair and put on display here as part of a promotional gimmick.

Michigan City (population 39,000) is the end of the line for Indiana's portion of Highway 12. It's a fair-sized city but don't let that put you off—it has some charming areas and is well known for its summer stock theater groups. Michigan City was the site of a substantial Potawatomi village in 1675. First stop should be at the *La Porte County Convention and Visitors Bureau*, 1503 S. Meer Road, (219) 872-5055.

Crunched for time? Head just north of Highway 12 to the lakefront and Washington Park (admission) which has a beach, marina, coast guard station, free zoo, observation tower, band concerts in summer, and a lighthouse museum with various historical maritime items. The larger *Great Lakes Museum of Military History*, 360 Dunes Plaza, (219) 872-2702, is also along the lakeshore but not within Washington Park. This museum features displays of military detritus from the Revolutionary War to the Gulf War. Hours are 9 a.m.–4 p.m. Tuesday–Friday, from 10 a.m. Saturday. Admission.

Also downtown, just south of Highway 12 a few blocks, is the *Barker Mansion*. Built in 1857 by a railroad car tycoon, it boasts 38 opulent rooms that have been restored to period detail. Tours at 10 and 11:30 a.m. and 1 p.m. weekdays, also noon and 2 p.m. on weekends, June–October. Holiday tours on given weekends. Admission.

At the intersection of Highway 12 and Highway 35 in downtown Michigan City, drive southeast on Highway 35 for about 10 miles to Highway 2 in downtown La Porte. This town of 21,400 residents was once dubbed "the Door" because it was considered the gateway to the great prairies of the Midwest. Stop by the

Northern Indiana Harbor County/La Porte County Convention and Visitors Bureau, 1503 S. Meer Road, (800) 685-71714.

The *La Porte County Historical Society* Museum, Michigan Avenue at State Street, (219) 326-6808, has, among its historical memorabilia, one of the most impressive gun collections in the nation. Hours are 10 a.m.–4:30 p.m. Tuesday–Saturday.

Quick Trip Option: From Michigan City, you can venture north into Michigan's Harbor Country. Here exists a baker's dozen of tiny villages featuring sybaritic (and expensive) inns and restaurants and more antique shops than one would imagine possible. As you get closer to Benton Harbor, some lovely and opulent lakeside homes occasionally come into view.

From downtown La Porte, continue south on Highway 35 for 8 miles to Highway 6 at Kingsbury. Just after leaving La Porte, be sure to check out the *Door Prairie Museum*, 2405 Indiana Avenue, (219) 326-1337. It's well known for its excellent—and extensive—antique auto display and its full-scale diorama of three street scenes from the nineteenth century. Hours are 10 a.m.–4:30 p.m. Tuesday–Saturday, from noon Sunday, April–December.

A Few Tidbits about the National Lakeshore

The principal site of the processing plants—around which the city of Gary would grow—was literally reclaimed from Lake Michigan–soaked swampland using enormous pumps and spreaders. Tons of fertile soil had to be trucked in and laid atop the area's prodigious white sands in order for landscapers to create a "town look."

One hiking trail in the lakeshore, the Great Sauk, parallels the Native American footpath connecting Detroit with the western Potawatomi regions. The Potawatomi signed peace treaties with the U.S. in the early nineteenth century but were eventually betrayed by President Andrew Jackson and forcibly relocated to Kansas in 1838 along a march known as the Trail of Death.

Hikers in Indiana Dunes State Park will also find the 1,500-acre Dunes State Nature Preserve, which contains more species of trees than any area of comparable size in the Midwest.

Be careful of swimming in the area. West Beach can have dangerous rip tides when north winds blow!

Best bets for birders include the incredible (and cacophonous) semiannual congregation of blackbirds at the corner of Beverly Drive and State Park Road, goldfinches along the South Shore right of way, and the great blue heron, often sighted throughout the park's boundaries.

July Fourth and Labor Day are good days to visit Hesston, a tiny village about 10 miles east of Michigan City, when huge steam-powered agricultural equipment is on display.

Michigan City was the site of a large Potawatomi village. Famed Jesuit explorer Jacques Marquette visited here and preached in 1675.

The forests met the prairies at Little Door Village, southwest of La Porte. One traveler described the grass as so tall that it stood higher than a man on horseback.

Sliding down the Sahara-like Mount Baldy at the Indiana Dunes National Lakeshore.

In Kingsbury, head east on Hupp Road to the *Kingsbury State Fish and Wildlife Area,* (219) 393-3612, which has over 6,000 acres of prime wildlife viewing. Once part of the epic Kankakee Marsh, which was later drained for agricultural purposes, this restored habitat has hordes of deer. But birds are what really draw visitors; you'll have a good chance to see herons and egrets. Note that this site was also once home to a U.S. Army munitions plant and there are still hazardous spots, so check with the office before tramping off into the underbrush. A primitive campground is here. Hunting and fishing are also available.

Back at the intersection of Highway 35 and Highway 6, head west on Highway 6 for about 12 straight-as-an-arrow miles. When Highway 6 turns north, continue west on County Road 600N for 3 miles to its intersection with Highway 2. Turn left (south) and proceed about 8 miles to Valparaiso.

In Valparaiso, at the intersection of Highway 2 and Highway 130, take 130, which becomes Lincolnway, into the downtown area. This trim community of 24,300 folks in Indiana's famed "popcorn belt" is dominated by Valparaiso University, dubbed the "poor man's Harvard." Along Lincolnway, you'll pass the university, but your first stop should be at the *Greater Valparaiso Chamber of Commerce,* 150 W. Lincolnway, (219) 462-1105.

Be sure to set aside some time to walk around the square and take in the town-and-gown atmosphere. You can get excellent brochures detailing historic district walks; if the office is closed, stop by the library, 103 Jefferson Street. A highlight is the city's *Memorial Opera House,* 104 Indiana Avenue, more than a century old and still a jewel in the downtown landscape. You can have oodles of fun at the *Porter County Historical Society Old Jail Museum,* (219) 465-3595, 152 S. Franklin Street, which has lots of historical treasures. Hours are 1–4 p.m. Tuesday–Friday.

Double back east on Highway 130 to Sturdy Road at the eastern edge of the Valparaiso University campus. The university is the main draw to the town, and the chief attraction of this handsome campus is the *Brauer Museum of Art,* which houses a collection of American realist paintings. The *Church of the Resurrection* is the world's largest college church; it's legendary for its precise acoustics. Guided tours are available from 8 a.m. to 10:30 p.m. daily; call (219) 464-5112 for information.

From Sturdy Road, go south a short distance to Highway 30; turn right (west) and proceed for about 16 miles to Merrillville. After about 12 miles into the trip, just north on County Road 800, you will come to *Deep River County Park,* 9410 Old Lincoln Highway, (219) 769-9030. The park is home to *Wood's Mill,* one of the largest and busiest mills in the nineteenth century. It has been renovated and offers tourists an up-close gander at the inner machinations of an extant stone mill. Hiking trails meander about the park. The park and mill are open 10 a.m. to 5 p.m. daily and are free.

Merrillville was once a primary stop for settlers heading west; at one time over a dozen trails branched out from the community. For such a modest town there sure are lots of highlights here. First off, the *Star Plaza Theater*, at the junction of I-65 and Highway 30, (219) 769-6600, is a huge venue for nationally known performing artists. More subdued is the breathtaking cathedral of *Saints Constantine and Helen Greek Orthodox Church*; the 25 stained glass windows and 100-foot-wide rotunda are simply amazing. It's located along a city-state-sized plot of land along the 8000 block of Madison Street.

Lots of information is available at the *Chamber of Commerce*, 255 W. Eightieth Place, (219) 769-8180. Kids absolutely go bonkers for Indiana's premier waterpark, the *Deep River Waterpark*, 9001 E. Highway 30, (800) 928-7275. You'll find a lazy river, a wave pool, lots of waterslides (with supersonic speeds!), and a full array of land-based activities for the kiddies.

Go west on Highway 30 for 2.5 miles to Highway 55. Turn left and proceed into Crown Point. This town has one of the most stately and attractive courthouses you'll likely ever see, this one dating from 1878. In the early and mid-twentieth century, the place was regarded as somewhat of a midwestern version of Reno, Nevada, for its relaxed rules regarding marriage licenses. Celebrities like Ronald Reagan and Red Grange—among others—came here to get hitched. John Dillinger's most famous escapade—escaping with a fake gun made from wood and shoe polish—took place here as well. Best ice cream around is at *Valentino's* nearby. For a treat of a side trip, head southwest of town via Highway 55 to the Crown Point covered bridge and the arboretum and trails at *Lemon Lake County Park*, (219) 755-3685.

Return to Highway 55 and go north 9 miles to W. Forty-fifth Street in Ross. Turn left (west) and drive 3 miles into Griffith. On the southwest edge of Griffith is the site of one of Indiana's best-preserved pieces of prairie—*Hoosier Prairie Nature Preserve*. It's a spread of incredible diversity (over 300 species are contained here) and contains everything from tall-grass prairie to marsh and oak-savannah uplands. You'll find an excellent nature trail here. Not far away via Main Street is the *Oak Ridge Prairie County Park*, with jillions of songbirds and various critters like foxes and beavers.

The Carmelite Shrines in Munster, a respite along the road.

From Griffith, go west a short distance to Highway 41. Turn right (north) and drive about 3 miles to Ridge Road in Munster. Munster has a sacred site: the *Carmelite Shrines,* a series of 20 shrines linked via paths that offer a respite from highways and traffic. There's a small arboretum, too. Grounds are found along Ridge Road, one-half mile west of Highway 41, and can be toured 1–5 p.m. If someone's around, you can often get to see inside the buildings, where you'll find a replica of the Vatican's Private Audience Hall.

Return east on Ridge Road and go a short distance to Kennedy Avenue. Turn left (north) and go to the interchange with I-80/94 in Hammond. Here, you'll want to visit the *Lake County Interstate Visitors Center,* (800) ALL-LAKE, which is the home of the *John Dillinger Museum,* an interactive museum depicting the life and times of the notorious outlaw who escaped from the Crown Point jail. You'll find wax figures, an Essex Terraplane, and the wooden gun he used to escape the long arm of the law. It's great fun! Hours are 8 a.m.–8 p.m. daily.

Get on I-80/94 and drive east to I-65. Turn north and proceed to the interchange with I-90 and Highway 12/20 in Gary, the start of the tour.

"Great Lakes"—a Fitting Name

Indiana may lack epic stretches of Great Lake shoreline à la Wisconsin or Michigan, but it more than makes up for it in quality. Its precious stretch along the southern cusp of Lake Michigan is one of the Midwest's most scenic spots. Loads of tourists whip through, but it's amazing how little most folks actually know about one of the most important and fascinating bodies of water in the world.

Lake Michigan is the only Great Lake wholly within U.S. boundaries. It isn't the largest of the five; Lake Superior is the second-largest lake in the world (it has more surface area than Lake Baikal in Russia though the latter is more capacious) and, with three billion gallons of water, contains one-eighth of the world's freshwater and would take over a century to drain completely. Lake Michigan and its sister lakes account for nearly 20 percent of the planet's total fresh water; fifty million drink from its basins.

In terms of geology, the Great Lakes are actually quite young. They appeared in much of their present form some 2,000–5,000 years ago but the earliest geological workings started about half a billion years ago, with successive volcanic shifting of terra firma during the pre-Cambrian period. Essentially, the Great Lakes as they exist today were formed by the lurchings of the Canadian Shield during the Paleozoic period. Ancient seas rose and retreated; glacial advances carved up the Midwest, laying the foundation for lake beds, helped along by glacial streams and rivers. Both Lakes Michigan and Superior were once part of one enormous glacial lake, Lake Nipissing, which even subsumed Lake Huron.

Environmental issues are particularly relevant to Lake Michigan, and Indiana, the gateway to the lake, has had its share of problems. Part of the Rust Belt, postwar northern Indiana was as gritty and industrial as any region of the United States. Great for the economy, bad for the environment.

Industrial effluents were the primary cause—factories dumping at will, though all citizens were pretty much to blame. Even today old batteries and freezers can be pulled from lake shorelines. Helter-skelter development chewed up crucial marshlands, which had heretofore acted as filters for toxic pollutants. At one point, some 75 percent of Great Lakes shoreline was hazardous for any use. Up to 20 billion pounds of pollutants were pumped into the Great Lakes annually before we wised up a bit.

The best thing that ever happened to the Great Lakes was the Clean Water Act of 1972. Far from a perfect piece of legislation, it nonetheless spurred the Midwest to take stock of its environmental needs; the Great Lakes were at the top of the cleanup list. A dozen hydrocarbons, pesticides, paper mill and other waste, and agricultural waste are the peskiest toxins still polluting the Great Lakes. Waste effluents from as far away as Russia are claimed to be falling into the Great Lakes. Due to the fact that the groundwater in the Great Lakes region is not renewable, very little of Lake Michigan is in an active hydrologic cycle. The lethal ingredients read like the periodic chart: PCBs, DDT, HCB, mercury, OC5, and pernicious chemicals like chlordane, dieldrin, and toxaphene. DDT and PCBs are perhaps the most dangerous, as they leach out of industrial fluids and are ingested by small fish, which are in turn eaten by larger fish and thus the vicious cycle has begun. Humans may be at the "top" of this food chain, but we may not wish to be.

Though dead zones still exist in the Great Lakes, all isn't lost. Sportfishing has become a billion-dollar industry and the Clean Water Act really did clean up the lakes overall. A 1986 council of Great Lakes governors signed a ban on all discharges. Intertribal agencies, the EPA, and Canada have also begun cooperating to clean things up. Scientists claim that DDT and PCB contamination in human milk has been reduced by 90 percent. Mercury, cynics counter, is up since 1972. Also, some scientists worry about the quick rise in Great Lakes water temperatures, perhaps owing to global warming. No one disputes the dropping of water levels and the absolute invasion of nonnative species. Worse, the federal government has been pushing since 2000 to do exploratory drilling for oil in Lake Michigan and even proponents have to wring their hands at the thought of a major oil spill in the Great Lakes.

Still, the one thing most people will need to think about is consuming fish they've caught. For the most part, your fish will be safe, since most Great Lakes fish—except Lake Superior trout—aren't commercially marketed. The feds say trout is safe to eat, while others claim that people risk a one-in-ten chance of developing cancer by eating one meal of large lake trout per week. Most dangerous are these large trout and salmon, both of which are fatty and can grow old. As a general rule, never eat a fish over 30 inches long. Children and pregnant women should always think twice about eating these fish. Skinning, trimming, and filleting all fatty tissue can help.

Tour 19
North from Indianapolis

Indianapolis–Zionsville–Lebanon–Carmel–Noblesville–Anderson–Fishers–Indianapolis

Distance: 127.5 miles

Indianapolis offers tons of worthy sights for the traveler but don't forget the surrounding districts. To the north you can experience endless streets of Victorian charm before spinning off to one of the state's best living history museums. We get an amusing look at an assortment of dolls, then perhaps take in an Indianapolis Colts practice session before we head to the quiet solitude of the state's smallest state park, an example of a prehistoric mound-building culture.

From downtown Indianapolis, drive north on Martin Luther King Boulevard, which then becomes Michigan Road, to I-465 (a total of 10 miles). Continue past the interstate on Highway 421 north, going for 2.5 miles to Highway 334. Turn left and go into Zionsville. This trim, picturesque little community hearkens to a bygone time with its fabled Brick Street historic district; the lights are gas lamps and the roads are brick-paved. The town arose as a railroad hub and drew a cultured population. Abraham Lincoln stopped to greet supporters on his way to his first inauguration on February 11, 1861, and was quoted as saying, "I would like to spend more time here, but there is an event to take place in Washington which cannot start until I get there." A monument now marks the spot in Lincoln Park.

Stop by the *Greater Zionsville Chamber of Commerce,* 135 S. Elm Street, (317) 873-3836, for free brochures and self-guided tour maps of the Brick Street district. Shopaholics have a field day in Zionsville, to be sure; the streets are absolutely lined with antique shops, galleries, and boutiques of all sorts. Gingerbread Victorian architecture adds to the effect. You could also stop by the *P. H. Sullivan Museum and Genealogy Library,* 225 W. Hawthorne Street, (317) 873-4900, to see its displays and exhibits pertaining to regional history. Hours are 10 a.m.–4 p.m. Tuesday–Saturday, mid-January to mid-December.

Return to Highway 421, turn left, and go about 6 miles to Highway 32. Turn left (west) and go for 9 miles into downtown Lebanon. The *Boone County Courthouse* is truly a spectacle. The leviathan pillars of the courthouse, which dates from the early 1900s, are three stories high

and weigh 50 tons. They're purported to be the largest hand-hewn limestone monoliths in the United States.

From Lebanon, return east on Highway 32 and cruise for 19 miles to Highway 31. Turn south and drive for 5 miles to Carmel. Carmel was reportedly the spot of the first automated traffic light in America. This fun little community sure has taken to the saying "It's a small world after all." Carmel is home to the *Museum of Miniature Houses,* 111 E. Main Street, (317) 575-9466, a repository of antique and contemporary dollhouses, room boxes, vignettes, accessories, traveling exhibits, special collections, and seasonal displays. Even those not into dolls and dollhouses will learn something and come away appreciating this fascinating art. You can see an antique dollhouse dating from 1861 and a large, scratch-built replica of a Cincinnati home created by the grown-up child who grew up there. Hours are 11 a.m.– 4 p.m. Wednesday–Saturday; from 1 p.m. Sunday.

Double back to Highway 32, turn right, and continue for 7 miles to downtown Noblesville. More Victorian gingerbread awaits you in Noblesville. Your best bet is to wander awhile around the town square, which is dominated by the old *Hamilton County Courthouse,* another beautiful example of ornate courthouse architecture, this one dating from 1878. Also on the square is the *Hamilton County Museum of History,* which features the restored *Sheriff's Residence and Jail. Stoneycreek Farm,* two miles east on Highway 38, (317) 773-3344, is a nineteenth-century farm with gardens, restored buildings, and animals. Hours are 10 a.m.–5 p.m. Monday-Saturday.

From downtown Noblesville, head east on Highway 32 for 20 miles to downtown Anderson. This busy industrial city lies amid glacial residual topography on the site of an erstwhile Delaware Indian village. Its name comes from a somewhat-mangled transliteration of the name of a local chief—Kikthawenund, which supposedly translates into English as "Captain Anderson." Like many central Indiana communities, it owes its exis-

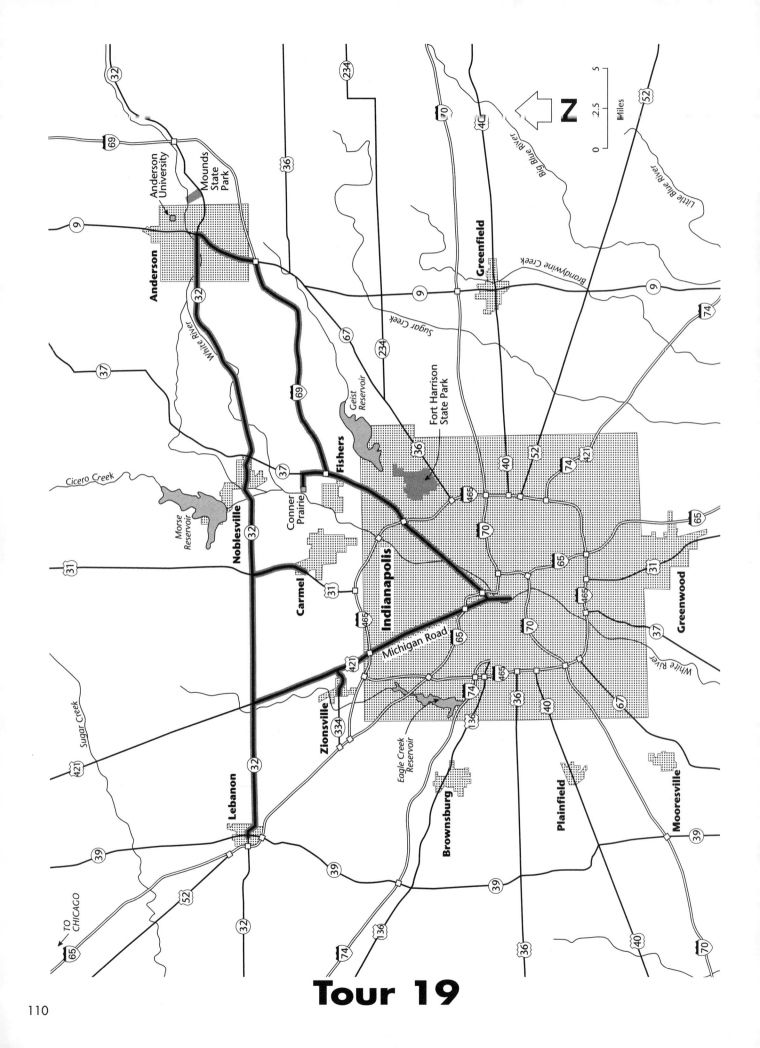

Tour 19

tence to abundant natural gas reservoirs that allowed companies access to cheap power before they went dry in 1912; at one time it even had the moniker Queen of the Gas Belt The city is known today for being the site of Mounds State Park, the state's smallest state park, and the summer home of the National Football League's Indianapolis Colts, who practice on the Anderson University campus. The *Anderson/Madison County Convention and Visitors Bureau,* 6335 S. Scatterfield Road, (765) 643-5633, www.madtourism.com, has all the information on local sights you might need.

For starters, you can take a stroll around the lovely downtown historic districts; the highlight is *Historic Eighth Street,* an 11-block stretch of refurbished Victorian opulence, right down to the historic gas lamps. The historic *Paramount Theater,* 1124 Meridian Plaza, was designed by architect John Eberson. The hallmark, its ballroom, is a wondrous piece of eye-candy. You can experience projected astronomical shows or just lap up the Moorish influences of the interiors; its generally open business hours on weekdays.

Gruenewald Historic House, 626 Main Street, (765) 646-5771, is a 12-room Second Empire House which housed a successful German immigrant saloonkeeper. It has the Gay Nineties period stuff down quite well. Hours are 10 a.m.–3 p.m. Tuesday–Friday, 9 a.m.–2 p.m. Saturday, April 1–mid-December. Admission.

The *U.S. Merchant Marine Museum,* 1230 Jackson Street, (765) 643-6305, is devoted to the seamen who never seem to get credit for the ultimate victory in World War II. See uniforms, ship models, photographs, and more and gain a better understanding of these heroes. Hours are 1–4 p.m. Tuesday–Friday. Admission. More martial-themed stuff like half-tracks, tanks, and trucks is found at the *Military Armor Museum,* 2330 Crystal St., (765) 649-TANK. Hours are 1–4 p.m. Tuesday, Thursday, and Saturday.

Anderson is also the home of *Anderson University,* (765) 649-9071, which houses a set of Holy Land artifacts in its School of Theology. You'll also want to explore the campus's art gallery and bird collection.

On Highway 32 east of town about four miles, *Mounds State Park* is the state's smallest park and the site of burial earthworks of a prehistoric mound culture. A somber place to reflect on the anthropology of the area, the site was the home of a band of Adena-Hopewell Indians. The tallest mound is nine feet high and nearly a quarter mile in circumference. A network of fine trails leads out

An explosion of color that awaits travelers in Indiana's state parks and wildlife preserves.

into the White River valley; the canoeing is excellent. The park also offers a swimming pool, fishing, cross-country skiing, and camping.

From downtown Anderson, take Pendleton Road (Business Highway 9) southwest 5 miles to I-69; turn west on I-69 and go 18 miles to Highway 37. Turn north on 37 and proceed 1 mile to *Conner Prairie*. Located in Fishers, this complex, 13400 Allisonville Road, (317) 776-6006, is one of central Indiana's most visited spots. It's a living history museum superbly realized, where you truly become part of history. Time travel to 1836 to a place called Prairietown, and have garbed docents show you what life was like then. You can shoot the breeze with the town constable or the doctor, then maybe have a shot at candle making or bread baking the hard way. The original Conner family home, in stately 1823 Federal style, was one of the first brick houses in the region and stands as a museum. The newest addition to Conner Prairie is the rural crossroads site, with covered bridge, Quaker meeting house, and district school. Other spots are a log trading post and reconstructed frontier garden. For a glimpse at a period of Indiana's—and the nation's—treasured past, this is a real treat. Hours are 9:30 a.m.–5 p.m. Tuesday–Saturday, from 11 a.m. Sunday. Admission.

Return to I-69 via Highway 37. Drive southwest on I-69 for about 15 miles back into downtown Indianapolis.

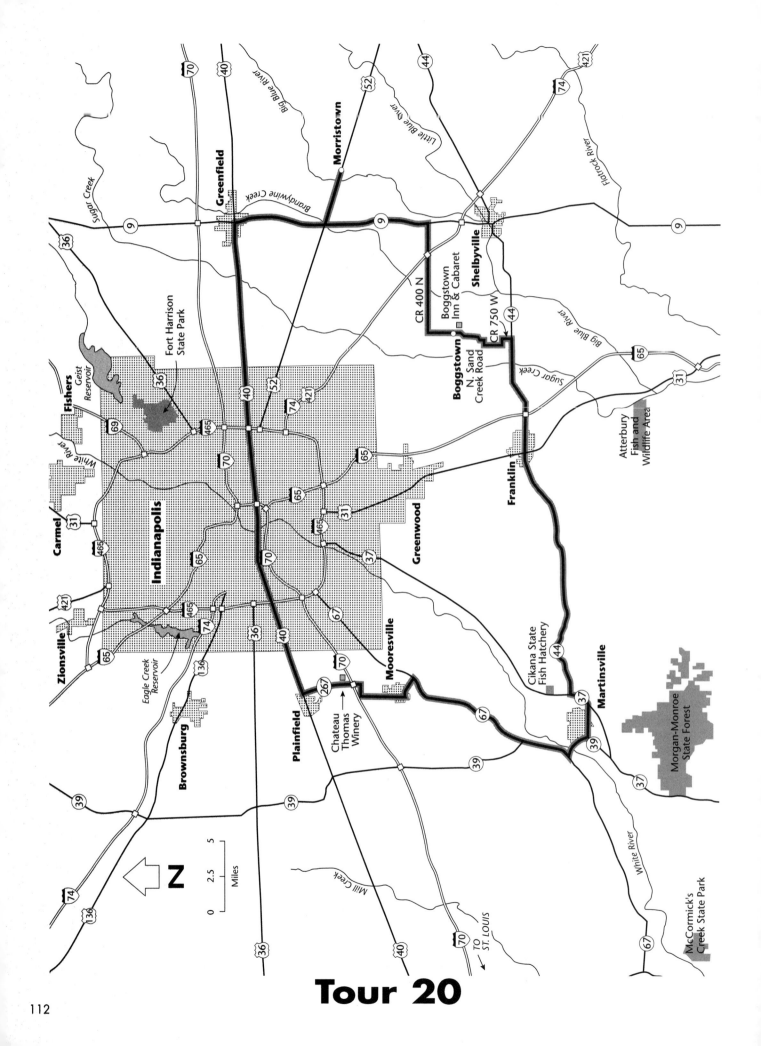

Tour 20

Tour 20
South and East
from Indianapolis

Indianapolis–Plainfield–Mooresville–Martinsville–Franklin–Boggstown–Morristown–Greenfield–Indianapolis

Distance: 120 miles

This tour explores the byways south and east of Indianapolis. We start by experiencing a boutique winery and a center of Islamic faith in North America. We have fun experimenting with gravity near Mooresville and maybe take a gander at the stars. We learn more than we thought there was to know about goldfish before we roll through classic agrarian stretches to dance the night away with feel-good ragtime music in Boggstown. One of Indiana's most treasured spots—beloved native son James Whitcomb Riley's home—is next as we visit Greenfield, a major stop on the old National Road. We'll then cruise back into Indy on this most venerable of roads.

To start this tour, head southwest from downtown Indianapolis via W. Washington Street, which is also Highway 40. Proceed to Highway 267 at Plainfield, driving a total of about 15 miles. Plainfield is best known as the entry point for Indianapolis Raceway Park. The biggest attraction for road trippers is likely the *Chateau Thomas Winery,* 6291 Cambridge Way, south of town, (317) 837-WINE. Tours are offered and free tastings of vinifera wines are the highlights. Hours are 10 a.m.–9 p.m. Monday–Thursday and till 10 p.m. Friday–Saturday; noon–7 p.m. Sunday. There is another draw to little Plainfield. The *Islamic Center of North America,* Center Street, (317) 839-8157, has served as a cultural and educational center for North America's Muslims and non-Muslims alike. The center's staff has acted in concert with the U.S. government and military as liaison with the Muslim cultures of the world. With the horrors of September 11, 2001, and all the anger that followed, a place like this is even more important now. Stop by for a visit.

At Highway 267, turn left and head south for 7 miles to Mooresville. One of the odder attractions around is Gravity Hill, south of Mooresville via Highway 42. Here you can enjoy a strange ride at a spot that seemingly defies physical laws. Put your car in neutral and, inexplicably, find yourself seeming to coast backward up the slope for nearly a quarter mile! Also in Mooresville is the *Goethe Link Observatory,* (317) 855-6911 (it's under the auspices of Indiana University's Astronomy Depart-

Some classic rural Indiana architecture, here outside Boggstown.

ment), home to a 36-inch reflector and 10-inch refractor telescopes. Public tours are possible but must be reserved by phone. Contiguous are lovely gardens—the *Link Daffodil Gardens*—about 15 acres wildly splashed like an artist's palette. It makes for a wonderful walk. Late April is the best time to go.

Continue south on Highway 267 for 13 winding miles to Highway 39. Turn left and drive a short distance to Martinsville. This community was legendary in the nineteenth century for its therapeutic artesian springs; it even garnered the moniker Artesian City. Springs were piped to several sanatoria treating arthritis, rheumatism, and other ailments. (It also was the hometown of two Hoosier governors.) Waters are important today as well, but for a different reason. The *Cikana State Fish Hatchery,* (765) 342-5527, a two-unit facility, annually produces astonishing amounts of fish for the state's anglers: 20 million walleye fry and 150,000 channel catfish, for example. There are about 35 earthen ponds in both units. Hours are 8 a.m.–5 p.m. Monday through Friday. Tours can be arranged.

Quick Trip Option: For a change of pace from the urban traffic and suburban sprawl you left behind, check out the *Morgan-Monroe State Forest,* 6220 Forest Road, (765) 342-4026, an enormous expanse of scenic rolling hills and hardwood canopies southeast of Martinsville. From Highway 37, there are several roads leading into this 26,680-acre tract, which has everything a nature lover would want: lakes, rivers, camping (some primitive backcountry sites as well as developed sites), fishing, hiking trails, hunting, a nature preserve with marked trails, and a log cabin.

In Martinsville, drive a short distance to Highway 37, which runs along the southeastern edge of town. Take 37 a short distance to Highway 44, turn right (east) and cruise for about 25 miles to Franklin. This is another charming town that is home to a fine liberal arts institution, Franklin College, founded in 1834. (What is it about Indiana and its abundance of quality colleges tucked away in idyllic settings?) The town also boasts of some well-preserved architectural gems, some in the Neo-Classical style. To get a better feel for other local lore, visit the *Johnson County Museum of History,* 135 N. Main, (317) 736-4655, 9 a.m.–4 p.m. Monday–Friday.

Continue east on Highway 44 for 7 miles to County Road 750W. Turn left, then left again at County Road 100S, right at County Road 775, and finally a left at N. Sand Creek Road. You should be in Boggstown. But why? Well, this dot on the map is a hoot, quite literally. For nearly two decades this unassuming little burg has been the scene of some serious hootenannies at the *Boggstown Inn & Cabaret,* on Boggstown Road, (317) 835-2020, self-described aptly as a "slice of Americana" bar none. Yup, pretty much on the mark. It's hard to believe this place exists after you've spent a half-hour or so getting lost on the rural roads around here just looking for it. But then voila! there it is, along with a dozen or so belching tour buses parked out front. It's live entertainment that brings folks here. You may get dueling pianos, you might get banjos, or you might get a Broadway-esque revival or even karaoke. Most often you could call the music "feel-good ragtime" (who doesn't enjoy a washboard performance?). You're expected to sing along and join in the fun. And there's food. The whole shebang opens up at 6 p.m.; the music and fun start not long after. Charges vary according to what is on tap. It's open Wednesday through Saturday; you may have to reserve more than a month in advance for dinners but you can often get a seat at the Sunday

brunch. Not surprisingly, due to the inn's popularity, Boggstown is now the home of the weeklong Hoosier Ragtime Festival, held the first week of August.

From Boggstown, go north 1.5 miles to County Road 400N. Turn east and drive 7.5 miles to Highway 9, passing I-74 along the way. Turn left (north) on Highway 9 and motor 10 miles to Highway 52. Turn right and head east for 6 miles into Morristown. This community is well known for its fertile fields; in the first half of the twentieth century its canning factory was one of the largest in the state and images of wagons heaped high with sweet corn are still vivid today. The nearby Blue River was immortalized by *The Bears of Blue River,* a children's tale by Shelbyville author Charles Major. The *Kopper Kettle Inn,* 135 W. Main Street, (765) 763-6767, is a legendary eatery; housed in a stately mansion filled tastefully with antiques. It's not chic or high cuisine; it's just great food in a wonderful atmosphere. Reservations are highly recommended.

Go back west on Highway 52 to Highway 9 and turn right. Drive north for 9.5 miles to Highway 40 in Greenfield. Greenfield is a tomato-growing and processing center and home to one of the state's most cherished historic spots—*James Whitcomb Riley's Birthplace and Museum,* 250 W. Main Street, (317) 462-8539. James Whitcomb Riley was born on October 7, 1849, and would ultimately become known as the Hoosier Poet for his odes to the state. His dialect poetry was a significant contribution to the Midwestern literary canon; you may recall reading "When the Frost Is on the Punkin" in elementary school. Hours are 10 a.m.–4 p.m. Tuesday–Saturday, 1–4 p.m. Sunday, May–October. Admission.

The city's *James Whitcomb Riley Memorial Park* on the east side of town preserves the Old Swimmin' Hole of Riley's poems. (He loved the town back and once called Greenfield the "best town outside heaven.") In early October the town celebrates its favorite son's birthday with the *Riley Festival,* one of the largest festivals in the state. A touching highlight is the Parade of Flowers, when local schoolchildren place bouquets at the foot of Riley's statue downtown.

Don't forget that Greenfield is bisected by Highway 40, the National Road, the granddaddy of the country's highways (see Tour 10).

For some scenic side trips, check out the many round barns in surrounding Hancock County. One of them is the largest in the state and is now a bed and breakfast, the Round Barn Inn B&B in McCordsville, northwest of Greenfield.

In Greenfield, head west on Highway 40 for 14 miles to I-465, where 40 becomes E. Washington Street. It's another 6 miles past I-465 until you're back in downtown Indianapolis.

What's a Hoosier?

Ah, the eternal question. What, exactly, is a Hoosier? Well, it depends on whom you ask. One theory holds that a foreman—named Hoosier—on the Louisville and Portland Canal hired only Indiana workers. Another says that it comes from the "Who's there?" response to early settlers knocking on farmhouse doors. Still others say that it comes from "hushing" or talking down an adversary. There are countless other versions. Actually, the word could stem from "hoozer," a word from England used generally to mean any outdoorsman or woodsmen. It may have had pejorative meanings at one time but no longer, certainly not for anyone from these parts.

PERSONAL NOTES

PERSONAL NOTES

PERSONAL NOTES

MORE GREAT TITLES FROM TRAILS BOOKS AND PRAIRIE OAK PRESS

Activity Guides

Great Cross-Country Ski Trails: Wisconsin, Minnesota, Michigan, and Ontario, Wm. Chad McGrath
Paddling Southern Wisconsin: 82 Great Trips by Canoe and Kayak, Mike Svob
Paddling Northern Wisconsin: 82 Great Trips by Canoe and Kayak, Mike Svob
Paddling Illinois: 64 Great Trips by Canoe and Kayak, Mike Svob
Wisconsin Golf Getaways: A Guide to More Than 200 Great Courses and Fun Things to Do, Jeff Mayers and Jerry Poling
Wisconsin Underground: A Guide to Caves, Mines, and Tunnels in and around the Badger State, Doris Green
Great Wisconsin Walks: 45 Strolls, Rambles, Hikes, and Treks, Wm. Chad McGrath
Great Minnesota Walks: 49 Strolls, Rambles, Hikes, and Treks, Wm. Chad McGrath

Travel Guides

Great Indiana Weekend Adventures, Sally McKinney
Great Little Museums of the Midwest, Christine des Garennes
Classic Wisconsin Weekend Adventures, Michael Bie
In Lincoln's Footsteps, Don Davenport
Sacred Sites of Wisconsin, John-Brian and Teresa Paprock
Great Iowa Weekend Adventures, Mike Whye
Tastes of Minnesota: A Food Lover's Tour, Donna Tabbert Long
Great Minnesota Weekend Adventures, Beth Gauper
Historical Wisconsin Getaways: Touring the Badger State's Past, Sharyn Alden
The Great Wisconsin Touring Book: 30 Spectacular Auto Tours, Gary Knowles
Wisconsin Family Weekends: 20 Fun Trips for You and the Kids, Susan Lampert Smith
County Parks of Wisconsin, Revised Edition, Jeannette and Chet Bell
Up North Wisconsin: A Region for All Seasons, Sharyn Alden
Great Wisconsin Taverns: 101 Distinctive Badger Bars, Dennis Boyer
Great Weekend Adventures, the Editors of Wisconsin Trails

Home and Garden

Creating a Perennial Garden in the Midwest, Joan Severa
Bountiful Wisconsin: 110 Favorite Recipes, Terese Allen
Foods That Made Wisconsin Famous, Richard J. Baumann

Photo Essays

The Spirit of Door County: A Photographic Essay, Darryl R. Beers
Wisconsin Lighthouses: A Photographic and Historical Guide, Ken and Barb Wardius
Wisconsin Waterfalls, Patrick Lisi

Nature Essays

Wild Wisconsin Notebook, James Buchholz
Driftless Stories, John Motoviloff

For more information, phone, write, or e-mail us.

Trails Books
P.O. Box 317 • Black Earth, WI 53515
(800) 236-8088 • e-mail: books@wistrails.com
www.trailsbooks.com